AF262752

still

First published in Great Britain in 2025 by Ilex,
a division of Octopus Publishing Group Ltd
Carmelite House, 50 Victoria Embankment
London, EC4Y 0DZ
www.octopusbooks.co.uk
www.octopusbooksusa.com

An Hachette UK Company
www.hachette.co.uk

The authorized representative in the EEA is
Hachette Ireland, 8 Castlecourt Centre,
Dublin 15, D15 XTP3, Ireland
(email: info@hbgi.ie)

Distributed in the US by Hachette Book Group
1290 Avenue of the Americas, 4th & 5th Floors
New York, NY 10104

Distributed in Canada by Canadian Manda Group
664 Annette Street, Toronto, Ontario MS62C8

ISBN 978-1-84091-923-3

A CIP catalogue record for this book
is available from the British Library

Printed and bound in China.

10 9 8 7 6 5 4 3 2 1

Publisher: Alison Starling
Commissioning Editor: Richard Collins
Managing Editor: Rachel Silverlight
Assistant Editor: Stephanie Selçuk-Frank
Art Director: Ben Gardiner
Design: JC Lanaway
Senior Production Manager: Peter Hunt

still

a mindful practice for
photographers

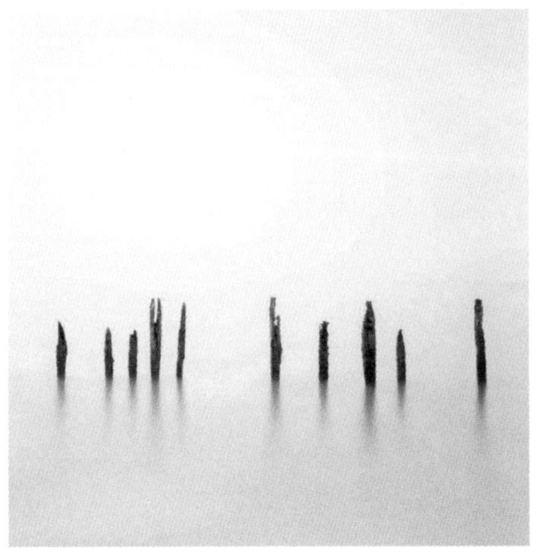

PAUL SANDERS

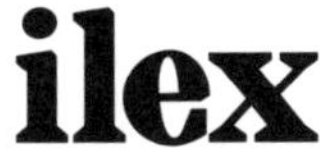

CONTENTS

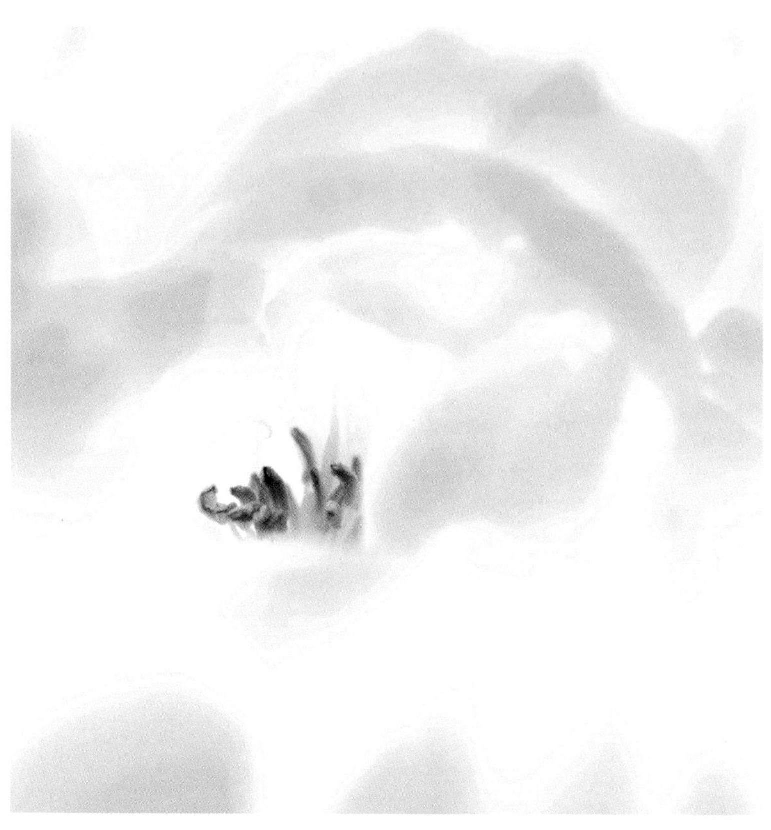

And off I would go making pictures around
the garden, of nothing in particular.

—

introduction: my story

When I was 14, my dad bought a Practika MTL3 single-lens reflex film camera with a 50mm lens. I was warned that under no circumstances was I touch it, play with it or even look at it – it was expensive and needed careful handling!

Of course, I was curious, so while my parents were out doing the weekly food shop one day, I made my way upstairs, found the shiny silver box at the back of my dad's wardrobe, unpacked the camera and flicked through the instructions. I learned how to carefully rewind my dad's film and insert my 24-exposure black-and-white film from school, and off I would go making pictures around the garden, of nothing in particular – just enjoying the process of looking through the lens, bringing the subjects into focus and clicking away. When I heard the car turning into our driveway I would rush upstairs, rewind my film and put my dad's roll of film back into the camera, hastily winding the film forwards to the frame number that I had memorized.

My dad never knew I borrowed his camera. He was always slightly baffled by the multiple exposures that showed my mum superimposed onto a tree or landscape, but he always put this down to a fault with the camera rather than to his son's inability to count properly. Meanwhile, from the very first moment I picked up that camera, I knew I wanted to be a photographer.

My teachers had other ideas, sadly. I was not very academic, was never top of the class and had to have extra maths lessons on a Saturday to make sense of quadratic equations and fractions. I was told in no uncertain terms that I didn't have what it took to be a photographer; my careers advisors all told me that my poor performance in key subjects pointed to someone who'd be better off working in a factory or shop than in the highly competitive and technical field of photography.

Their negativity probably spurred me on; I have always had a need to prove myself. I found a Saturday job in a camera shop, largely so I could get a discount on film and cameras. At the same time, I did a college course in art and photography, though I struggled – I gained a D in my O-level photography examination and failed my A level! I hated being in education; I wanted to learn on the job and be surrounded by real photographers.

My lucky break came when I met a photographer who was working at our local athletics club photographing a race meeting. I started chatting and asking so many questions that he ended up taking me under his wing. I dropped out of art college and worked with him for free, just to get the experience. In time, I made myself pretty indispensable, and when his paid assistant left, I jumped at the chance to fill the gap. And so, at the age of 18, I found myself photographing glamour and fashion calendars in Spain as well as working on all manner of commercial jobs. Finally, I was living my dream.

Of course, things aren't always rosy – I ended up spending more money than I earned and was soon faced with a visit to the bank manager accompanied by Dad. I needed to get a more regular income, so when a job opened up at the *Daventry Express* in Northamptonshire in the English East Midlands, I decided to go for it.

To say that decision changed my life would be an understatement. I was presented with a very battered Nikon FM2, a couple of lenses, a pea-green Vauxhall Astra car and a diary filled with 15 to 20 jobs per day all over the county. I loved seeing my work printed in the newspaper at the end of each week, and I knew that this was what I really wanted to do: I wanted to be at the forefront of news photography.

With luck and connections, I joined a press agency in Birmingham supplying pictures to the national press and magazines, making my way up the ladder to become the deputy picture editor at the *Manchester Evening News*, then the UK assignments editor for Reuters, and eventually I was approached by *The Times*. It was a dream come true. When I had started at the *Daventry Express*, I had made a list of the things I wanted to achieve in my career, and working for *The Times* was at the top.

In April 2004 I was made picture editor of *The Times*. I had achieved my ambition and reached the top of my personal mountain. Naturally, I threw myself into this role, working all the hours I could. Blessed with an incredible team of picture researchers and photographers, I wanted *The Times* to be known as the best photographic newspaper in the UK, not just as its paper of record.

The job of picture editing a national newspaper is huge. Every day there would be a tsunami of photographs – roughly twenty thousand – to look through, of which we would eventually use only around 250. On a busy day, such as a royal wedding or the Oscars, or when the Olympics or the FIFA World Cup was on, that number would be more like forty to fifty thousand photos. At the same time, budgets needed to be met, photographers assigned and future projects planned. I had the very best team around me but gradually I began to feel the pinch.

In the world of newspapers you are judged in hindsight. Pictures that were

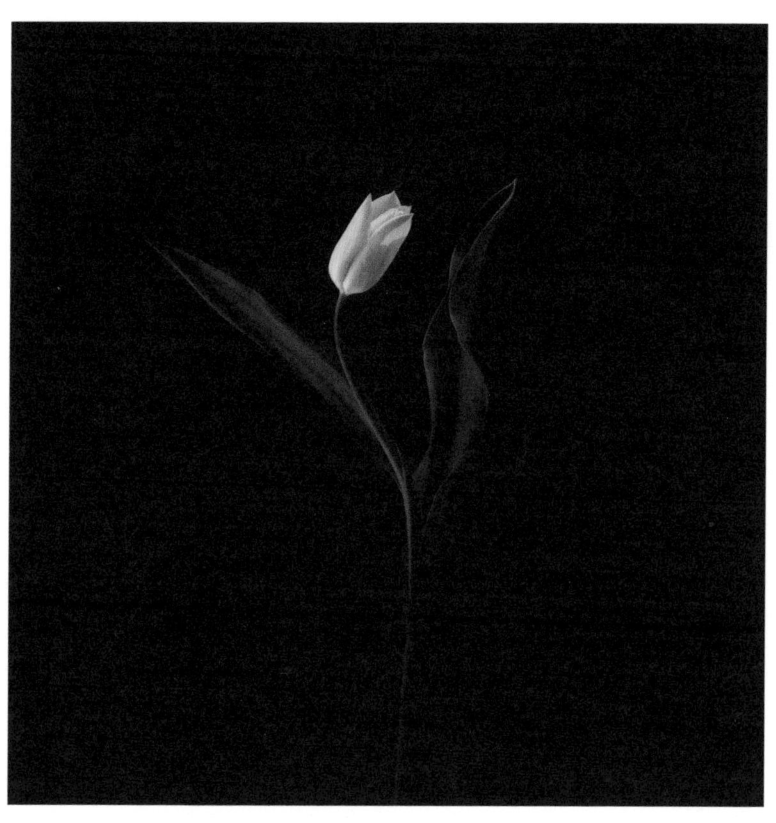

Gradually I lost sight
of who I was.

—

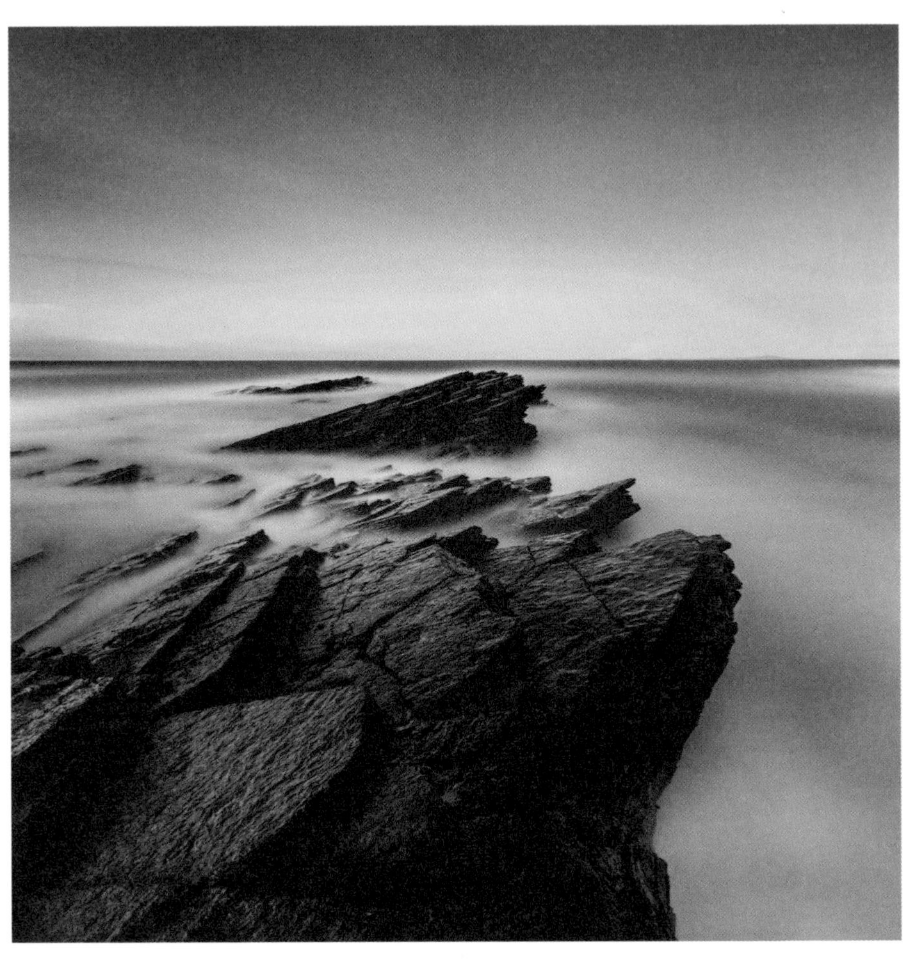

rejected by senior editorial staff are paraded in front of you in rival publications, with questions about why we didn't have it, see it or couldn't afford it. Unfortunately, the newspaper world is rife with toxicity – with fierce battles of one-upmanship, and internal power struggles in which too many are willing to trample on everyone and anyone to climb the greasy pole and get what they want. Long hours and cancelled holidays took their toll on my personal and family life, and gradually I lost sight of who I was and became just the picture editor of *The Times*.

In July 2008 one of my photographers, Richard Mills, took his own life while on assignment for me in Zimbabwe. While I know I wasn't responsible for his death, one of the senior editors at the time directly told me, 'You've killed him.'

That stuck with me then, and it still does. Could I have done things differently? I honestly don't know. Richard lived and worked from his home in Scotland, occasionally popping into the office when needed in London or on his way through to Heathrow. When I saw him in person, he was larger than life, always joking and the centre of conversation. I didn't know that, underneath all the bravado, Richard was struggling.

From that point on, I became overprotective of my team while caring less about how much I was taking on myself. I was trying to please everyone. A round or two of redundancies and cuts didn't help, as the remainder of my team took on more and more of the work. With everyone feeling the strain, I ended up working late into the night, worrying about the morning front page, about budgets, projects, my marriage.

My wheels came off in 2011. What had started with a few sleepless nights had become insomnia. I also started to self-harm, cutting myself to try to express the internal pain I was feeling. I spiralled into depression but was still trying to hide everything from everyone. Like many men of my age and background, I just tried to carry on regardless. But then, one morning, walking to the office, I got as far as a coffee shop in St Katherine's Docks and couldn't take another step. I was in tears, breathless; my vision blurred. I didn't know what was going on.

I was signed off work for a period of time, and when I came back to the office nothing had changed except that I was now damaged goods, and treated as such. I took the decision to leave *The Times* and finally walked out of the office after serving my notice on 30 December 2011.

If I thought things would get better from that point, I was totally mistaken. *The Times* had defined and anchored me; now I was lost and adrift from everything I had been and achieved. My marriage had also ended just before Christmas that same year, and my wife left with our young son.

I felt as though I was in a storm. The world around me seemed to be turning too fast, as though out of control, and I constantly felt as if I was being suffocated. Self-harm was now a feature of my daily life; my fingernails were often dark with blood from the damage I was inflicting on myself. I was lost, with no idea who I was or what I wanted, and I was cut off from anyone who had cared for me. I felt I had failed. The teachers at school who had said I couldn't make it as a photographer had been right; I had been given my dream job and left it, my marriage was over and I couldn't bear to be with my son in case he viewed me as a failure.

And so, I made a plan to take my own life. My first attempt was planned to look like a cycling accident. I drove to the French Alps and in pouring rain cycled up the Col de la Croix-de-Fer. When you do a lot of cycling, you learn little tricks like releasing the tension on your brakes while climbing hills to avoid them dragging on the wheel rims. My plan was to get to the top, then turn around and ride back down, but without retensioning my brakes. I knew that, as soon as I reached a tricky corner on the descent, I would fly off my bike and the result would be called a tragic cycling 'accident'. People would be sad for a bit, but at least my life insurance would pay up.

On reaching the top I stopped and had a coffee at the little café there. Just as I was finishing my coffee, my mum called my phone and I picked up. 'Don't do anything stupid!' she said. I headed back down that mountain at the slowest speed I have ever cycled, in tears, broken.

The second time I tried to end my life was in 2013, this time at Beachy Head in East Sussex. I had a clear plan: I would go to the cliff edge, pretend to be making photographs, and when no one was walking along the nearby footpath, I would jump. This time, my mum didn't call. I have been a Christian for many years and my faith in God is strong, but at that moment I felt even He couldn't save me.

I was standing there crying, asking for forgiveness, and was about to step forward when a man appeared and asked whether I was okay, if he could help or if I wanted to talk. All my energy disappeared, and I crumpled on to the ground and cried like

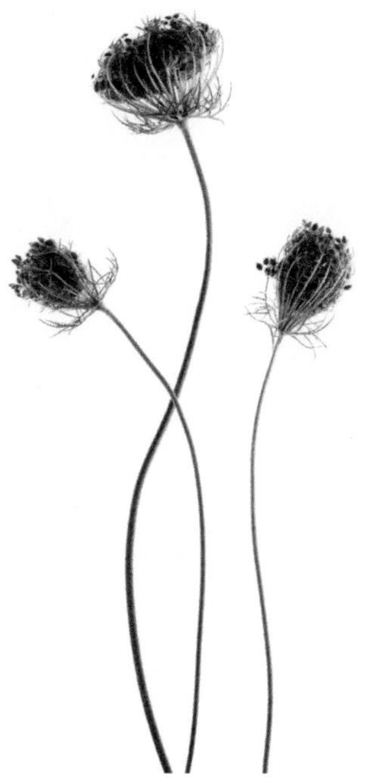

I used photography to help my recovery,
photographing flowers, which essentially helped
me to open discussions about the state of my
emotions, and how I felt about who I was.

—

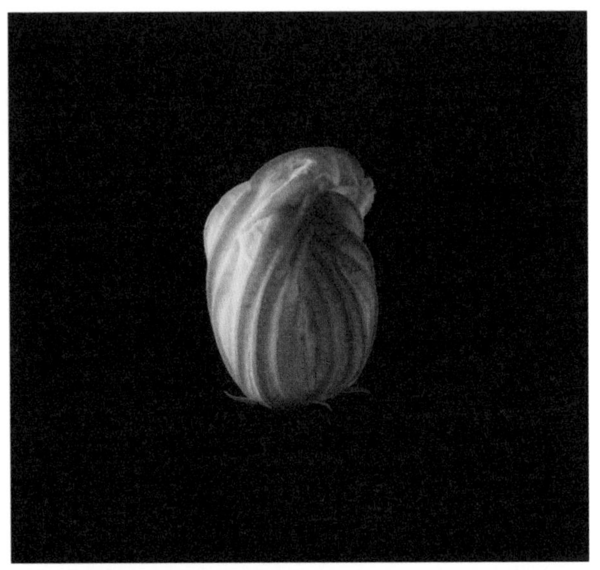

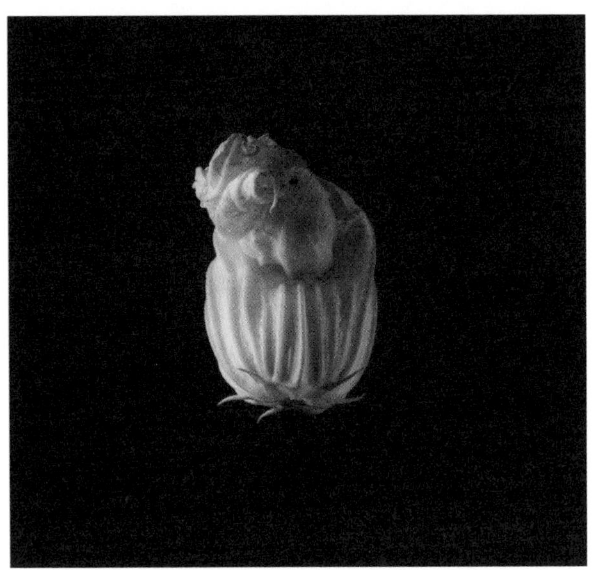

I never have before. I have no idea where he came from or even what his name was, but his intervention stopped me taking action that would have devastated my family and friends.

After that, I had a visit from the police and social services. A care plan, an emergency action plan and a recovery plan were put in place, and the NHS doctors, therapists and nurses proved amazing and non-judgemental. From that point on, I started receiving the most incredible care and support. My therapist helped me start to unpack all of the things that had led to that moment on the cliff top. Because I found it hard to talk about my feelings, she asked me to discuss one of my images, and this led to the vital realization that I could express my feelings best through my photography.

There were two main ways I used photography to help my recovery. One was by using long-exposure photography – this technique involves leaving the shutter open for a long time, which has the effect of smoothing out water, blurring clouds and giving a soft calm, almost meditative effect to images. The second was by photographing flowers, which essentially helped me to open discussions about the state of my emotions, and how I felt about who I was.

My therapist encouraged me to create lists of things I noticed, things that made me smile. She explained how important it is not to compare yourself with others but to move from moment to moment with the intention of being fully present. This was a huge light-bulb moment for me; I needed to photograph things that I noticed, things that gave me little bits of joy; I needed to pay attention to the world around me, not looking backwards at what had happened but appreciating the present moment with gratitude and love.

Since that time, I have adopted a more mindful approach to my photography. This approach is about slowing down, removing the pressure to obtain a certain result, and enjoying the pleasure of the whole process as something catches my eye and I pause to make a photograph.

The key phrase in all this is 'my photography'. I have no desire to please others with my images – I photograph just what I enjoy. If I don't get lots of likes on social media, that's fine – these days I use Instagram as a personal journal, writing what was going through my head at the time of making the photograph.

The power of photography to help us slow down, pay attention and notice more, so that we suddenly see something that only we could ever have noticed, at that particular time and place, has not only changed my life – it has saved my life.

1

photography
& mindfulness

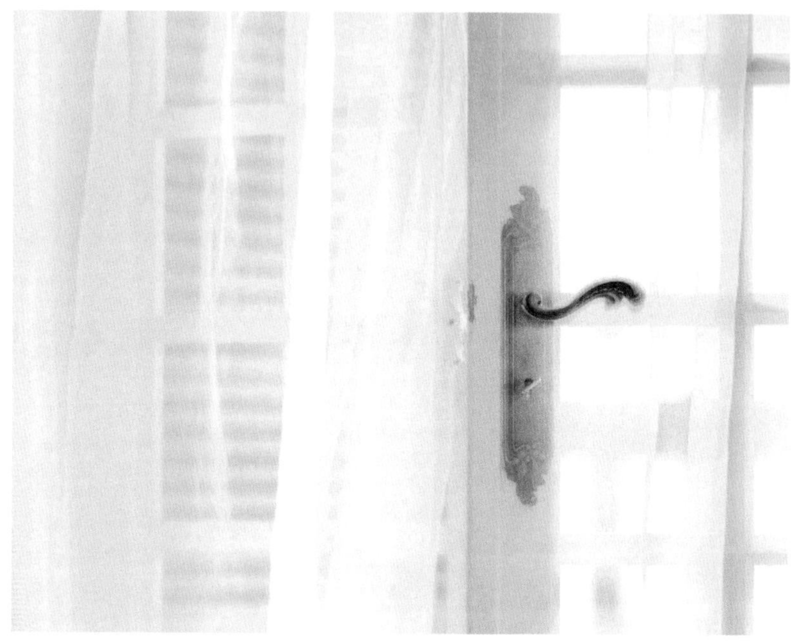

'A photograph is neither taken nor seized by force. It offers itself up. It is the photo that takes you. One must not *take* photos.'

—

Henri Cartier-Bresson

a mindful practice for photographers

Mindfulness is about being present in the moment. The practice is currently in vogue, but it isn't new.

The roots of mindfulness reach back into Hinduism and Buddhism, its tenets gradually transferring across to the West via teachers, such as Jon Kabat-Zinn, who have applied the key principles to Western culture and lifestyles as a way of reducing people's stress and helping them to find an inner peace. Although mindfulness is rooted in Eastern religious culture, it is largely taught in a secular way in the West – you don't need to have a faith or an interest in religion to practise its principles.

Kabat-Zinn defines mindfulness as 'paying attention in a particular way, on purpose, in the present moment without judgement'. Can you think of anything else that fits so perfectly with photography? My definition of mindful photography is even simpler: it means paying attention to what and where you are without judgement or ambition.

When photographers such as Henri Cartier-Bresson talk about the experience of the photographic moment, this is a mindful approach to photography. In this view, photographs are neither made nor taken. They are received by the photographer who is paying attention, who is able to notice the unique beauty in a fleeting moment because they are not attached to a preconceived outcome. Mindful photography is about being curious – asking questions, the most important of which is *why*. Why am I intrigued by this? Why is this fascinating? Why did I stop at this spot?

For many, photography is about the search for perfection, and everything is judged against this impossible benchmark as they try to please an ever-wider public through social media. But life, people, nature aren't perfect; they are perfectly imperfect and, because of their consequent uniqueness, are beautiful, intriguing and inspiring.

Mindful photography is based on acceptance, gratitude and non-attachment. When we are attached to a specific outcome or set of criteria – such as lighting or weather conditions, the appearance of a subject, our desire for riches, fame or awards, and so on – we risk missing what is right in front of our eyes. Letting go of the things we think we want allows us to approach the world more openly, and this, in turn, expands our creativity.

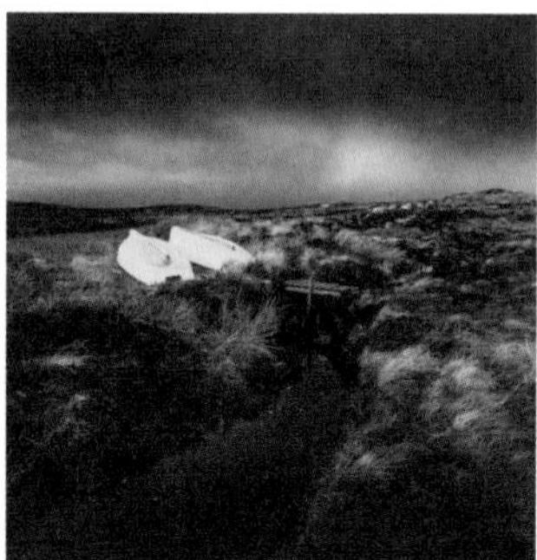

With my background as a news photographer, my approach to photography is about producing an accurate account of a particular moment. I'm not saying that manipulating a scene or image before or after capture is wrong, but, for me, the goal is to celebrate what is present rather than wishing for less of this, more of that, better light, one more tree, and so on.

Contemplative photography brings contentment not only with your photography but also in a broader sense. This is because the better you become at observing the world around you, the more you will appreciate how rich life is. The joy of starting to accept what you are given in nature is that it helps you to accept the imperfections in yourself. Gradually, over a period of paying attention and making pictures, you may even come to doubt the relevance of words like 'flaw' and 'imperfection', when everything in nature has its place.

We've likely all seen an image that we consider truly superb, or have an idea in our mind of what our perfect shot would look like, but comparing our work to an ideal standard often leads to disappointment and loss of enjoyment in our craft. Mindfulness in photography is not about attaining any real or imaginary standard; it is about learning to enjoy the process in its own right.

You will, of course, like some images more than others – that's OK. When I go out making pictures, I always come back and choose my favourite. Lighting, atmosphere, composition – all manner of tiny things might make you choose one as your best of the day, and it's worth taking the time to consider what makes you like one image more than another. What isn't helpful is labelling your images as 'good' or 'bad', because this reduces the whole process to a simplistic judgement.

If you take the judgement out of photography, you start to make pictures that you enjoy, and you become more aware of the things that intrigue and inspire you – that you simply want to sit and spend time with. The picture almost becomes irrelevant to the greater process.

Imagine you go to a well-known photographic location to make a certain image. You've planned it, worked out the sun, checked the weather forecast, studied maps...the whole works, but when you get there, it's cloudy. Instantly, you embark on a downward spiral of discontent, feeling that you're wasting time and energy.

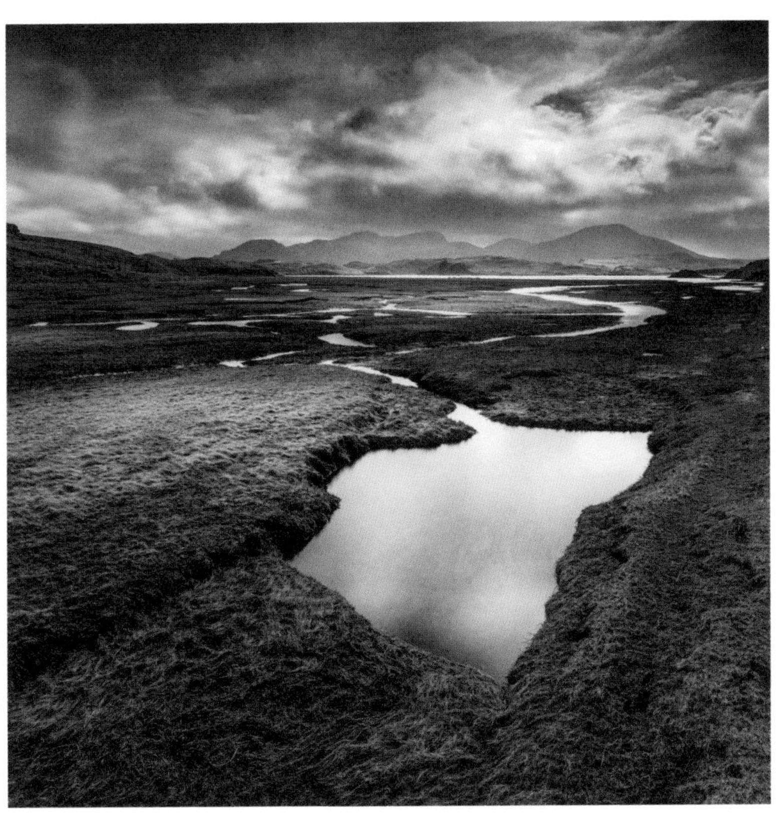

The better you become at observing the
world around you, the more you will
appreciate how rich life is.

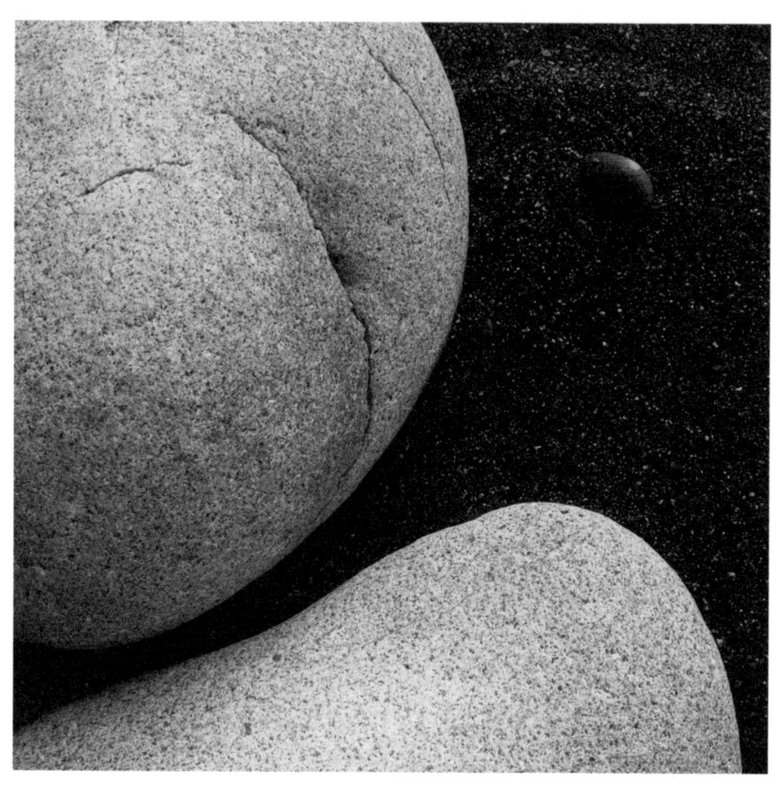

All sorts of very random, seemingly
ordinary things will become the most
extraordinary subjects of your
photography.

—

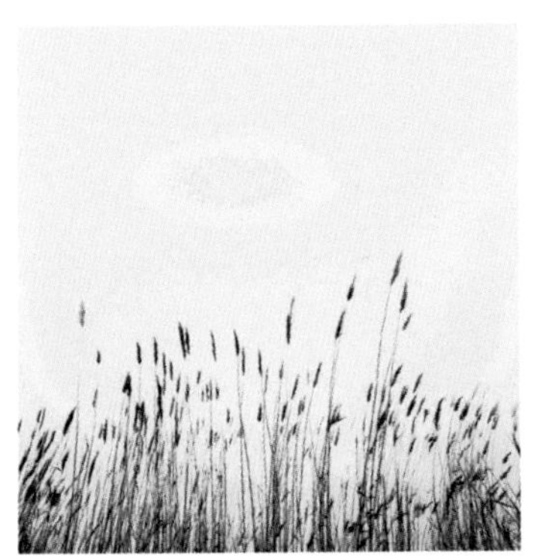

Now imagine you've arrived at the location and the sky has clouded over, but instead of the flood of disappointment, you look at the scene, open your mind and enjoy the fact that you are there. You sit with your flask of coffee listening to the birds, and as you notice the wind blowing through the grasses, you become fascinated by the movement and the sound of their whispers. Eventually, you wander over to take a closer look, and finally you take out your camera to photograph this phenomenon, this moment, which called uniquely to you.

Whether it wins an award or gets lots of social media likes is not important. Feeling fulfilled in the moment, enjoying the experience and making an image that resembles what captured your attention are the most uplifting reasons for being a photographer.

Another benefit of this approach is that it produces original work rather than reproducing the same views of the same tired locations. You start finding inspiration in the shadows on your wall or the movement of leaves on trees, and all sorts of very random, seemingly ordinary things will become the most extraordinary subjects of your photography.

A MINDFUL PROCESS

The way I work is always the same, and it starts before I leave home. I check my bag to make sure everything I might need is in it, and that I know exactly where everything is. The better prepared you are, the less distracted you will be fiddling about with kit and looking for things once you get to the location.

On arrival, I like to begin by spending a while without my camera. As photographers, we instantly start assessing a scene for photographic potential without giving the other 80 percent of our senses time to adjust to the change of pace and environment. I like to close my eyes, sit or stand still, and tune in to all the sensations. Sometimes I will note down all the things I'm aware of, including how I feel. This helps ground me in a place, slowing me down to a more contemplative mode and diverting the impulse to look for particular outcomes.

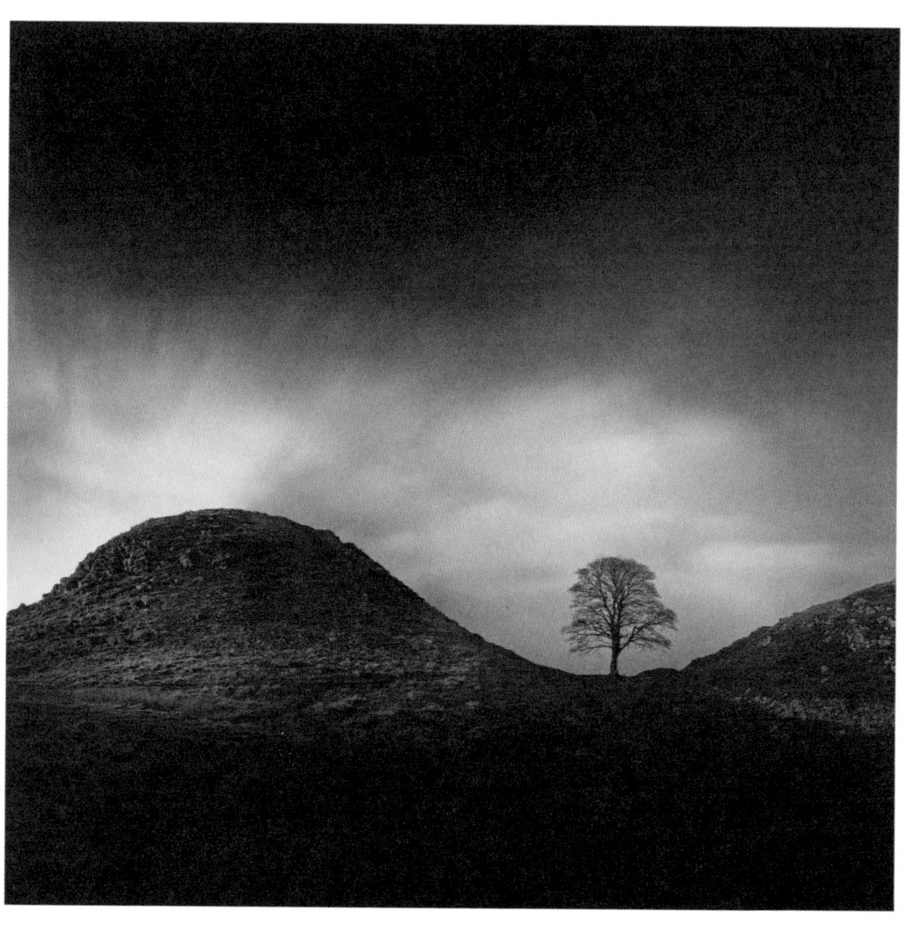

As my awareness settles on something, I start to explore it, moving around it, perhaps touching it, and trying to see it as if I'm seeing it for the first time– looking as a child might look. I will ask myself what it was about the subject that caught my attention, and explore that, too. This process is about spending time appreciating the subtleties of your subject – enjoy the process of looking, and don't be impatient.

By this point, a photograph may be starting to form in your mind's eye, but keep in touch with reality and resist composing an imaginary image. Set your tripod up if you use one (I like to because it slows me down further) and make adjustments – moving your feet, changing the lens and so on – until what you see in the camera matches the view that attracted you. If anything is distracting you, try to adjust your own position rather than moving the subject.

If you can and want to, review the image, asking yourself: does this reflect what I feel, what I perceived, what I experienced? If it doesn't, spend a little more time looking and moving around your subject.

When you are done, say a quiet thank you and move on.

WHAT YOU NEED
- An open mind
- A childlike sense of wonder
- The ability to enjoy yourself even if you don't make a photograph
- A camera of any kind – your phone camera is fine

TIPS FOR SUCCESS
Less is more. Don't overcomplicate the image, but focus on capturing the essence of what you saw, keeping the composition simple. This guideline applies to equipment as well – too much kit only gets in the way.
Warm up first. I often start with a few simple exercises; for example, choosing a single colour and spending some time counting how many times I can see this colour in the location. Come with a few simple challenges that you can do anywhere to warm up, by looking for colour, line, shadow, texture and so on. Don't worry about making great images; just photograph the instances you spot.
Practise. It takes time to get used to this way of photographing. Gradually, it will become a way of seeing and a way of life. Be kind to yourself, and remember that photography is supposed to be a pleasurable experience!

ASSIGNMENT: COLOUR

Colour is all around us, and yet we often fail to notice it, or simply label it red, yellow, orange, purple, blue or green without seeing the subtleties.

This exercise is very simple; it can be used time and time again, and it demonstrates how well photography and mindfulness can work together to change your mindset.

For this exercise, start by sitting quietly for a moment, with your eyes closed, concentrating just on your breathing, following the sensation as the breath you inhale moves through your body.

Now ask yourself how you are feeling – I mean *really* feeling. Are you feeling angry, happy, sad, frustrated, stressed, exuberant, lonely, too busy, or something else? When you start to settle on a feeling, try to imagine it as a colour; nothing too specific, but just a general colour from the spectrum.

Now get up, and set the intention to notice the colour of your mood as you continue about your day. Whenever you see an example of the colour you have chosen, stop and spend a short time observing the colour: look at the way light the falls on it and how warm or cool the hue is; notice any patterns or textures, and how it interacts with any other nearby colours; observe how bright and saturated it is, whether it is an interesting shape, what the context is, and so on.

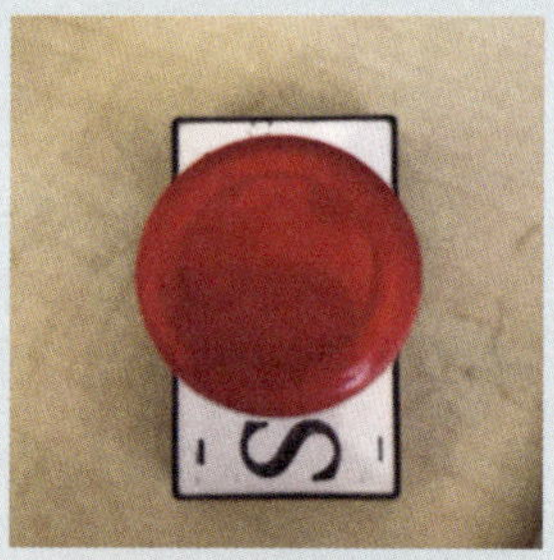

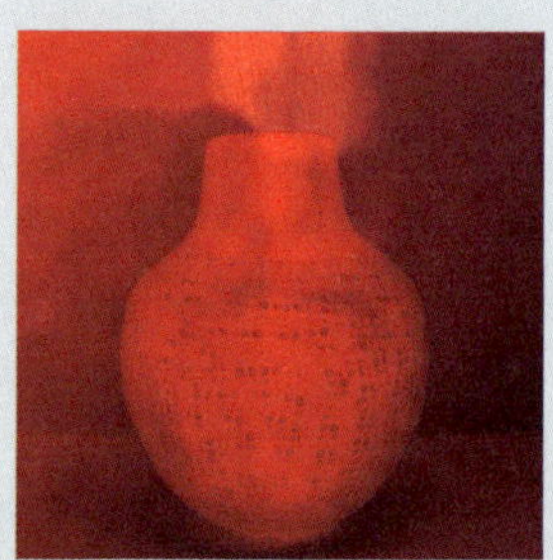

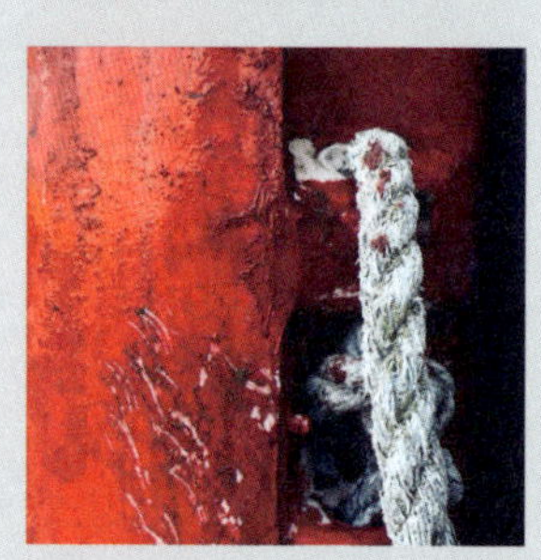

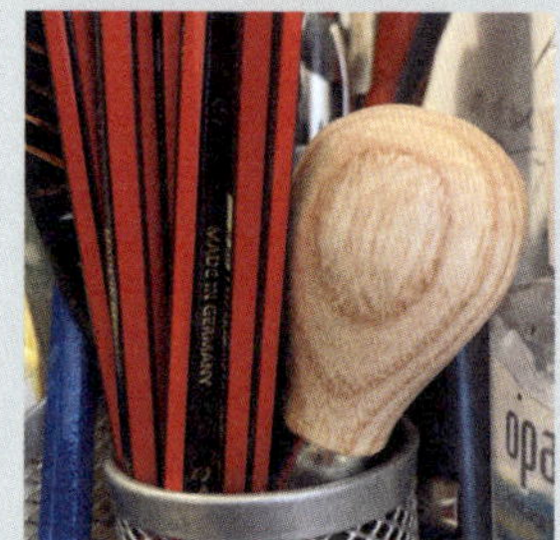

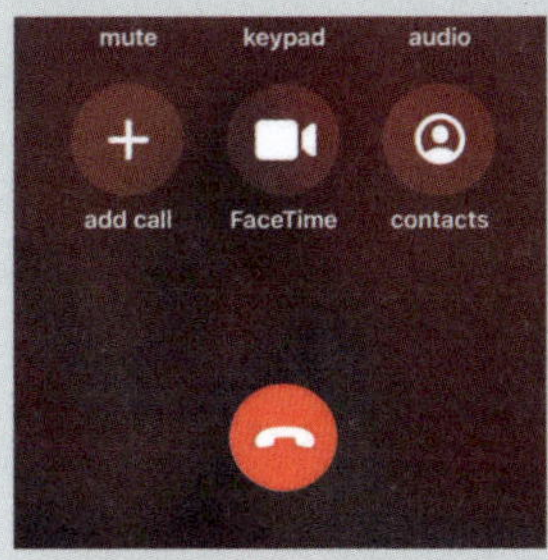

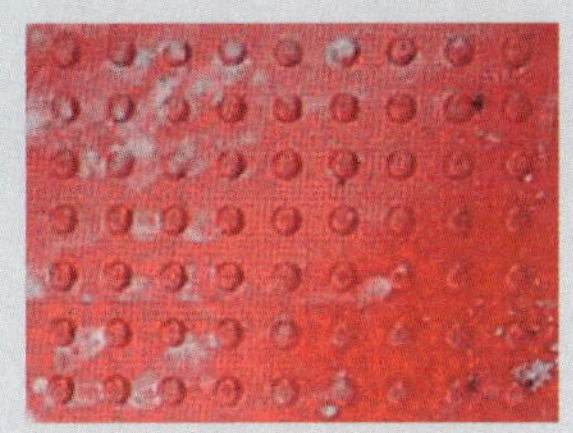

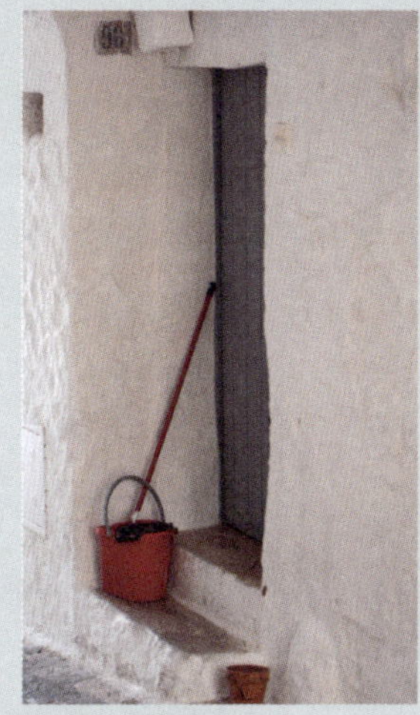

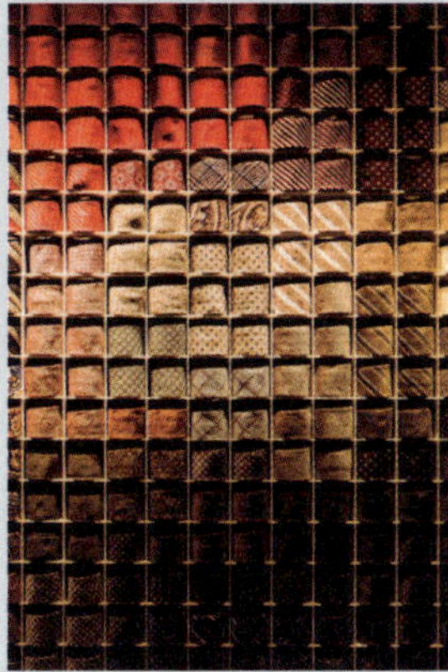

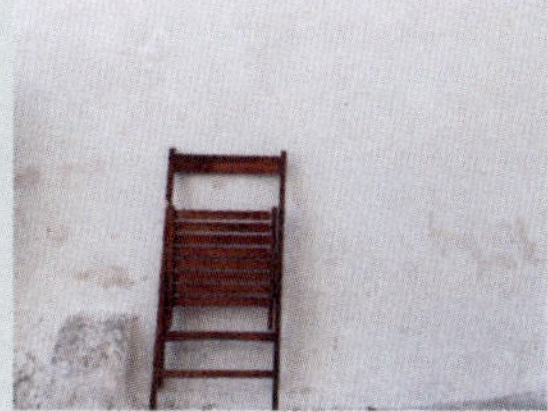

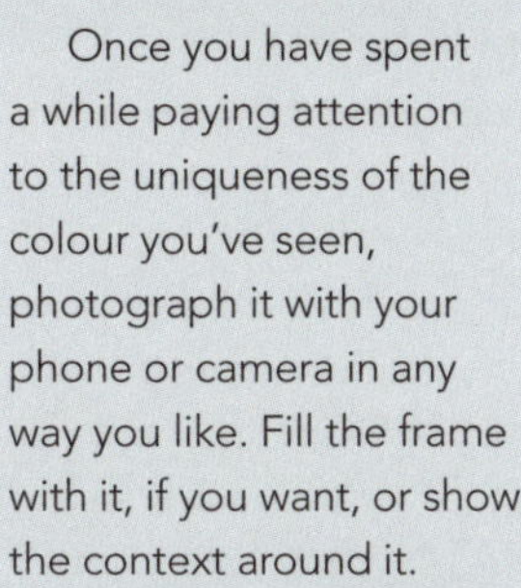

When you start to
settle on a feeling,
try to imagine it
as a colour.

—

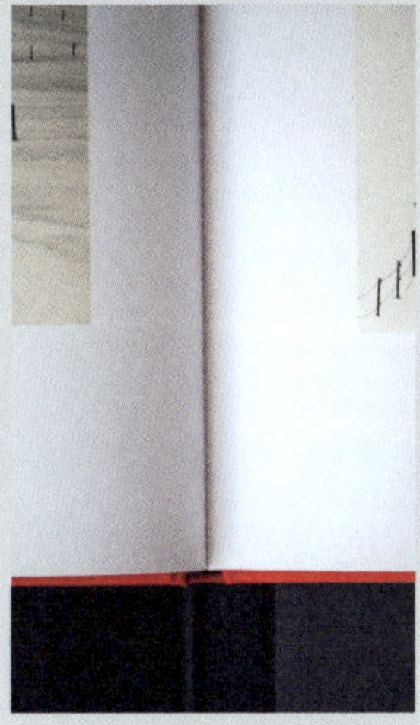

Once you have spent a while paying attention to the uniqueness of the colour you've seen, photograph it with your phone or camera in any way you like. Fill the frame with it, if you want, or show the context around it.

You will be surprised how many things of that colour you notice during the day – and likely for a few days after, too. I always think of this exercise as the visual equivalent of the ear worm – you know, that annoying tune you can't get out of your head. Apologies in advance! However, the benefits are worth it. What I enjoy most about this exercise is that it is impossible to hang on to any negative feelings when you're constantly distracted by beauty.

In the images shown here, I had chosen the colour red as I was feeling annoyed by something that day. By the end of the day my mind had shifted from annoyance to calm, as I marvelled at how much red I had found in so many unexpected places.

the language of photography

The language surrounding photography tends to be aggressive – we talk about shooting, capturing, framing, snapping and taking photographs. Similarly, photography is a very competitive industry, full of big egos.

During my newspaper years I, too, adopted an aggressive, competitive mindset about photography, but now this seems completely contrary to what I'm trying to do with my work.

For me, photography now comes from a place of vulnerability, of openness, and this has completely changed the way I see things. Photographs are not possessions but gifts that the photographer is granted as a reward for their patience, their stillness and their attention. We need a language of photography that better reflects a more receptive and collaborative way of seeing and being.

If we change the language we use, we may automatically think differently about our approach – we might become gentler, more grateful, and start noticing things more. Instead of 'taking' a picture or 'capturing' a scene, we can 'make' a picture or 'receive' a scene, for example.

This is also why I don't refer to photographs as 'good' or 'bad'. Sometimes the image doesn't come out as we hoped – maybe we missed the moment, or we don't yet have the technical skills – but photography is more than the resulting image. Was the time you spent with the subject all bad? Can such simplistic judgements do justice to what we are trying to achieve?

By taking the gentle and non-judgemental approach you will find yourself surprised by the subjects that reveal themselves to you. You can compare it to interactions with people: people don't tend to respond well to aggressive language or gestures; they will clam up and become defensive, if not becoming aggressive themselves. When we approach someone with kindness, however, and show genuine interest, it can lead to a memorable conversation.

By taking a gentler approach, you will also find yourself more tolerant of your own shortcomings, seeing the beauty in your flaws rather than damning yourself for them. In turn, this self-kindness will flow out to the people you interact with.

Gentleness and vulnerability are not weaknesses but superpowers. They can allow you to experience greater empathy and connection, and they will make you more aware of the presence of beauty and the uniqueness it shares with the world.

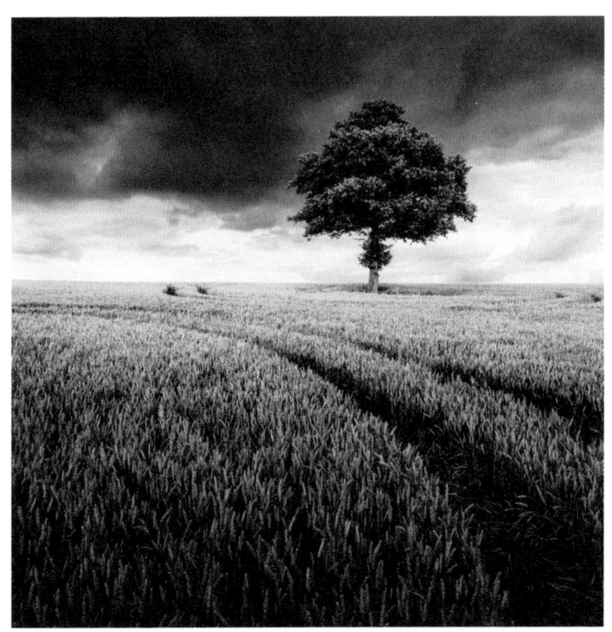

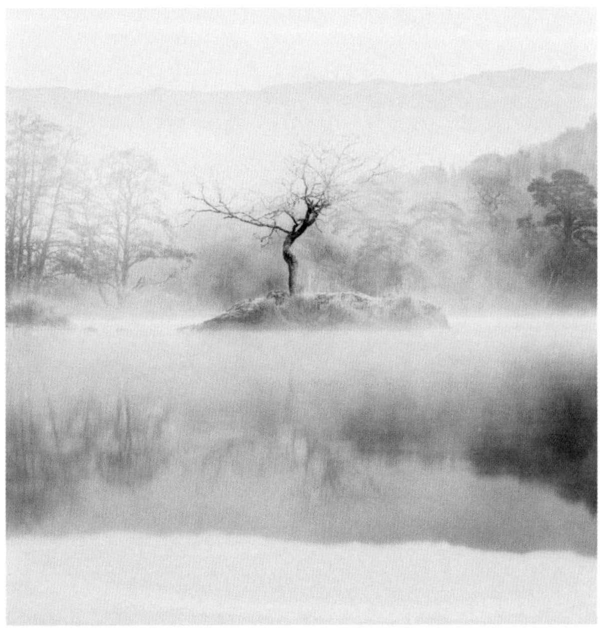

the universal language

Photography needs no translation. Every single person in the world can look at a photograph and decide whether they like it or not, what it says to them, and how they want to respond to it.

The ubiquity of the smart phone in today's world means that photography is now more accessible to more people than ever before. At the time of writing, there are almost five billion smart phone users across the globe, and around three hundred million images are uploaded to social media platforms every day.

Because the average attention span of people using social media has reduced to around 8 seconds, photography has become more powerful than the written word for communication. On the other hand, some researchers suggest that the actual time we engage with content is only 1.5 seconds – so what does this mean for how we are engaging with what we see? If I asked you which photographs you actively 'liked' on social media – as in clicking the heart symbol – could you remember as many as half of them?

When I worked at *The Times* I viewed on average about 20,000 images every day. If it was a big event like a royal wedding, the Academy Awards, the Olympics or a World Cup, that number might be five times as many. It was my job to look through all of those images and choose one for the front page. But now, I often find myself scrolling through one after another image for minutes or hours at a time, not really paying attention.

Instead of constantly fixating on social media, using your phone or digital camera intentionally, as a meditation tool and as a way of slowing down and stepping off the treadmill, reminds you to open your eyes and look at the world around you. This in turn helps you feel more connected, appreciative and contented in the world.

Making pictures for the sake of making pictures is a way of adding a richness to your day. It becomes a visual journal of things you enjoyed, that made you happy or feel inspired. There will be times, of course, when you make pictures of things that make you feel unhappy or angry – I encourage you to embrace these in the same way as the happier moments and images. I've found that not being afraid to photograph things that move me has allowed me to process grief and loss, anger and sadness, in a more rounded way.

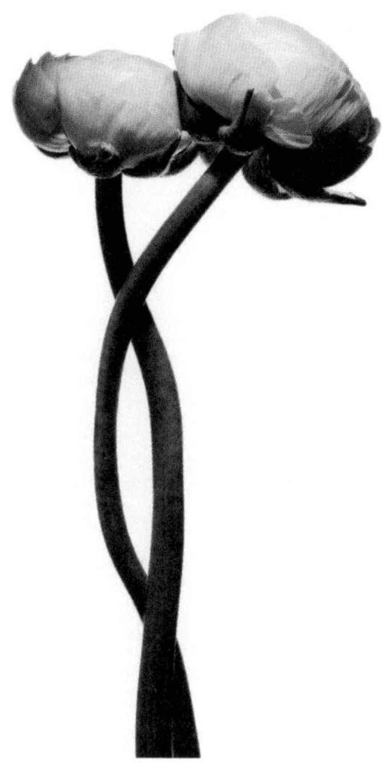

Making pictures for the sake of making pictures
is a way of adding richness to your day.

—

During my breakdown, many of the images I made were reflections of what was happening in my head – even though these images were of flowers. The process of finding equivalents or analogies in the flowers helped me both to understand and express the complexity of these feelings in an immediate, intuitive way.

This is how the language of photography can really help you to open up – at the same time as helping other people understand what you are experiencing.

distraction

We live in a world that demands our attention. An overabundance of sensory stimuli claims every second of our waking day and often crowds our minds as we try to sleep.

Now that we're connected to practically the whole world via the little devices we carry around with us and even wear, it is so easy to become overwhelmed by the vast quantities of information flooding through our lives like a digital tsunami. Phones constantly ping with messages, notifications and offers promoting things we don't need; with social media validations from people we don't know; with news rolling in 24 hours a day; and then the pressure of keeping on top of work and domestic chores, while keeping up with our families and friends... How many of us panic when we forget our phone? Do you find yourself constantly and inadvertently picking up your device and scrolling? Among this storm, the one person who needs your attention gets very little – and that is you.

I am one of those people who have been caught in the trap of distraction, of thinking I will do something only to wake up from a digital trance an hour later – procrastinating with another round of social media doom-scrolling rather than actually getting on with whatever I had planned to do. My phone tells me that, during an average day, I used to spend around four hours on social media, one hour reading the news, twenty minuteson emails, fifteen minutes answering texts and messages and only six minutes using the camera on my phone. I am meant to be a photographer, but I guarantee I spent even less time using my actual camera!

During my deepest periods of depression I would scroll all day, never consciously taking part in life, always looking for something to find but never knowing what I needed. At the time, it might feel like relaxing, like taking a break from the constant busyness of life, but these hours always felt hollow and empty.

What we need is to spend our most precious resource more wisely. Time is a resource we have only a finite amount of, none of us know how much we have been gifted with, and yet we squander so much of it doing something that adds little to no value to our lives.

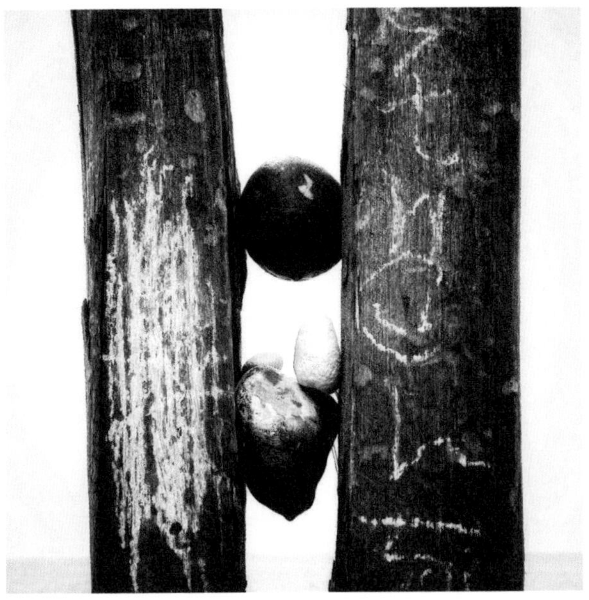

Time is a resource we have only a finite amount of.

—

Distraction has become an addiction. A 2022 report on social media use in the workplace estimated that 'employees spend around 40–45 minutes on social media during working hours for non-work-related purposes', reducing productivity by almost 10 percent.

Many psychologists and journalists have reported on the negative impact of social media on our attention spans as we scroll from one post or video to another, leaping from one platform to another with no end of new content to satisfy an unconscious craving for novelty.

And so much of the way we engage with social media is unconscious; the algorithms are purposely designed to keep us mindlessly scrolling. The distractions of the modern world are denying us the chance to fully live our lives by reducing the interpersonal, face-to-face relationships and meaningful activities that are important to our growth, not to mention how constant comparisons between our own and others' lives can damage our sense of self-worth. While there are obviously good things about modern technology and social media – being able to stay in touch with friends and relatives who live far away is hugely beneficial – perhaps we need to find a healthier way to enjoy these upsides.

We must also be careful not to let the overuse of technology rob us of real experience. These days, when you go to a concert or a major event, the number

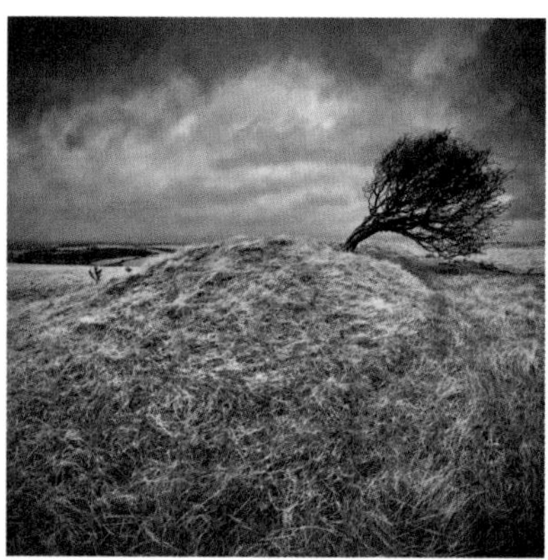

of people videoing, live-streaming or photographing the event is astounding. While it is great to be able to look back at things, the record of an event is not the same as the moment itself, and the compulsive need to capture it can damage not only our own experience of the moment but also that of those around us.

When we think about why we do this, sometimes it almost seems as if it's proof that we're after, especially if we post to social media – if your image or video isn't on social media, were you really there? Instead of filling our senses to create rich memories of these moments, we end up relying on our cameras, or on the validation of our followers, to give our experience meaning.

When I discovered my screen time usage, first I was shocked and then I was ashamed. How could I have been so wasteful? I work for myself, so time is valuable. I noticed then that there had been a decline in my work – not only in the number of photographs made but also in my ability to look properly and have my attention held by something.

I started to make changes after that. First, I made a conscious choice about how I started my day. Instead of instinctively reaching for my phone, I started to journal in the morning; just writing down a few thoughts, the half-remembered dreams, a short list of achievable to-do items, and so on. Taking my cue from *The Artist's Way* by

—

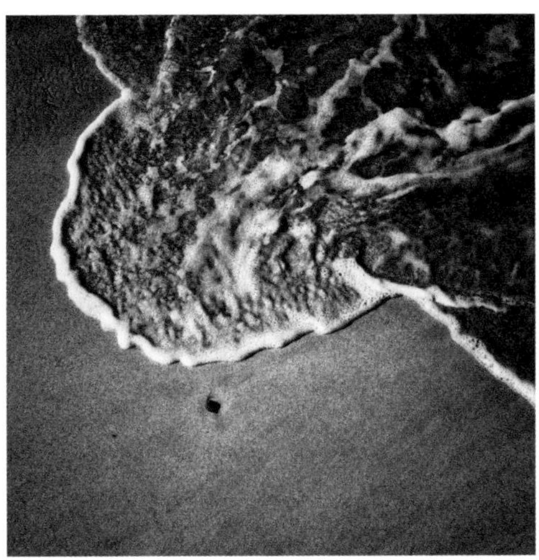

Julia Cameron, I found that writing a few pages of pure stream of consciousness every morning transformed my relationship with the world.

Limiting myself to answering emails only on my laptop instead of my phone also helped. I also weaned myself off the games I had become addicted to. My social media habits were the hardest to break. What seemed to work for me was only allowing myself a maximum of 20 minutes each morning (never first thing; I made myself wait at least an hour) and evening. As for news, I still look at the front pages and read the headlines, but I have decided I will allow news to reach me when it filters into my life, rather than letting it overshadow my life.

The first week of doing this I reclaimed over two hours, which I used to get out with my camera – to invest that time back into myself. After a month I found that I no longer missed social media. I've since taken to turning off all notifications on my phone apart from those from my immediate family.

After undertaking this experiment, I have discovered that I have more time to notice the beauty of the world and more attention for my partner, son and family. I am gradually becoming master of my time and attention again. Our modern lives need balance. We need to reclaim some of our attention and use our time with purpose, learning to pay attention to what is important and real to us.

expectations

With all the inspiring imagery we're exposed to via social media, it can
be easy to become disappointed if your photographs don't seem quite
as amazing as you wanted them to be.

There seems to be a need these days to achieve success almost instantly, and a tendency when things don't work out that way to abandon your efforts and try something else instead. When we watch videos, read articles and buy books on our hobby, sometimes we might be hoping we'll find the secret answer to make the pieces fall into place.

This book will not make you an overnight sensation – sorry! And it is not going to immediately unlock a new way of seeing the world, so that everything suddenly shines with wonder and light. What it will do is hopefully give you insights into how to enjoy your creativity without looking for or needing external validation. It will encourage you to practise, and not even want to reach the point where you know it all – and frankly you never can or will know it all.

Founder of the Mindfulness-Based Stress Reduction method Jon Kabat-Zinn said, 'It is not that mindfulness is the "answer" to all life's problems. Rather, it is that all life's problems can be seen more clearly through the lens of a clear mind.' Mindfulness and mindful photography are vehicles to managing the way we respond to the world around us. Rather than submit to the distractions that were stopping me truly experiencing the world, I made making photographs a daily practice. That is what I want to encourage you to do: to slow down enough to engage with what is happening right in front of your eyes; to form a habit of being curious and seeing the beauty in the world and even in the mundane moments of your everyday existence.

Having worked with the mental health charity Mind on several photography programmes, I have seen the results that making photographs can have on those suffering with depression, anxiety, burnout and stress. Any kind of art, inlcuding photography, is good for the body, mind and spirit. More than practically anything else you can do, making art leaves you feeling rewarded and uplifted, and provides a break from running the hamster wheel of troubling thoughts that keep us from being present and enjoying our lives.

Using our creativity also helps us to solve problems. Not only does the act of creation put us in a receptive state of mind, where the answers often seem to just come to us from out of the blue, but it also stimulates both sides of our brain – giving us new ways to look at and respond to problems in our art as well as in many different areas of our life.

When faced with a problem, I will often ask myself what it 'looks like': what shape it is; what texture it has; what colour it might be. Noting the answers I offer back to myself, I then go for a walk, looking for subjects connected to the visual prompts I have given myself. Gradually, my mind clears, and by approaching the issue from a more abstract angle, I can start to make sense of things in a calmer, less emotional way. (See the assignment on page 26.)

There is a saying, 'Life is not measured by the number of breaths you take, but by the moments that take your breath away', first used by Vicki Corona in 1989 in a pamphlet on the traditional dances of Tahiti. It is the richness of your experiences, not the material value of them, that is important. By making mindful photography a regular practice, you will start to find more of those moments in your normal day-to-day life – not because anything has changed in your material environment or circumstances, but because you will have become better at noticing how much value is to be found in the world all around you.

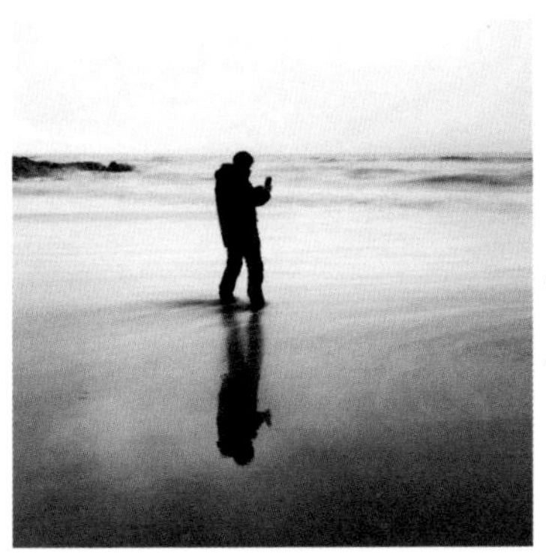

'It is not that mindfulness is the "answer" to all life's problems. Rather, it is that all life's problems can be seen more clearly through the lens of a clear mind.'

—

Jon Kabat-Zinn

ASSIGNMENT: ATTENTION

Whatever kind of camera you may be using – be it your phone camera or a top-of-the-line mirrorless model – and whatever your level of technical mastery, the most important skill in photography is your ability to see.

Seeing involves patience, effort and curiosity. It also involves a moment of physical (as well as mental) stillness, because every time we move, our perspective changes. This means that the length of time you could spend looking at something could potentially be endless. Often, we are in our heads when we think we are looking at something – allowing our imagination to come into play, seeing the 'what ifs' as we construct the image in our mind, or letting our curiosity be limited by things we know about or associate with the subject. It is surprisingly easy only to *imagine* the subject in front of you rather than seeing what is actually there; this is why I say seeing requires patience and effort.

We rush about our daily lives paying little attention to anything other than whatever our particular goal at that moment may be, practically blind to anything that isn't relevant to that task. It can be the same with the faces and places we see every day; things become so familiar and so taken for granted that it can take a conscious effort to stop and make yourself properly notice them again. In this way, photography can be an expression of love and gratitude.

Dorothea Lange said that photography can help us learn to see because it gives us a reason to stop and take the time to really look at something. However, it's a skill we can just as easily practise without a camera. In today's age, where photography has become

a form of note-taking – an easy substitute for truly noticing something – it can even be helpful to begin by separating yourself from that automatic response.

All this assignment requires is for you to spend a few minutes looking at something and then write down a list of ten things you noticed about your subject. Try to do this by hand – your handwriting is unique and personal to you, and a form of art in itself. Even if (like mine!) your writing is a scrawl, you will find it a lot easier to stay focused writing by hand than with a tablet or device.

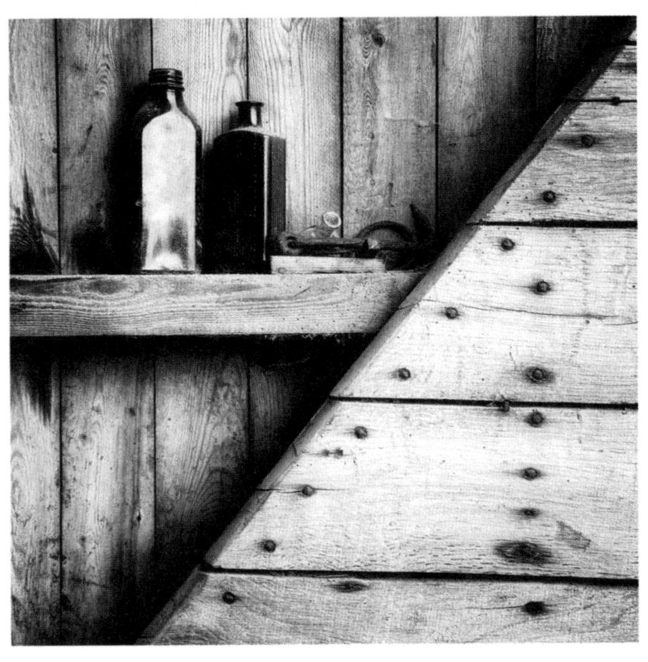

'The camera is an instrument that teaches
people how to see without a camera.'
—
Dorothea Lange

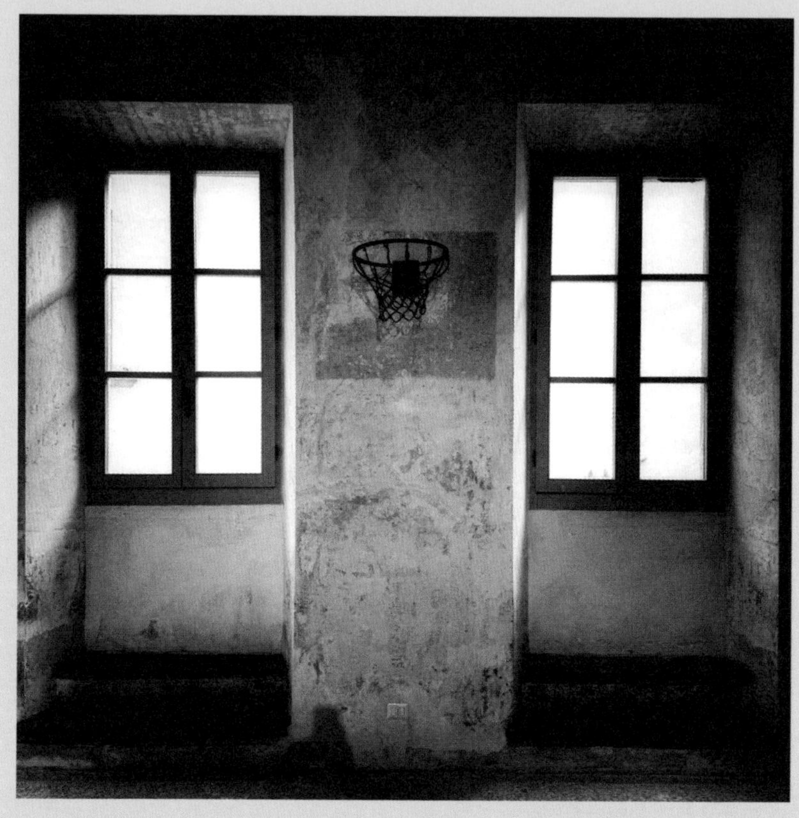

'You know there are moments such
as these when time stands still.'
—
Dorothea Lange

DAY ONE

Find a location you can easily go to every day for the next week. It might be your garden, the bus stop, the café where you buy your daily coffee, or even a particular window of your house – it doesn't matter how ordinary or mundane the place is.

Write down ten things you notice around you; just the first ten things you see. For example, sitting in my garden, my list might go like this: trees, lawn, rosebush, garden gate, chair on lawn, hedge, shed, lawnmower, dog sitting on the lawn, bin by the gate. That's it.

DAY TWO

Same location, different day. Write down ten new things. For example: daisies growing in the lawn, pink roses blooming, bees on the roses, garden gate is open, cushion on the chair, shadows from the trees, weeds growing between tiles, sparrows squabbling in the hedge, a wooden brush by the lawnmower, neighbour's cat on the lawn.

DAY THREE

There will probably be plenty of things you haven't noticed yet, but today, close your eyes and pay attention to the sounds that you encounter. You may hear birds, the wind in the trees, leaves rattling on the ground, rain on a window, the voices of people nearby… If you run out of sounds, what can you smell?

DAY FOUR

Now try bringing your sense of touch into the mix. What do you notice and what does it feel like? Perhaps it is the rough texture of an old wooden gate, the puckering paint on an old, rusty fence, the softness of grass, the prickly sharpness of the rose thorns… If you run out of textures, what can you smell or hear that you couldn't yesterday?

DAY FIVE

Now, using all your senses make your final list. So far, you have a list of ten things you noticed immediately, and thirty things you were initially only partially aware of. What has changed on this last day?

It's not a quiz, but if it was, the answer would be *everything*. There's an ancient saying attributed to Heraclitus that goes, 'You can't step in the same river twice.' Everything changes all the time, and so do we. It is because of this constant change that we can learn to come into awareness, pay attention and notice the beauty of even the most mundane of days and places.

2

we are all creative

what do you photograph for?

Until I left *The Times*, I had always photographed for a reason that I clearly understood. I made photographs to illustrate stories for art directors and picture editors. Working to a brief, the images had to work in certain formats and suit the style of the publications they might be used in.

Leaving full-time employment at the end of 2011, I suddenly didn't know what I wanted to photograph, or even whether I really enjoyed photography. But the realization that photography was how I communicated with the world, and how I explained my purpose and place in the world, changed the way I would photograph for ever.

For me, photography is about the relationship between a photographer and their subject. When we make an image, we are trying to show and share something about that subject: the thing we love about it; the thing that intrigues, excites or maybe even disturbs us; something we consider important or even urgent about it.

When I make a picture, I am trying to show something about the subject that has captivated me. It might be the curve of a river, the grandeur of a mountain range, the simple beauty of a feather held in a spider's web, the pattern of light and shadows on a wall in my home. They are

not images 'of' a phone box, a street sign, a tree, a lighthouse or whatever it might be. They are photographs 'about' these subjects that essentially communicate something about the way I feel about world, how it moves me and how I respond to it.

That's what I photograph for, but what about you? Perhaps you might want to one day be well known for your work, to have your work published or exhibited. You might be hoping to make a living from photography, or already be doing so, or to use your work to highlight social causes. Or perhaps you just like to record the things that fascinate you, and photography is the most convenient and accessible way of doing that.

There is nothing wrong with any of the above, but looking deeper, what is it for? What is it that drives you to go out with your camera in the first place? What is it that makes you stop and look closer, put your camera to your eye and press the button to make an image of it?

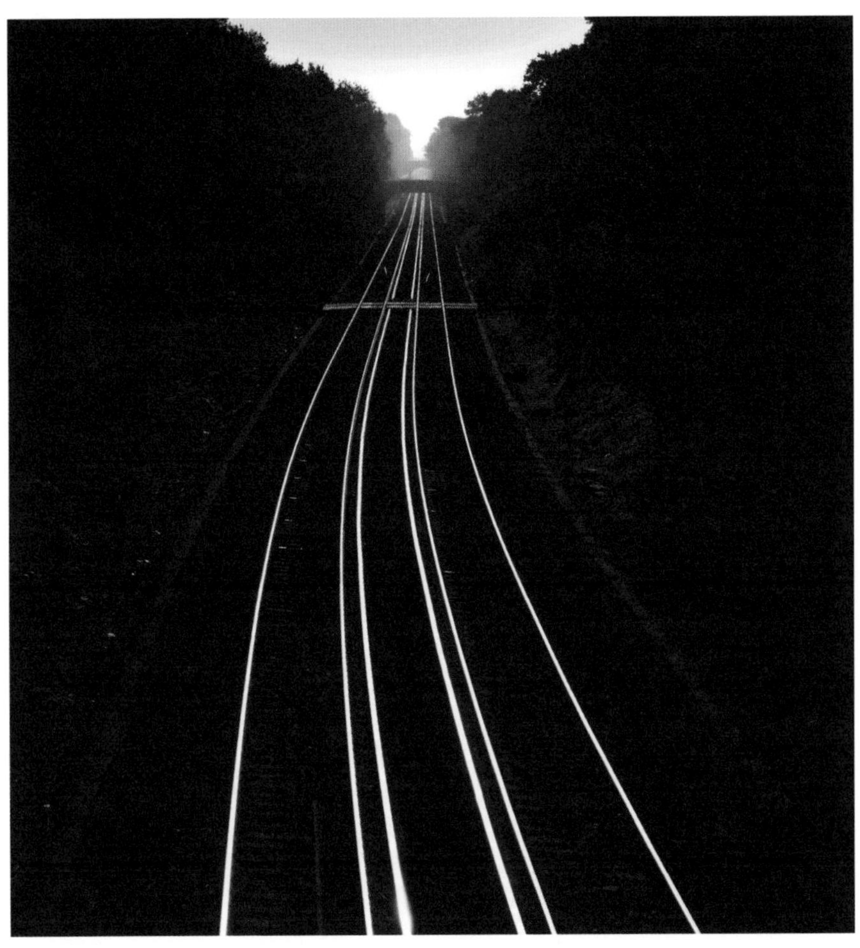

45   what do you photograph for?

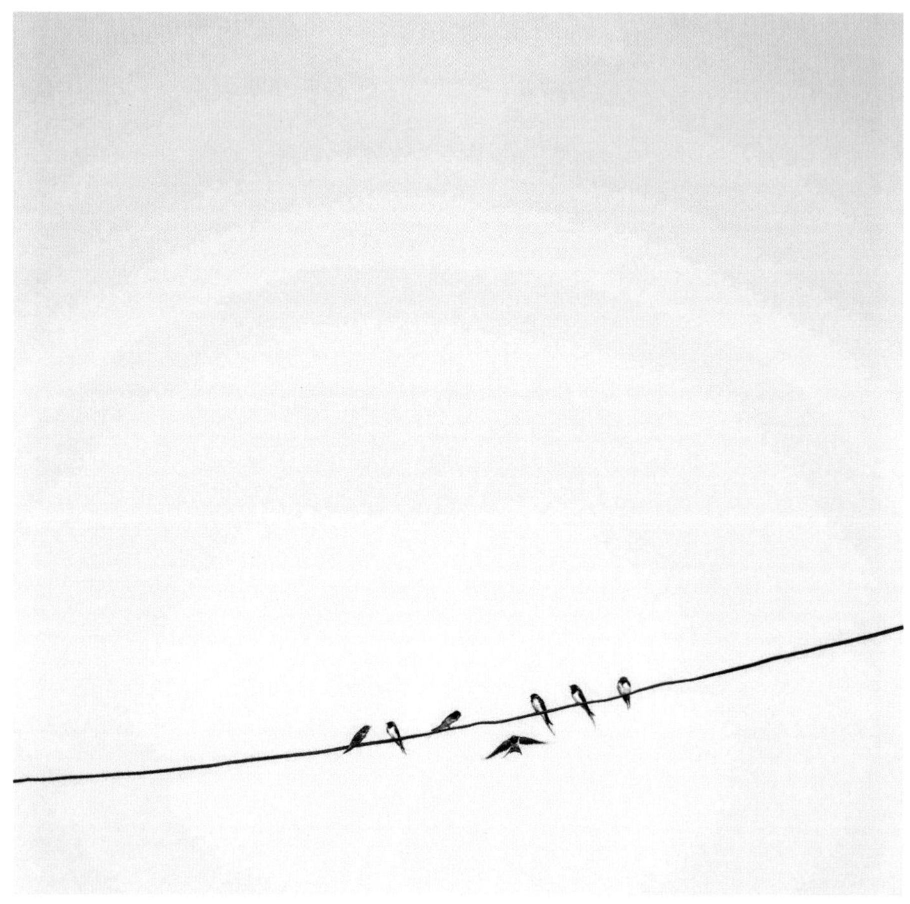

The war photographer Don McCullin has said, 'Photography for me is not looking, it's feeling. If you can't feel what you're looking at, then you're never going to get others to feel anything when they look at your pictures.' It's true that when you look at McCullin's work, you cannot help be moved, appalled, left reeling by the power of his images. The photographs you make may not change the world or divide popular opinion, but you make them because you feel something, even if you aren't fully aware of it at the time.

Essentially, we photograph because we feel something we think is worth communicating. That might be awe or wonder; it might be disgust, revulsion or outrage; it might be humour, empathy or admiration. It is telling your truth as you see it. It is saying to the world: 'This is me, this is what I noticed, what touched me, how I feel today, what I consider important – in this moment, this is my truth.'

Whatever subject you like to photograph, in whatever style, learning to pay greater attention not only to it but also to yourself is important. Whether you are photographing only for yourself or for others as well, you can't hope to approach the truth and communicate that truth clearly unless you can tell yourself what it means to you. It is as important as having your own opinion on issues that matter and not just parroting others' views.

I once went through a spell of slavishly photographing scenes that others had already made pictures of. I stood in the same place and used similar equipment to achieve the magnificent shots I admired, but the images always left me cold. The reason was that there was nothing of me in the images – I didn't have to do anything apart from rock up and stand there. I asked no questions of myself or my own response to the scene. I stood there, pressed the shutter and walked away.

'Photography for me is not looking, it's feeling. If you can't feel what you're looking at, then you're never going to get others to feel anything when they look at your pictures.'

—

Don McCullin

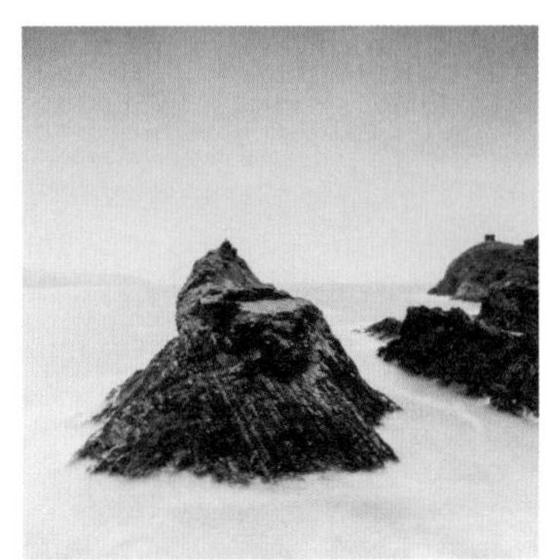

When I photograph now, I do so with my heart and soul, using every ounce of emotion I have in my body. It surprised me that the more I photographed in this way – attempting only to tell my truth – the more people responded.

I'm not entirely sure now why I was surprised. There are billions of people in the world, so it stands to reason that some of them will connect with the same things that move me, or find a truth of their own to relate to in an image – no matter how niche or specific to me it might feel. This is the beauty and power of art: to connect people via shared responses, and to help you realize you are never alone with your feelings.

This is why I believe it is important to be authentic when we make images; to be honest about who you are, what you see and how you see it. I don't like to erase the 'imperfections' or 'flaws' in my life or images because that is offering only a partial truth. I want to do better than that both for myself and for all those I share my work with. The images we make today are our legacy, our truth for generations to come.

There is responsibility in this, but if we take it, we are in the best position to understand the meaning not only of our work but also of our lives. Partly, therefore, I photograph to find peace within myself.

Why do you photograph?

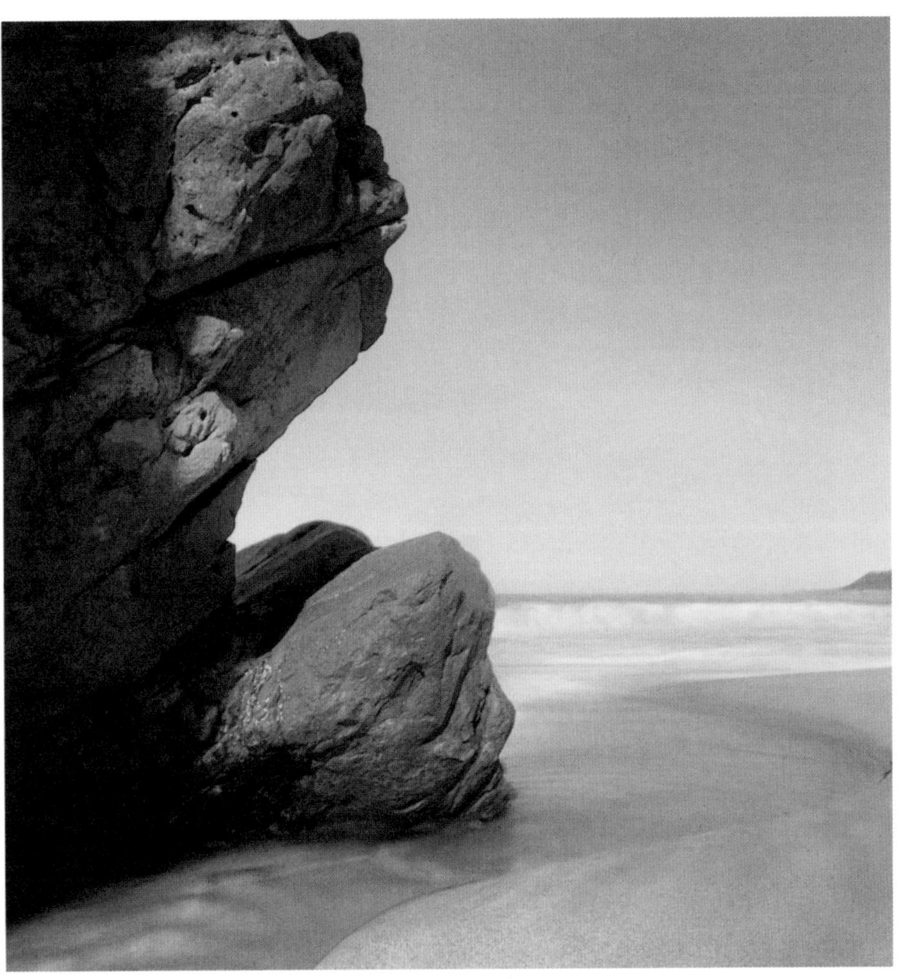

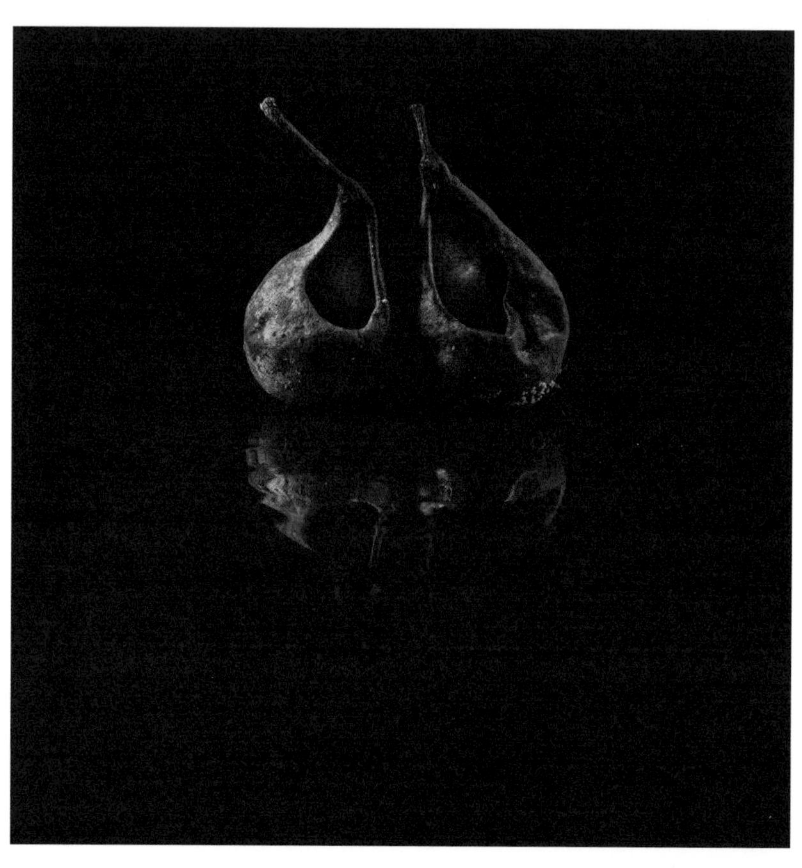

Learning to be gentle with yourself
will pay back dividends, including in
your photography.
—

social conditioning

Social conditioning is the process of learning to think, feel and act in ways that are approved by society or social groups. It would be hard to overstate the way this plays out in all of our lives.

It starts almost as soon as we are born, with our parents, grandparents and family friends all telling us what they believe is right: 'Colour inside the lines'; 'You need to do it like this if you want to get good grades'; 'Real boys don't cry...'

Of course, we can all benefit from learning from experience, and knowing the social conventions around different situations is important, but at the same time, the things that the authority figures in our lives tell us about how we should be, look and behave can embed themselves in our sense of self. Very quickly, we might decide we are not good at writing, that we're not creative enough to pursue an artistic career, that we don't have 'the eye' to take good photographs, and myriad other things.

The pressure of social conditioning probably peaks in our teenage years, when being accepted by our peers means not being picked last for a team or ostracized in the playground. If we abide by 'the rules', we are less likely to be bullied or humiliated because we don't stand out.

When out of school uniform (which they generally loathe), children often opt to wear another kind of uniform that their friends approve of – the same brand of trainers or jacket, a certain hairstyle, the attitudes they present to the world; they may even match the way they walk or carry their bags.

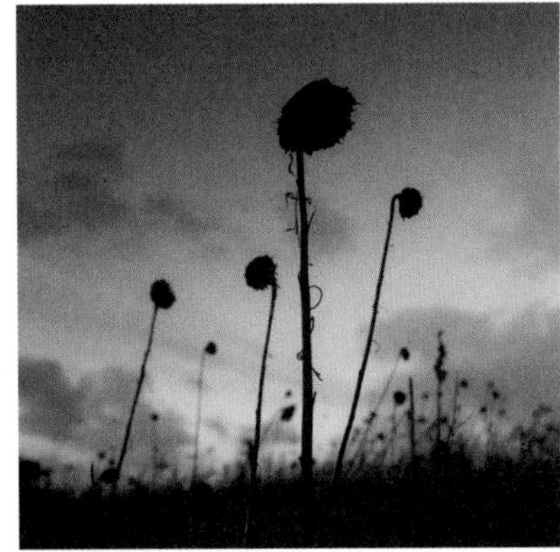

This instinct to fit in might not be as obvious in older generations – some people manage to shake it off as they get older, and some never seem to have acquired it in the first place – but it's usually just lurking in more insidious guises. It might be not speaking up when you disagree with a widely held opinion, not trying out a new hobby because none of your friends are interested in it, or feeling embarrassed about sharing a photo you made using a smart phone because you don't think people will consider it 'proper' photography.

Coupled to social conditioning is the question of self-confidence. In our teenage years, conforming with our peers is an easy way to avoid being called out for the choices we make around our tastes, interests and ideas about ourselves which are only just developing. You can usually identify the more confident members of a friendship group, because they will be the ones expressing more of their personality. This doesn't change with adulthood. Perhaps, in our head, we still hear the voice of a childhood detractor, ridiculing us for daring to believe we could be creative – which, as we have seen, just means being ourselves.

As with many other areas of our lives, social media generally hasn't helped things. It's made the pool of comparison infinitely wider, and in our desperation to be liked and approved of, we set ourselves up to second-guess what the whole internet likes and approves of. No wonder, then, that many people suffer from low self-esteem these days.

Once we start creating things, the joy this brings us can be a self-reinforcing process that will itself build our confidence. However, in order to stop worrying and start making, we need at least a little bit of belief in ourselves in the first place.

When I first started going to therapy, I was at a particularly low point in terms of self-confidence. My therapist always challenged my negative self-beliefs by asking me questions that forced me to be more realistic about myself. Whenever I said something negative about myself, she challenged me by asking whether what I had just said was objectively true, beyond any doubt. The answer was invariably no – it was never absolutely 100 percent true. She then got me to write down the things I felt I was good at – a self-gratitude list. What I included was definitely a bit woolly to start with – things like 'I am good at breathing in and out', 'I'm good at listening' and 'I make nice coffee' – but it's okay to start small when you are working to re-establish your confidence and shake off the negative voice that comes from your social conditioning. Even in writing this book, I've had to sit myself down and write some positive things about myself.

Learning to be gentle with yourself will pay back dividends, including in your

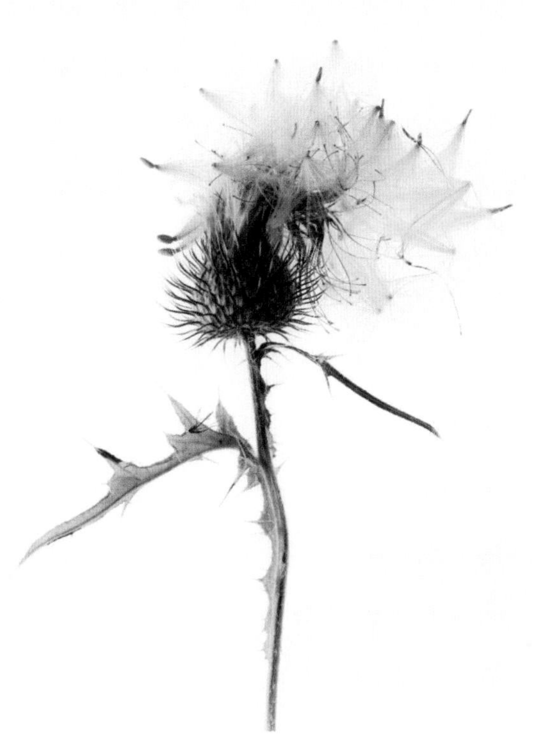

photography. If you are kind to yourself, you are less likely to approach your subjects with a harsh or judgemental attitude. I now find it impossible to think of any subject as 'not good enough'. Just as with self-reflection, if I'm disappointed with what a scene, location or subject is offering, it's because I'm coming to it with too many of my own expectations instead of taking the time to really see my subject and notice its qualities. Now, I look at each fresh subject as having its own unique being with quirks and scars that speak of its particular experiences in life and give it its personality.

Give yourself permission to photograph the world as you see it without worrying about anyone else's approval.

Very few great photographers worried about what others would think of their work – many didn't share their images or even develop the finished rolls of film, because for them it was all about the process and the act of seeing.

And we like their images not because they conform to convention, and repeat pre-approved ideas, but because they stand out from it. They show us something new about the world, something we hadn't thought of before, something we recognize as true.

We can do that with our images, too. All those traits that we tried to downplay in our school years – the things about us that make us different – are what will allow us to make art that other people might connect with.

The first step is to give yourself permission to express yourself in any way you wish. This sounds easy, and in essence it is, but it is also challenging.

My first suggestion is to write a letter to yourself, giving yourself permission to approach your photography (or art more broadly) in a way that pleases you. If others enjoy it, that's a bonus, but as long as you enjoy it, that is all that matters.

The magic of written permission is incredible. Write the letter by hand, put it in an envelope and address it to yourself. You could even go as far as posting it to yourself! Then, keep the letter in your camera bag or handbag, notebook or

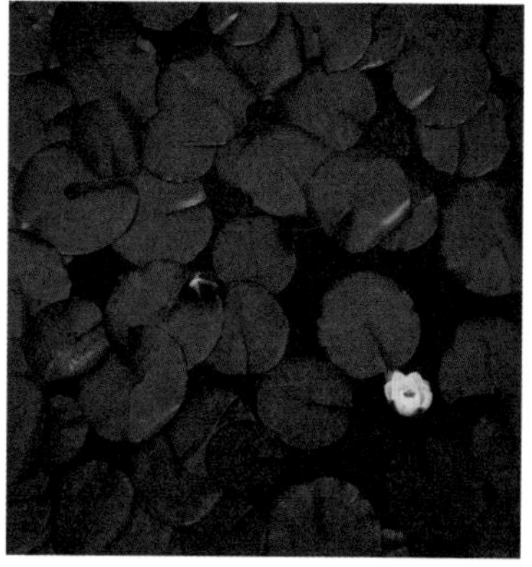

wallet so that you always have it with
you whenever you go out to make
photographs. I often refer to mine
(written in 2016) when I'm out making
pictures and find myself wondering how
and what others might photograph in
the same location.

My second suggestion is a ten-minute
challenge, for which you will need a timer
with an alarm – your phone is perfect.
Set the timer for one minute and start
walking. When the timer goes off, reset it
for another minute, and without moving
your feet, make a picture of something
– anything that catches your eye – before
the timer goes off again. Repeat the
process until you have five photos in five
different locations.

When engaged in this simple exercise
you will rarely be in position to make
pictures of obviously photogenic subjects;
instead, you will start to make pictures
of things that catch your eye. By asking
yourself why that view, that subject,
caught your attention, you will begin to
develop confidence in your photographic
eye without even thinking about it.

The other thing this exercise is great
for is getting you used to stopping and
looking without being worried about
what anyone else thinks. That said, these
days we are so familiar with people
photographing all sorts of things that
chances are no one will take any notice
of you anyway.

a word about creativity (or, am I good enough?)

'But I'm rubbish at taking pictures!' is something I've often heard when someone has been asked to take a photo on somebody else's behalf. Even if our reaction is less extreme, we may still experience a pang of terror when someone gives us this responsibility. In our minds, we've failed to meet their expectations before we've even tried.

It is very easy to form poor opinions of our own creative skills, especially as we get older, because we don't want to look like failures – or idiots for trying and failing. Our inhibitions around creativity can become so pronounced that we are afraid to ask the basic questions to get ourselves started.

This has become even more prevalent with so many images being shared on social media. Suddenly, everyone looks like a pro photographer or a model – how can we compete? Of course, deep down we know that our friends and the people we follow online share only their best shots, which they may have spent hours editing beforehand. We don't see the retakes, the closed eyes, the sloping horizons or gurning faces.

The same is true of professional photographers working at the highest levels. *Magnum Contact Sheets* by Kristen Lubben is a compilation of work

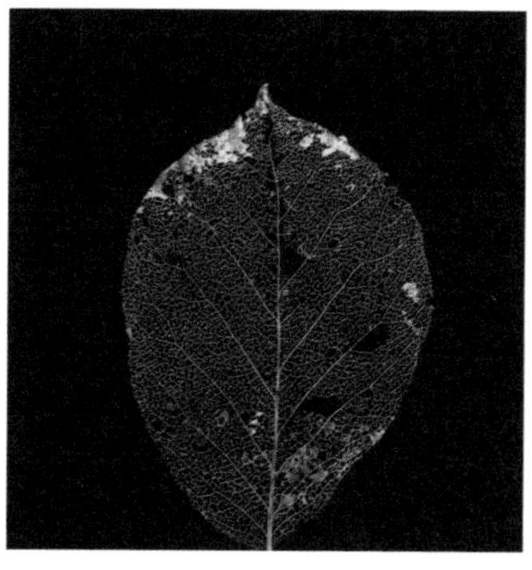

from the world's finest photographers. The book shows every frame they made around some of their best-known works – it's eye-opening to see how they arrive at the shot that defines a moment.

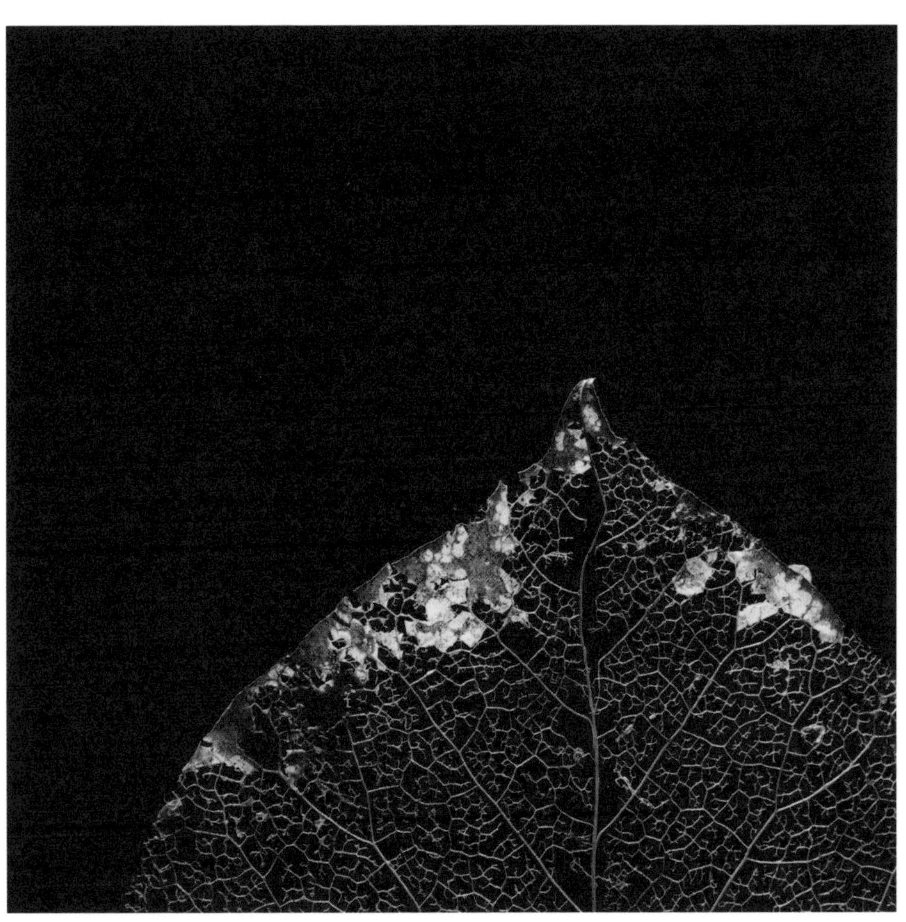

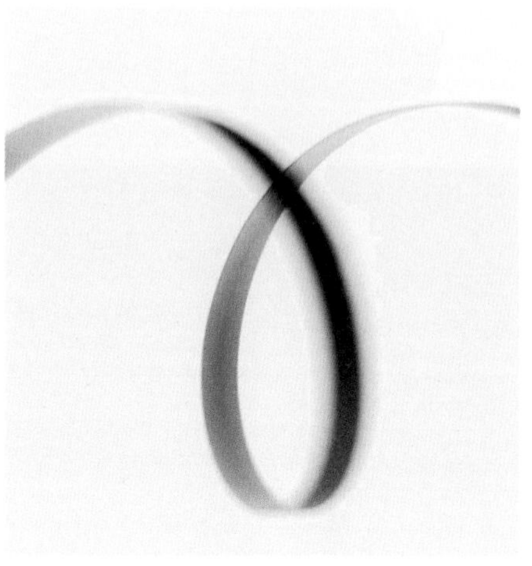

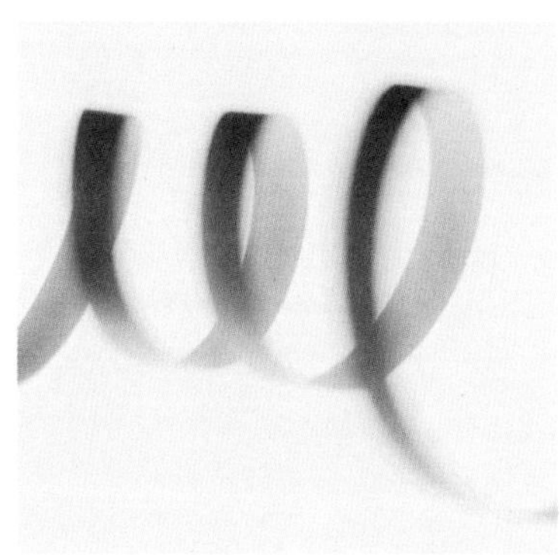

But let's unpack creativity a little. The *Oxford English Dictionary* defines creativity as the ability to transcend traditional ideas, rules, patterns, relationships and the like, and to create meaningful new ideas, forms, methods and interpretations.

Judgements around the *quality* of what we produce may come later, but creativity itself isn't defined in terms of 'good' and 'bad'. Essentially, being creative means to produce something original. And since every one of us is unique, it means the best way to find our creativity isn't by looking at what other people are doing and comparing our work to theirs, but by spending time discovering what we like to look at and make.

You and I are different: we've had different parents, friends, educations and experiences at work, and we've come from different cultures – even if that means only that the neighbourhoods you have lived in have been different from the ones I have. It therefore stands to reason that we will see the world differently and be attracted to different subjects.

When I see something that catches my eye, I know it is uniquely for me. Even if someone else sees it at the same time, or even if it's been photographed many times before, I will photograph it differently, according to the particular thing I have noticed about it and the particular way I choose to frame it.

Forgetting about technical aspects for a moment, half the art of photography is learning to actively see the world around us (we'll talk more about this in Chapter 3), but the other half of it is about learning to see ourselves – what we like, and what moves us in one way or another. Ask yourself:

- Do I enjoy making pictures?
- What do I enjoy making pictures of?
- What do I enjoy about making pictures?

The first one might seem like a given, but it's worth checking in with yourself.

Producing images you or others consider brilliant isn't nearly as important as enjoying the process. Technique comes with practice; the more pictures you make, the better you will become at handling your equipment, and the more innovative and effective your images will become as you start to challenge yourself.

By asking yourself what subjects you most enjoy photographing, and what you enjoy most about the process, not only are you making it a lot easier for yourself to answer that first question with a 'Yes', but you are also beginning the serious work of learning what you want to show or see or say in your art. The very first thing you should ask yourself is: 'What caused me to stop?' It might be light hitting a leaf, the enigma of a path curving out of view, the meeting of two flowers... Whatever it was that caught your eye, this is what you are photographing.

Not everyone will like your images or find the same things interesting as you do, but that is the point.

Wherever your photography journey takes you, I am an advocate of keeping things simple and building strong foundations. The act of seeing something that moves you and being able to make a picture of it is the start of a creative adventure that never stops giving.

ASSIGNMENT: IT'S CHILD'S PLAY

We are all born creative, and every one of us has creativity flowing in our veins. Reconnecting with our inner child can release this creativity.

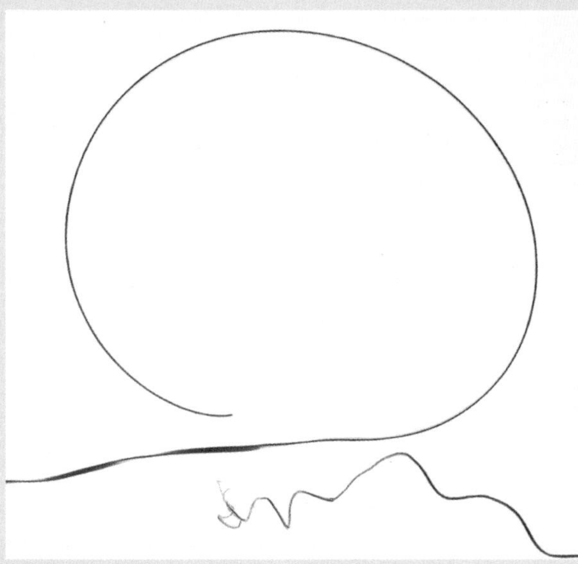

So many of us think we are not creative, or that we don't take good photos. But these ideas are just the confines of our social conditioning speaking.

The American photographer Minor White once said: 'Innocence of eye has a quality of its own. It means to see as a child sees, with freshness and acknowledgment of the wonder.' As we get older, we typically become more self-conscious about our creative endeavours, and grow more concerned about people judging what we do as childish or amateurish, or that they may laugh or mock us. Sometimes, this imagined pressure can be so great that it stops us from creating at all, and when we try creating something, it can prevent us from taking any pleasure in doing so.

Learning to see with a child's wonder means losing the inhibitions you've built up like walls around you to protect yourself against others' judgement and criticism. It means letting yourself be excited by the world around you; letting yourself look with such curiosity that a quick glance simply isn't enough, and you have to explore further, in any way that seems right.

For me, photography is about the relationship I have with the subject. And this works only when there is a meaningful connection between us. To reach that point, I often like to ask my subject questions such as 'What are you trying to share with me?' This is where a childlike attitude can be helpful – to look at something I might have seen hundreds of times before as though it's the first time I've ever noticed it.

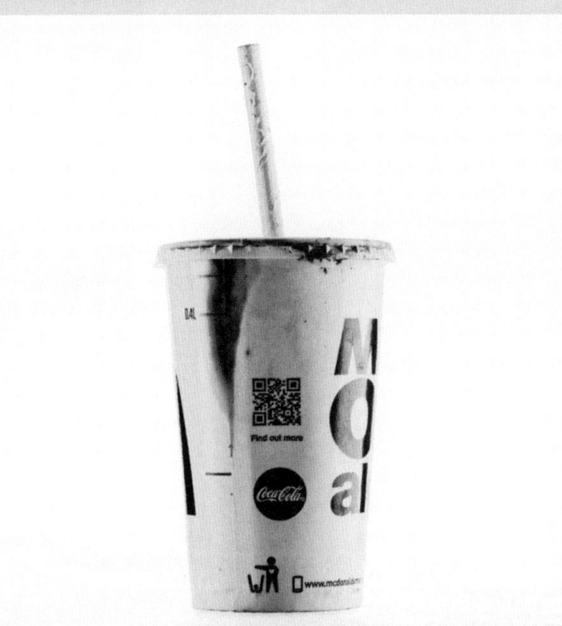

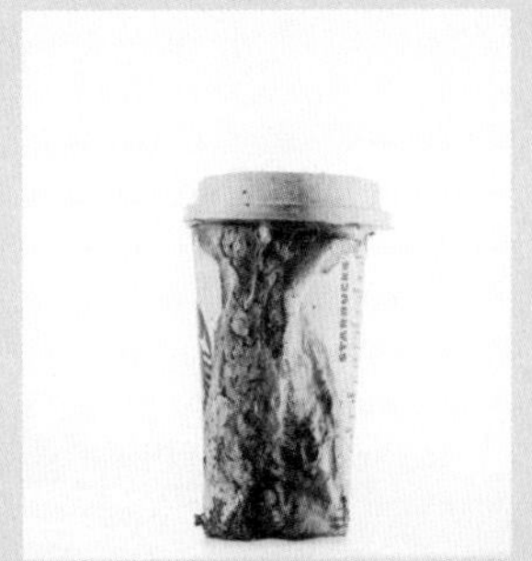

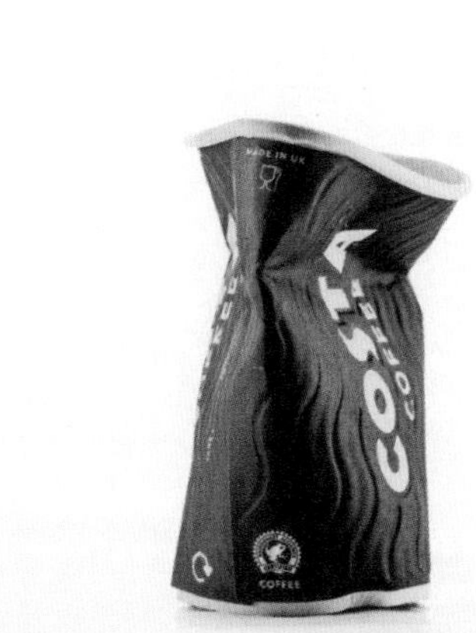

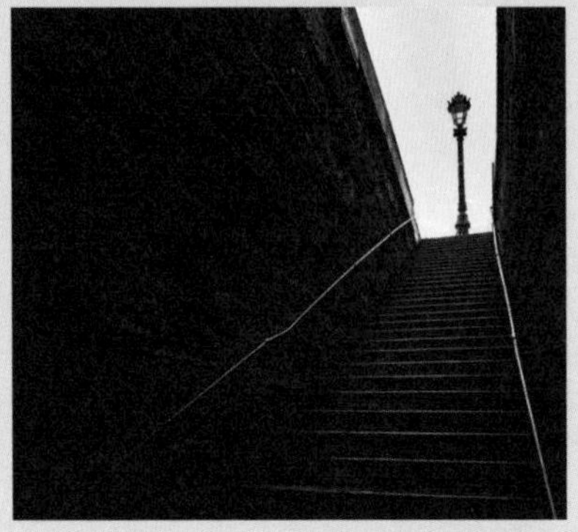 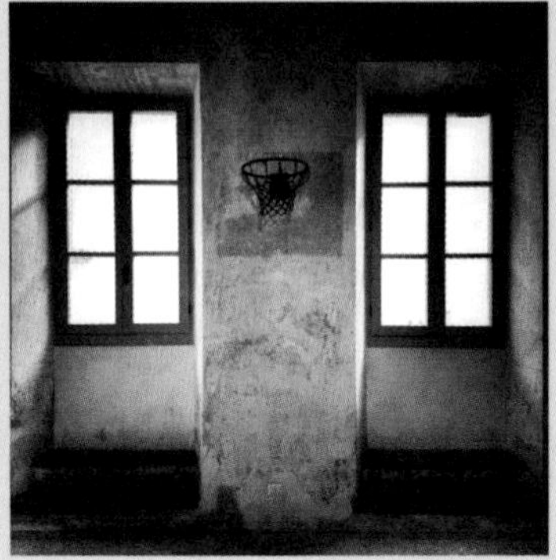

One quite literal way you can embrace the child's perspective is to try shooting only from a lower position. Adults see the world from a perspective of between approximately 1.5m and 1.8m (4ft 11in and 5ft 11in) from the ground. What if you were to lie down to make pictures, get on your hands and knees, or sit down? If you crouch down in a crowded place, you will likely feel somewhat intimated by the size of those around you and the speed at which they are moving, and I guarantee you will also notice a lot of new things because of this change in perspective.

Alternatively, you could stand on a chair or ladder to see what the world looks like from a giant's point of view.

This might sound silly, but I often suggest to clients taking part in my workshops that they adjust their height to suit the subject. Rather than photograph a dog from their own height, they could try putting themselves in the dog's shoes, so to speak, and seeing how the world looks from its perspective. The same goes for children, grass, flowers and many other subjects. It is astonishing how such a small change can get you out of your own thoughts and help you connect with a subject in a new way.

In any case, photography should be fun and playful. There are far too many photographers who take themselves too seriously, who forget to smile and enjoy their art. Making a picture can be as simple as 'I saw this and liked it enough to stop, pause and try to capture the thing I liked about it in an image.' It doesn't have to have a meaning deeper than this – although photography made this way often does carry a deep meaning or convey a sense of metaphor.

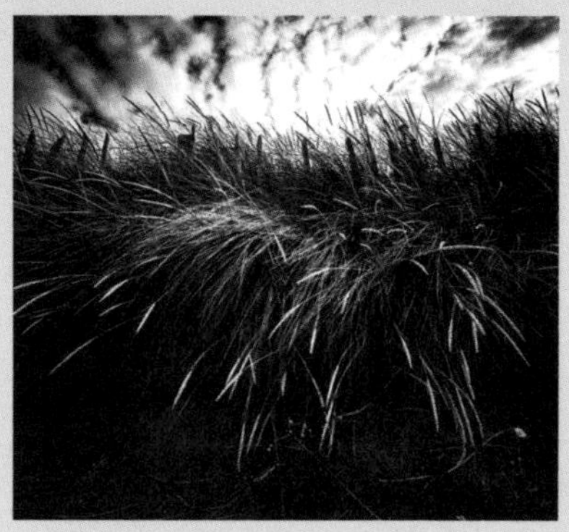 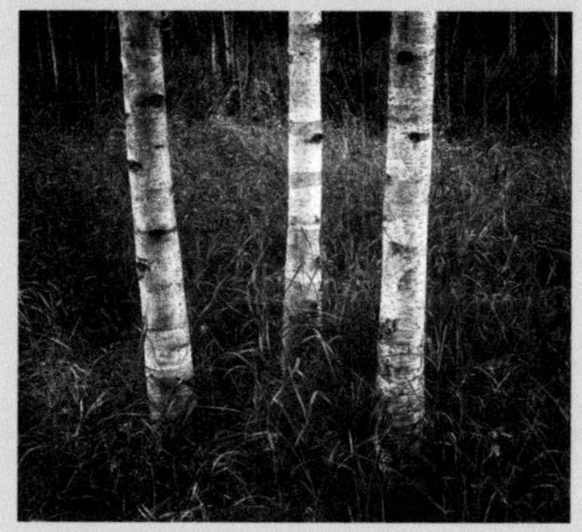

Children are often very open when they create or play; frequently, they expose their worries or fears through games. As adults, we learn to hide negative emotions, putting on armour to face the world. But what if we embraced our vulnerability and learned to express it in a creative way?

When we make a photograph, we are opening ourselves to the possibility of being moved by something. When we share that photograph, we are sharing something about ourselves. That is pretty vulnerable, but it's powerful, too.

'Vulnerability is
the birthplace of innovation,
creativity and change.'
—
Brené Brown

equipment – and how to use it

Photographic equipment can be a thorny subject, since practically every photographer has an opinion on what camera to use, which lens to shoot with and what kit you should always carry. My philosophy, however, is very simple: I believe the best camera is the one you have with you – that's why most of my photography, including the images in this book, is made with my phone, and I'm not remotely ashamed of that.

For me, photography is responding to something that catches your eye or your heart; the equipment you have is only a means of storing that moment until you decide what to do with it.

Modern smartphones have an incredible array of tools to make photography more accessible to those daunted by knobs and dials – myself included. Smartphone technology is also improving all the time. In recent years, while the basic interface and software haven't changed that much, phone manufacturers have been investing a great deal of attention in upgrading the capacities of their lenses and sensors.

Whatever camera you use, the more comfortable you are with it, the more confident you will be in responding to something when it happens. In an ideal situation, your tools will become an extension of yourself, so you use them automatically and they don't get in the way of the connection between you and your subject.

For this reason, I always want to encourage people to learn the basics of photography and become familiar with the controls offered by their camera, no matter how untechnical they consider themselves. This is not going to be an instruction book on how to operate your camera – not only do I not have the room, but, if you are anything like me, you will learn by doing rather than reading. If you want to delve more deeply into any aspect of photography, the rabbit hole will be potentially endless, but here are the things I think you need to know if you are to get the most out of your art. This advice will be relevant to any kind of camera you use.

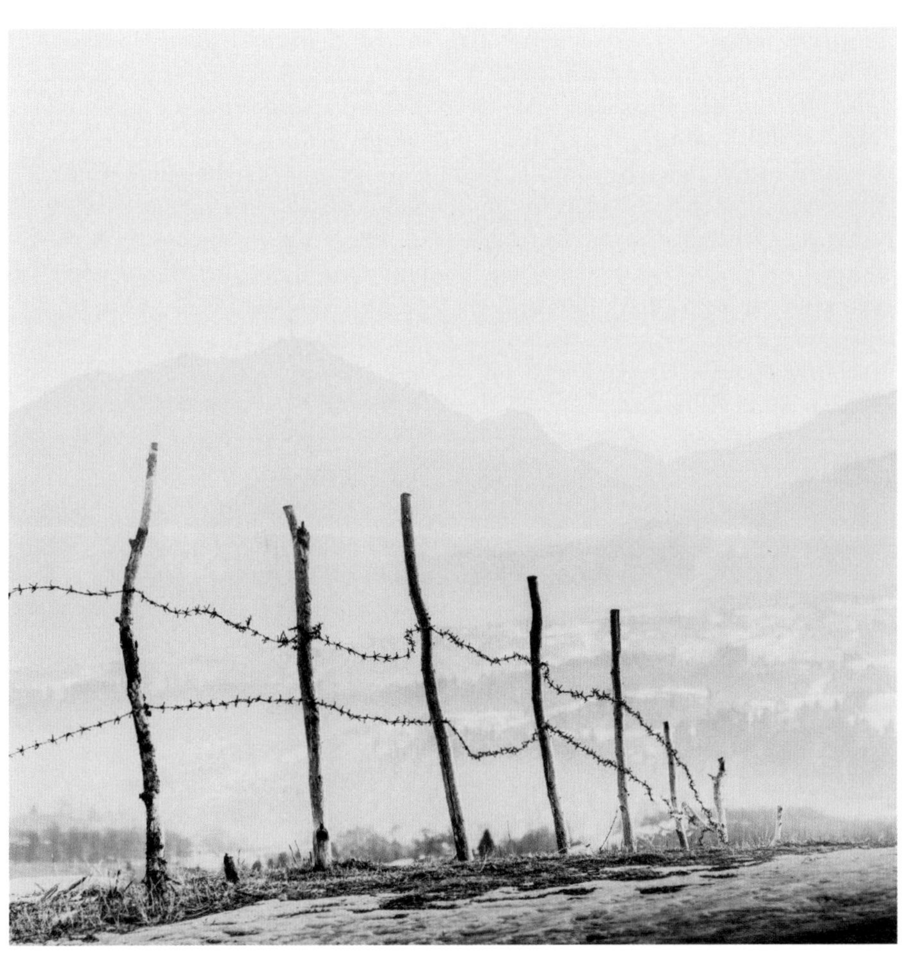

 equipment – and how to use it

Learning to compose your image to focus on the subject – to include what you want and exclude what you find distracting – is a huge step in the right direction. Move your body and explore different distances and angles to photograph your subject from. As we have seen, just the simple act of changing your position can give you a radically new perspective (see pages 60–3). You can also try cropping existing images to explore new compositions, although heavy crops will affect the image quality.

There's an idea that, in good photography, everything has to be sharp. However, a little softness can suggest movement, add to atmosphere or blur out distracting elements. How much of a scene is in focus depends on the aperture of your camera as well as the distance between elements you're photographing. A wide-open aperture gives a shallow depth of field, meaning less is in focus, helping to isolate a subject in a scene. A narrow aperture will have the reverse effect.

Sometimes, when there's not much light in a scene, you might need to support your camera with a tripod or by propping it up and using the timer function (or a remote trigger) to make your photograph. The longer the shutter is open, the more chance that any movement from either the subject or the person holding the camera will introduce blur.

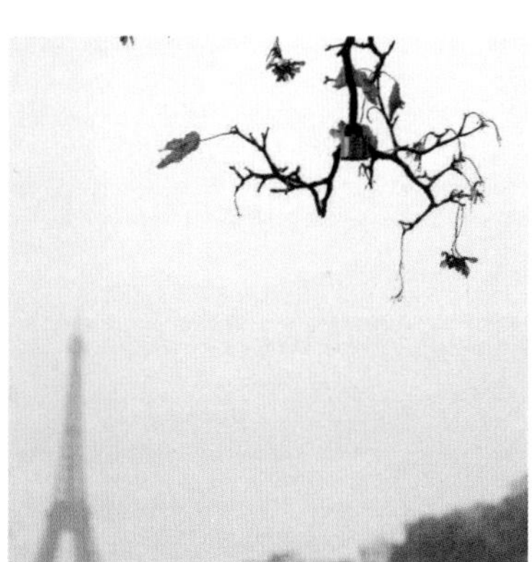

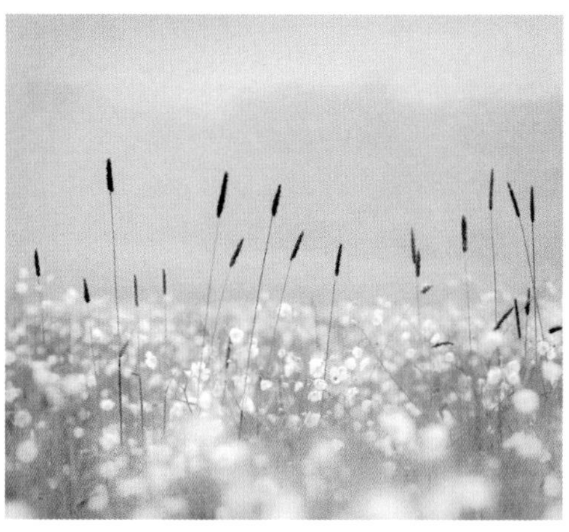

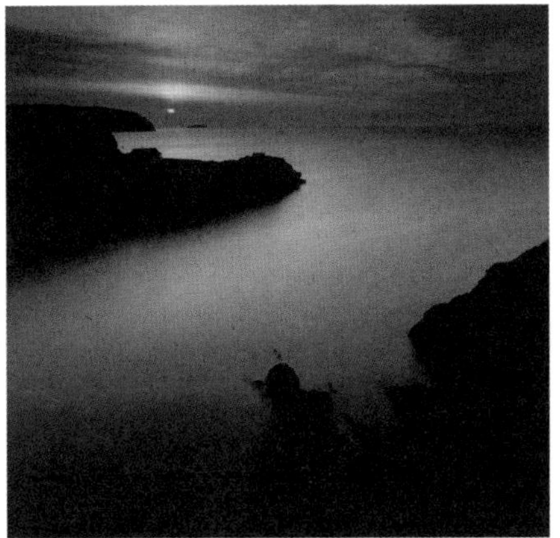 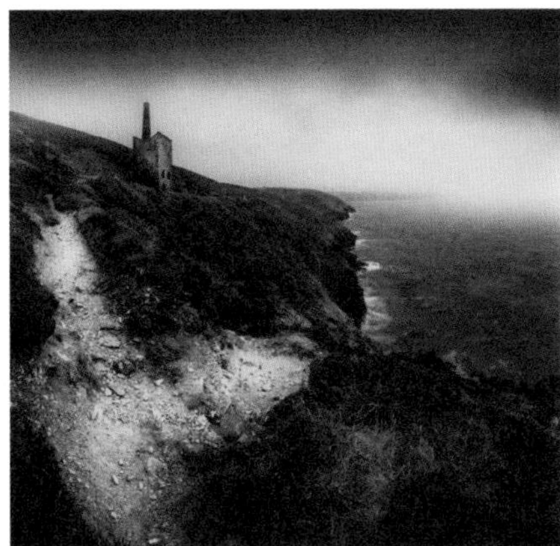

EXPOSURE

Controlling how light or dark your image appears is the next step along the way. How dark or light an image is, and whether it has high contrast or consists of similar tones, greatly affects how it will be viewed. Overall brighter or paler shots can appear more cheerful or peaceful, while darker or more shadowy shots can seem intimate or oppressive. A high contrast between light and dark, known as *chiaroscuro*, can be dramatic or sculptural – you can use areas of shadow and light to direct a viewer's attention. Bear in mind that the camera records information in a different way from the human eye; working out how your camera sees the world is a big step in terms of learning how to make the images you want.

See pages 108–15 for more on light.

LENSES

While lenses might be some photographers' favourite subject of discussion, the most important thing to know about them is that different focal lengths affect how much of a scene is included in the frame (known as the field of view). The three basic focal lengths are:

- **Telephoto:** A long focal length (at least 85mm) with a narrow field of view is great for picking out a subject at some distance.
- **Medium/50mm:** A street photographer's favourite. The field of view of a 50mm lens is seen as the closest to the human eye, therefore giving the most 'natural' representation.
- **Wide-angle:** As the name suggests, the shortest focal length gives the widest view of the scene. Opposite to a telephoto lens's ability to isolate, this can give a scene an immersive feel.

SMARTPHONES AND LENSES

Traditionally, smartphones had just one lens which – because the phone is flat and the focal length is necessarily very short – was a wide-angle lens. These days, however, many phones come with additional lenses that offer longer focal lengths, and there are also special adaptors you can buy. While all lenses will have their limitations, it can be a great thing to challenge yourself to work within those limits and get the most out of the lens you have. On the other hand, adding extra lenses to your kitbag means having extra decisions to make, which can often confuse things.

LEARN TO ENJOY IT

Even if you have a state-of-the-art mirrorless camera you want to master, there is no shame in using its fully automatic mode to begin with. You will still be learning about these concepts, but without having to worry about all the dials and settings and options available to you. Concentrate first on getting comfortable with the basics, so that your equipment starts to feel like an extension of yourself, rather than a cumbersome tool.

Remember that photography should be a pleasure. We all want to be experts immediately, but I recommend that you take a moment to enjoy where you're at right now. Being a beginner can be the very best part of the journey, because there's a beautiful sense of possibility when you are just setting out. The fun part of being a beginner is just experimenting, asking yourself what might happen if you try shooting like this or try doing that. It can be much harder to maintain this openness when you're well established in your craft and think you already know what you're doing.

I would also encourage you to make photographs every day. By far, this is the best way to learn. The more photographs you make, the more quickly you will gain experience, confidence and technique.

Every image you make is a valuable part of the process, so never be afraid of trying things out. By their nature, experiments aren't supposed to work every time, so embrace the mistakes and supposed failures as well as the successes – that is the key to learning.

I've been making pictures since I was 14. That's a pretty long time now, yet I am still constantly learning new things, and I love nothing more than making a mistake. There are no better learning opportunities than the mistakes we make – as long as we can see them this way. (See more on constructive criticism on pages 184–7.)

USE YOUR HEART

My final piece of advice about equipment is to photograph from your heart, not your head. Technical prowess doesn't naturally result in a great photograph, and vice versa. Take a look at Robert Capa's

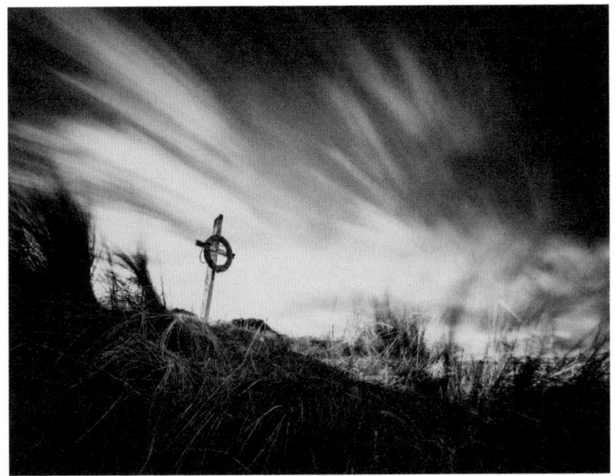

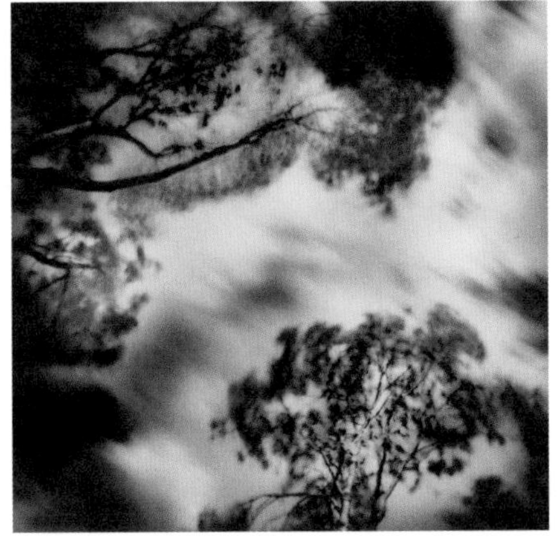

photographs of the D-Day landings on
Omaha Beach: they are blurry and at
odd angles; some are too dark and others
too light – not for nothing did he title
his memoir *Slightly Out of Focus* – yet
they profoundly convey the essence of
the experience. These images inspired
the beginning of Steven Spielberg's film
Saving Private Ryan, and Capa has
been referred to as the 'greatest war
photographer ever'.

Photography is emotional. Yes, there
are technical aspects to it, but just as with
any form of communication, no amount
of technical precision can make up for
a lack of feeling, and no technical
'imperfection' ever prevents someone
from being moved when an image
resonates with something true.

ASSIGNMENT: GET FAMILIAR

Here's a set of exercises that you can work through to start mastering your equipment with minimal effort.

Using whatever camera you like, try making a series of pictures of a simple, static subject, such as a flower or a jug. The subject and camera will remain the same, but all the images will be different. Ideally, do this assignment in daylight.

1 Position your subject so that it is in the centre of the frame, and make a photo with any framing you like.

2 Repeat step 1, but turn your camera 90 degrees – so, if your first photo was made in a portrait orientation, it will now be landscape, and vice versa.

3 Approach your subject from the same angle, but this time place your subject anywhere but the centre of the frame. Try it at the extreme edge of the frame, in a top or bottom corner, or a third of the way in. You can turn your camera portrait or landscape as you choose.

4 Now, identify which direction the light is coming from (e.g. the sun or a window) and move either your subject or your own position to make an image from the opposite angle to before, or as close as possible. If you were photographing towards the sun, for example, now try standing between the sun and your subject.

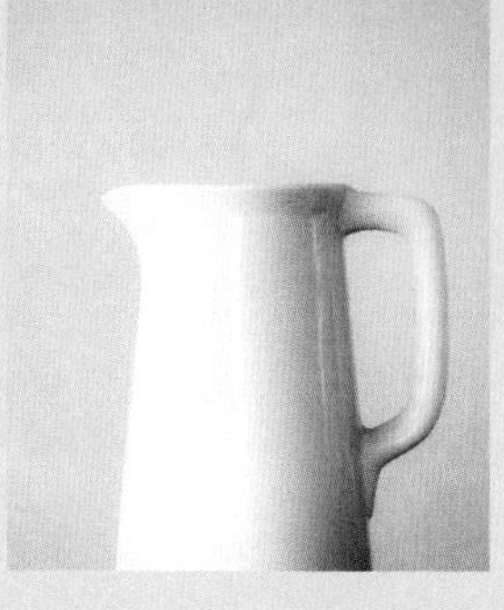

5 From whatever position you like, try making the image appear lighter and darker with your in-camera tools. On most modern phones, you can do this via the screen by tapping the screen and sliding your finger up and down. On a DSLR/mirrorless camera, there will be an exposure compensation dial; the + increases the exposure and makes the image lighter, and the − decreases the exposure and makes it darker.

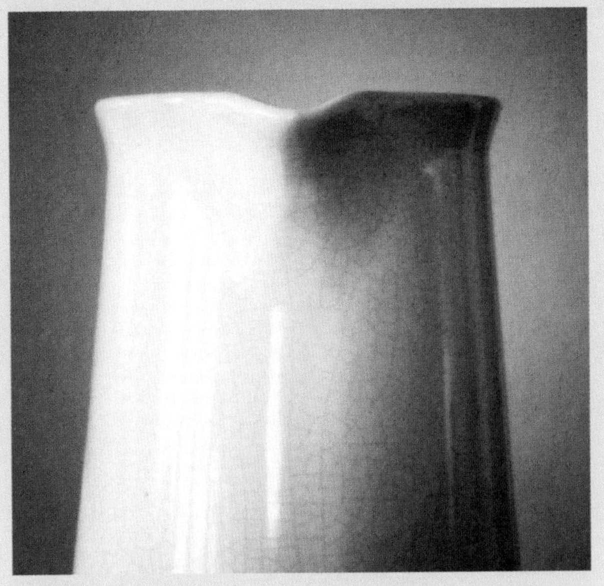

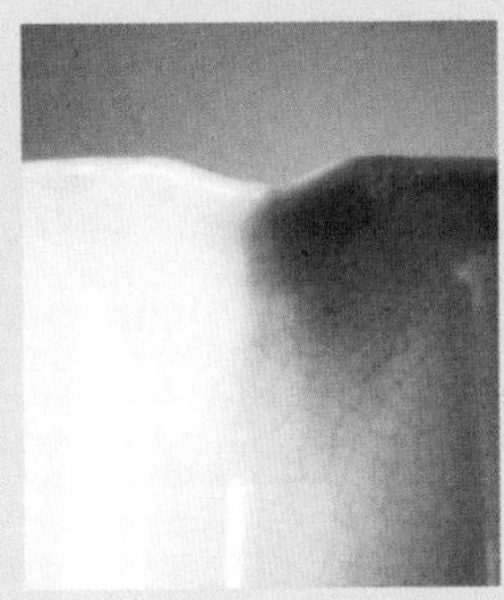

6 Now try changing the point of focus. In automatic mode, your camera or phone will try to focus on your subject, which it will identify either by its contrast from the background or from its central position (if you have chosen to centre it). On a phone, you can change the point of focus by tapping a different area in the screen; on a camera, you will need to set it to Manual Focus, and adjust the lens's focus ring. If you're fairly close to your subject, the effect may be minimal – but what if you get even closer or take a few steps back? Do you notice any change?

7 How much of a scene is in focus is known as the depth of field, and you can manipulate this when you want to make your subject stand out against a busy, distracting background. On a camera, set the dial to Aperture Priority mode (Av) and adjust the aperture (using the ring or buttons) from the highest number (e.g. f/22) to the lowest (e.g. f/1.4), making an image at each increment. You will notice that the lower the f-number, the less of the scene is in focus. This is an optical effect linked to the aperture size, which you can reproduce on a phone camera by switching to Portrait mode.

Just like that, you have learned some of the key concepts of photography. You can repeat this exercise and add to it in any way you like. To get the most from it, try keeping a journal or just make some notes on what you've learned from each image you made. What choice of framing and orientation did you prefer and why? What did you notice about the quality of the light at different angles, and what was the effect on the image?

Take the exercise further in little steps. Try zooming in or experimenting with editing the image afterwards, by adjusting the crop or exposure, making it black and white or adding a colour cast. Try the same exercise at night, holding your device very still or setting it up on a tripod or makeshift support and setting a

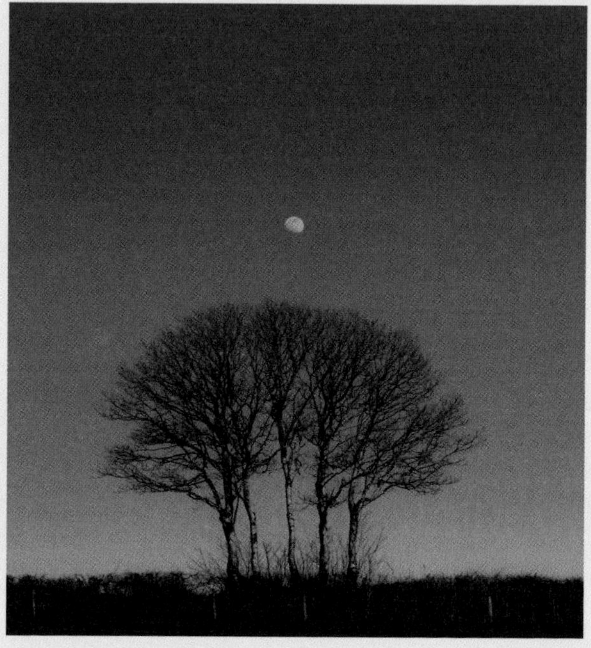

timer. Try adding some artificial lights. Just experiment – you won't break anything, and you will soon become confident at using your equipment in all sorts of settings and scenarios.

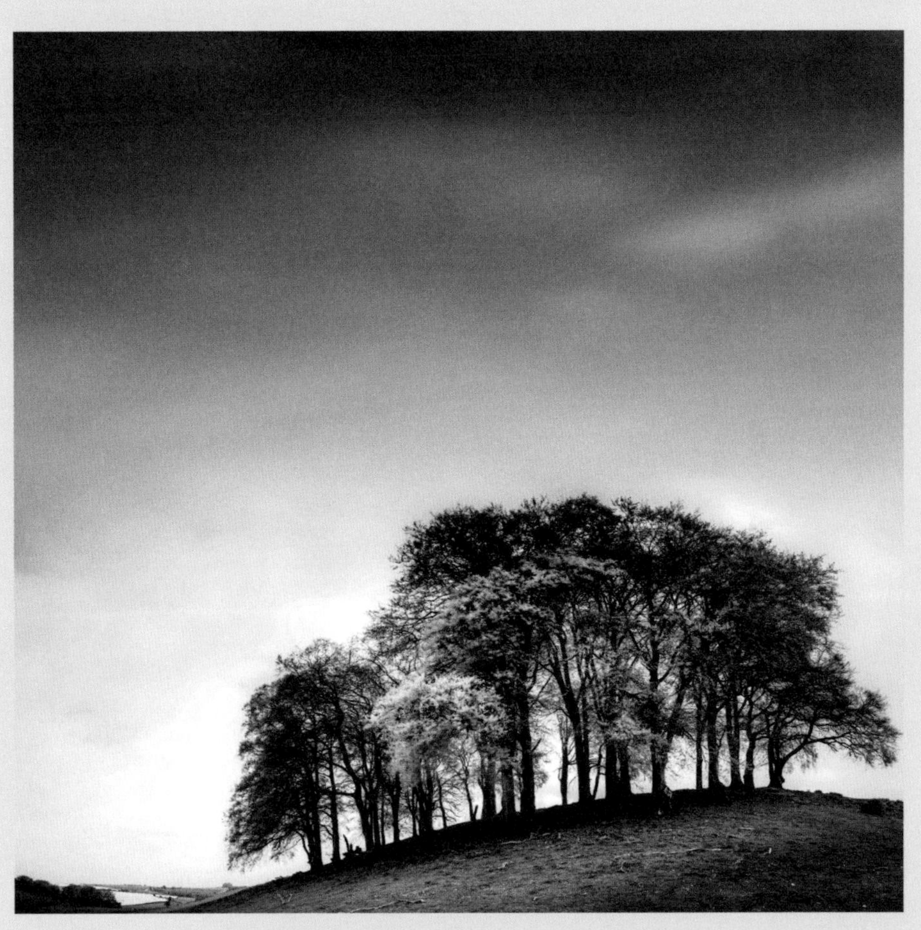

Just experiment – you won't break anything.
—

3

learning to see

the key skill of photography

It might seem odd or obvious to say that seeing is the key skill of photography. What can that mean, when those of us who are blessed with sight use our eyes every day?

In our daily lives, as we move through the world, most of the time we're not paying much attention to the things around us. Our surroundings are generally so familiar that we can navigate through them while looking down at our phones or lost in thought, only tuning in with annoyance when we bump into someone or something. One of the reasons adverts use every trick in the book to be 'eye-catching' is for exactly this reason – it's no small feat to capture our attention long enough for us to absorb the information a brand wants to communicate about its product.

Seeing cannot be just a cursory glance. In the sense I am talking about, seeing involves patience, effort, curiosity and stillness. It requires us to choose to spend a while contemplating something outside ourselves.

It is also a self-reflective state. Seeing means discerning what is important to you among all the visual noise and confusion. When you see something that makes you want to reach for your phone or camera, even if your first thought is 'That would make a great photograph!', if you examine your reactions more deeply, you will realize that there was something that came even before that: a gut reaction.

Seeing means learning about yourself too – discovering what your heart truly resonates with.

—

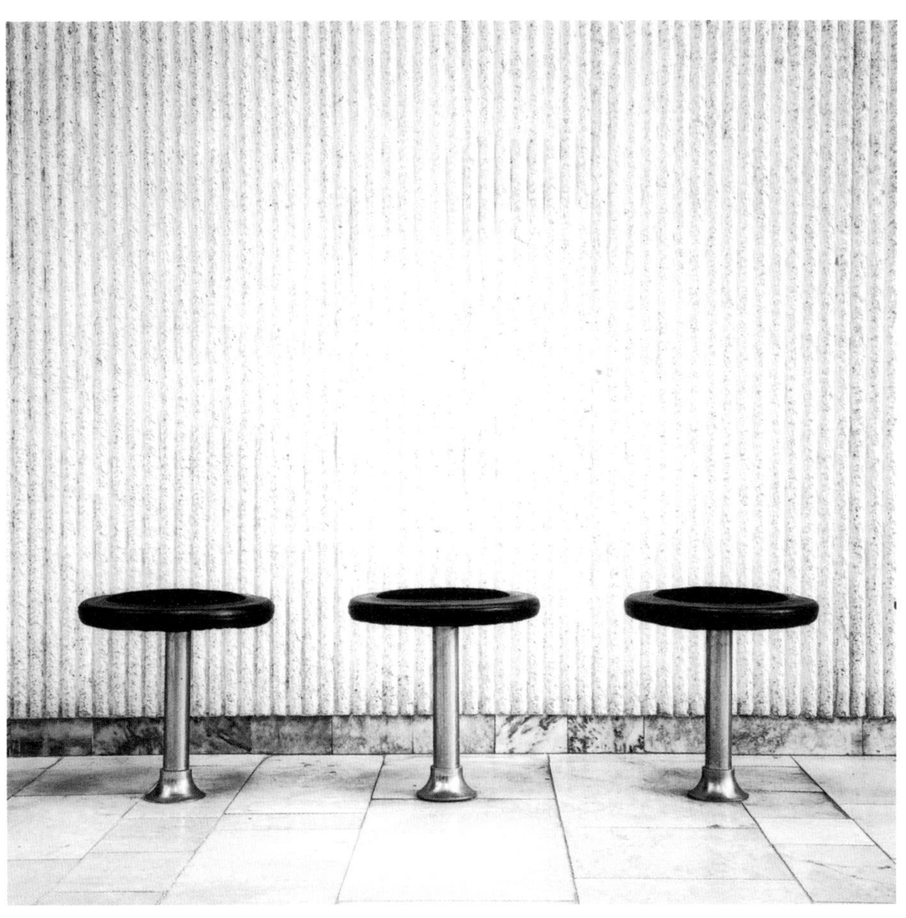

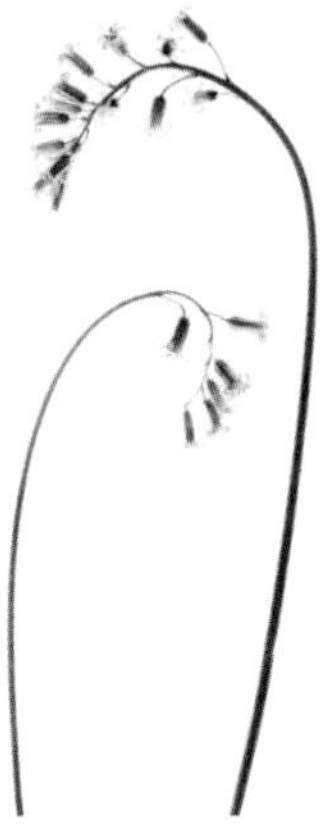

Seeing with regard to mindful photography is really allowing yourself to be fascinated by something – not to be entertained or seek reward or kudos but, much like a good conversation, just for the value of the exchange. It involves cultivating a restful, reflective state of mind, allowing you and your subject to just be – without the need for anything else. This reflective way of seeing is calming, allowing both your mind and body to slow down from the hyperstimulated state we often find ourselves in.

All this sounds straightforward, but it takes effort to calm our habitual, fidgety need to be doing something, and to quiet the inner voices that get in the way of our paying proper attention.

Often, we will be in our heads when we think we are seeing, allowing our imagination to come into play. It is very easy to imagine what you are seeing in front of you as opposed to what is actually there. When we think we are seeing something but get home to find our images are disappointing, this is the result of looking and then allowing the imagination to draw us an image of the ideal. The camera can see only what it has been pointed at; we have to drive it, to make the effort to see what it is showing us rather than expect it to conjure up the vision inside our head.

My mum would often comment that
the photographs she made of me and my
brother on our summer holiday were not
how she remembered those times. In her
mind's eye, she saw us close on the beach
with our buckets and spades, making
sandcastles together, all laughter and
smiles. The photographs do show us
making sandcastles, but we look tiny,
lost in a huge beach, and much farther
away than she had thought.

One of the wonderful things about
the human brain is that it will effectively
'zoom in' for you, making whatever you
are interested in seem bigger, brighter,
clearer than it really is. It edits the
distractions out so that you see what you
want to see; not the full picture but only
a partial and distorted view. It's also worth
noting that this works the other way, too
– when we focus on the negative aspects
of our life, editing out all the good things.

Seeing mindfully is about being
present to the moment as it really is.
It means looking beyond the first detail
that drew you in to become aware of your
subject as a whole, a being with shape
and volume, texture and colour, and,
potentially, a life all of its own. And it
means seeing your subject as something
that exists in an environment or context,
surrounded by other things. It takes
sustained attention to notice all the
distractions around your subject, how
close or far away it is, where the light

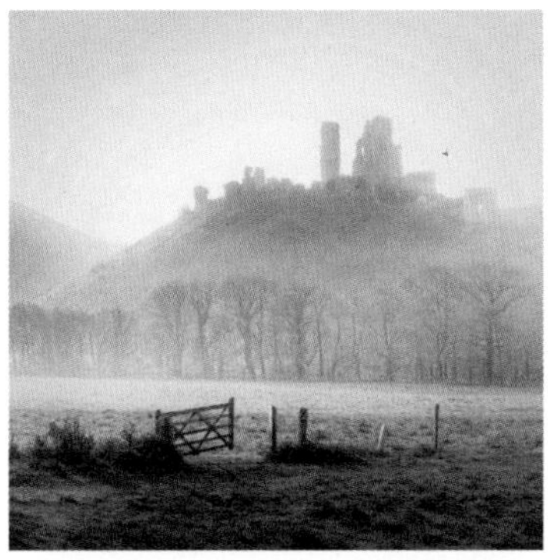

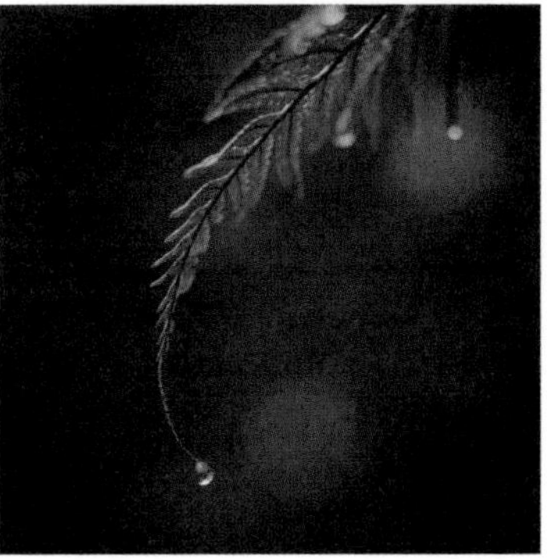

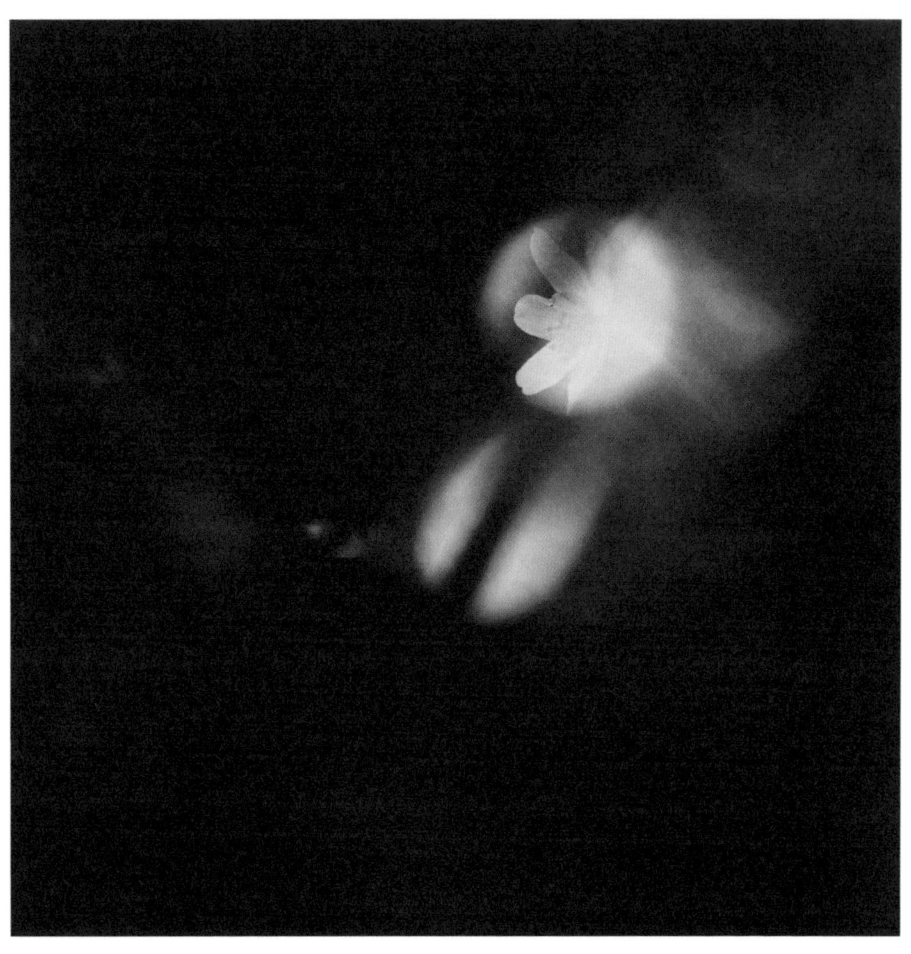

and shadows fall, what colours are really
present and all those details you would
miss at first glance.

Many people shy away from attempting
to really see because they worry about
'getting it wrong', not noticing the right
thing or seeing it in the right way. This is
why you often see photographers standing
in clusters around the same picturesque
view – because they know that image has
in a way been pre-approved. It might not
take much effort or input, but at least they
can be assured of having an image on their
camera that other people have already
judged worthy of seeing.

Seeing, as a personal act, is exposing
yourself – it makes you a bit vulnerable.

The pattern of shadows on a concrete
wall at the end of a car park is not a
conventionally beautiful subject. No one
else has probably bothered to photograph
it, and you may worry you will look odd
if you get your camera out to try to
photograph it. But you noticed it, and
it moved you. This moment was utterly
unique. In a world where people clamour
to find success via the validation of likes
and follows, the temptation is to repeat
what has been proven to work and to
avoid standing out. The uniqueness of
the individual's voice and vision gets lost
among the millions of pictures made
of the same places and subjects, shot
according to an approved aesthetic.

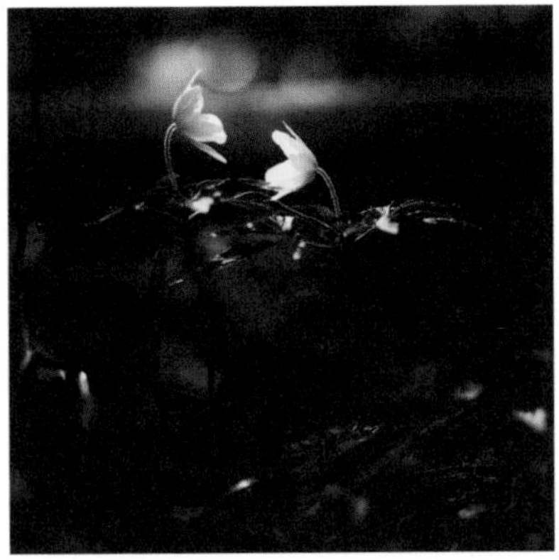

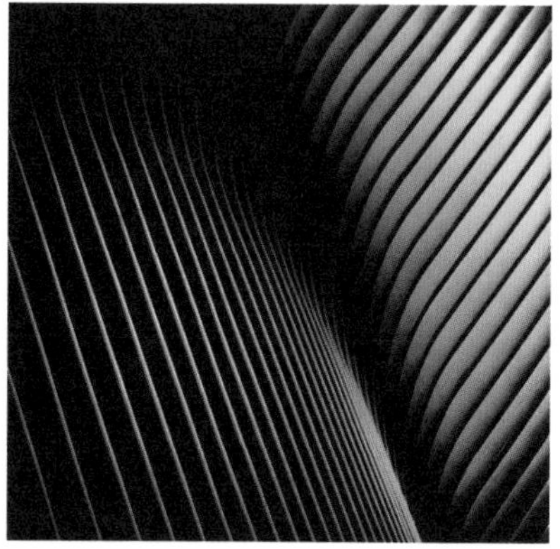 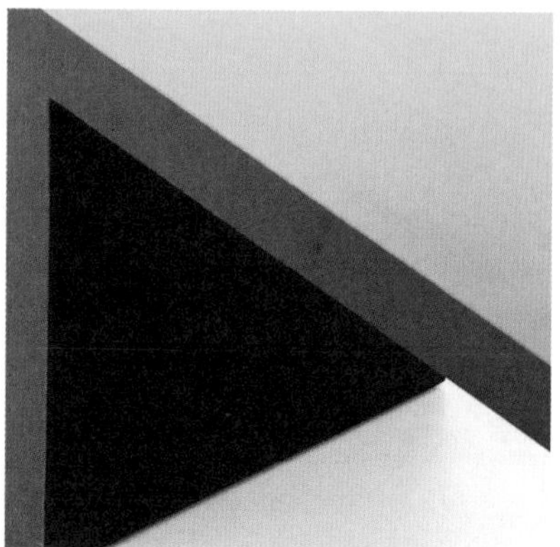

The first editor I worked for at *The Times* was a visionary, always encouraging photographers to stand out and pursue our own vision rather than attempt to copy whatever style or angle our competitors were using. This was brave for an editor, and a breath of fresh air. So many editors want to run the same material as their competitors because they don't want to be seen as missing the obvious. This editor wanted *The Times* to be unique, to challenge conventions rather than follow the crowd, to make being different a strength.

The same is true of photographers. When I look at the work of some of the great photographers – Ansel Adams (now one of the most copied photographers), Harry Callaghan, Minor White, Fay Godwin, Vivian Maier, Bill Brandt, Edward Weston, Nan Goldin, Adger Cowans and Robert Adams, to name but a few – what is clear is that they saw the world through their own eyes. They paid attention to the beauty that called to them and recorded it in a way that no one else could – and now they let us see it, too.

What if, instead of following the crowd, collecting locations and subjects as if we are trainspotting, we could be brave enough to pursue our own vision? Rather than repeating the same views and ideas over and over, the world could be filled with millions of different views. Each one would be as unique as the person who made the photograph; each one showing us something new, something we would never have thought of before – something that moved someone, and might well move others, too.

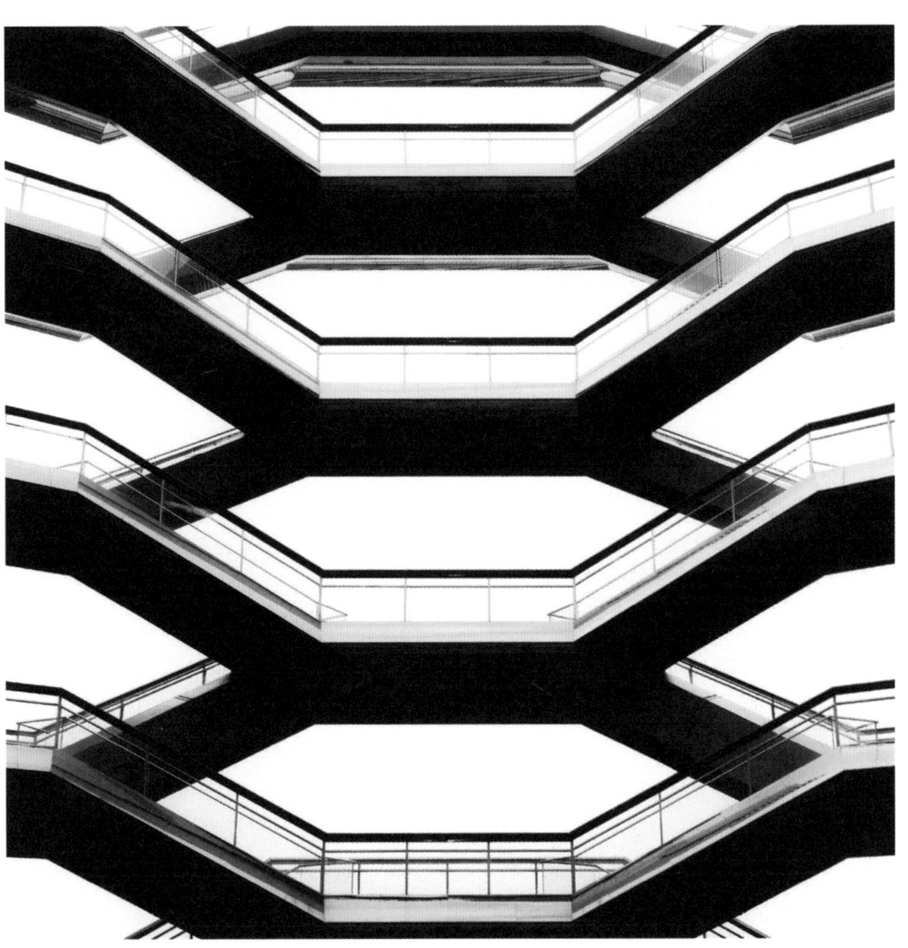

ASSIGNMENT: INVISIBLE BEAUTY

Many photographers travel the world in search of novel encounters and breathtaking scenes to photograph, and yet there is novelty and beauty all around us. This exercise is about finding an appreciation for all those little things we barely even notice in our day-to-day life.

For this exercise find one thing that you use everyday: a glass or mug; a kettle, toaster or pan; a bag or wallet – just something ordinary. Once you have selected your object, explore the feel of it with your fingertips, picking it up if you can. Feel the bulk and weight of it in your hands. Explore the form of it. Turn it around and look at it from every angle until you really begin to see it.

Place the item on a table worktop and look at how the light falls across it. Spend a while playing with the light, if you like.

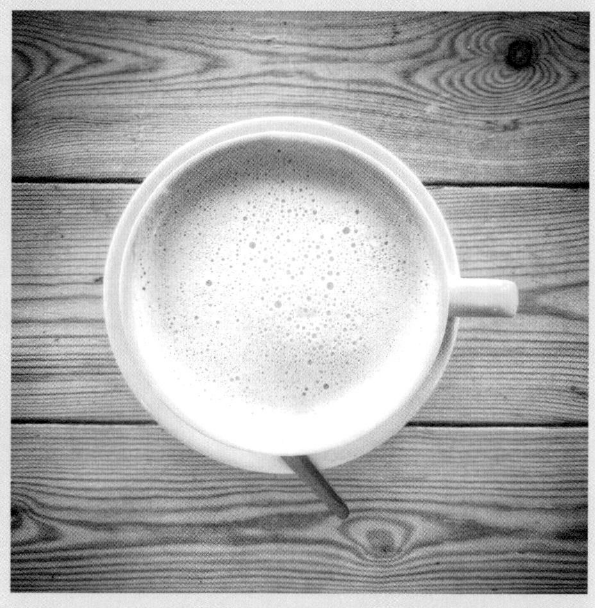

There is never nothing
to photograph.
—

Now it's time to photograph the item. What do you want to photograph about it? When you first chose your object, you probably saw it in terms of its function – as a glass, a kettle and so on – but then, as you looked more closely, you might have been drawn to the shape or texture, the light or shadow at its joins or folds. You can follow the same process with your camera, getting close and familiar, and finding fascination within the smallest details.

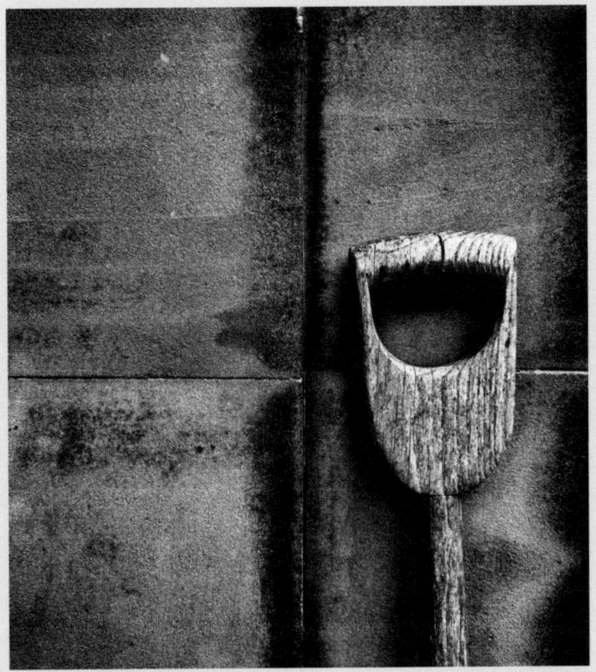

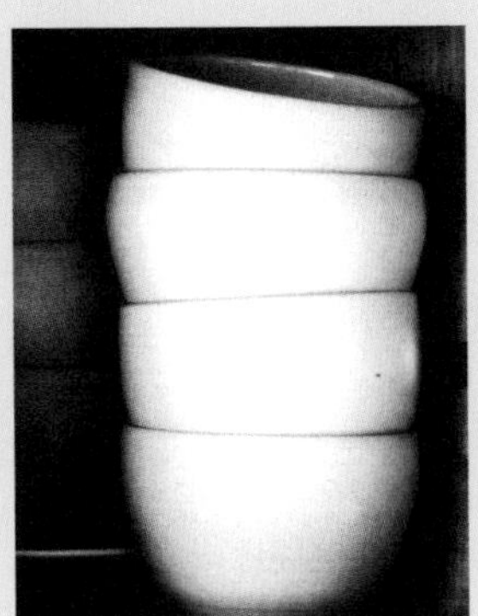

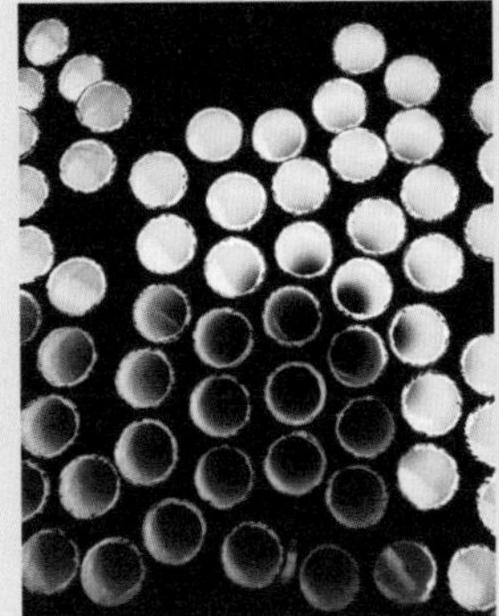

When you think you have finished, try to push yourself even further, finding a different angle or aspect to intrigue you.

This exercise will not only make you aware of the beauty contained in everyday items but will also make you realize that there is never nothing to photograph.

emptiness

It seems strange to start with a word that often has negative connotations, but emptiness is an important part of seeing.

As I mentioned earlier, when we set out to photograph, we often have preconceived ideas about the images we're going to return with. We might be imagining how the light will be glowing in our pictures, or how the shadows will sculpt our subject just so; we might be arranging the perfect composition in our mind's eye. We might even see ourselves winning praise and acclaim for the image we're about to take. In fact, I learned one of my biggest lessons about photography when I did just this.

In July 1996 I was working for a press agency in Manchester. On a bright Saturday morning, we received notice that a coded warning had been issued to evacuate the city centre because a bomb had been planted by the Irish Republican Army. To be honest, I got overexcited. I dashed into the city to find the police evacuating Deansgate – the city's main thoroughfare – and the surrounding streets. The story was happening around me, but I ran the opposite way to everyone else – I wanted something better. I thought that, if I could get to the area being evacuated, I would get the first pictures of the devastation right as it was occurring. In my head I was already collecting the Best News Image of the Year Award at several ceremonies!

I rounded the corner of St Ann's Alley onto Cross Street just as the lorry containing the explosive device blew up, and was promptly knocked off my feet. Rattled and showered in debris, I made a handful of images of the aftermath and sprinted back to the office.

The editor called me as soon as I'd returned, wanting a first-hand account of what I had seen. It was at this point that I realized I hadn't really seen what had happened. As soon as the film was processed, I scanned in my one usable frame, in which a huge plume of smoke and dust filled the image – the others were either out of focus or shaking and blurred. The image I chose was okay, and it was used on the front page.

I was still feeling quite pleased with myself when the editor called me downstairs. 'Where's the story in your photograph?' he asked. I stared at the image. News is about the response or impact of an event on people. In my desire to be different, better, bigger, I had forgotten to consider the most important thing. It was a realization that changed the way I worked from that moment on.

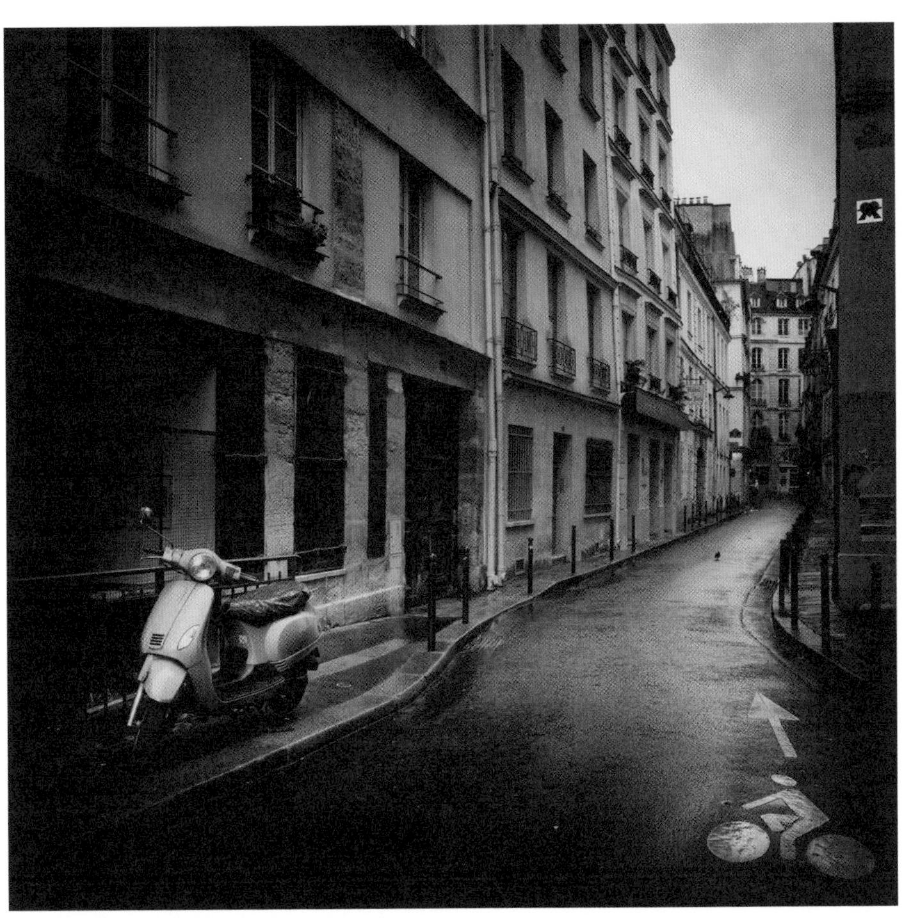

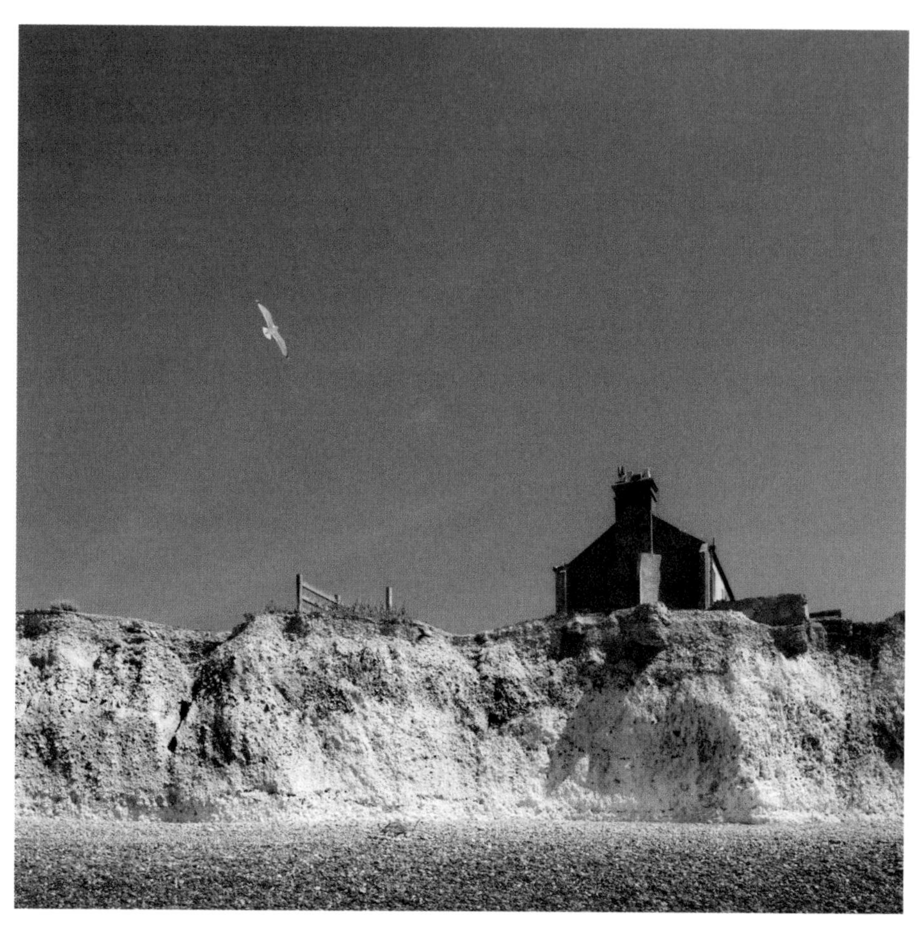

Emptiness is an important part of seeing.

—

Often, when we aspire to greatness
we actually miss the point, because we
are so taken with the ideas in our mind,
or striving so hard for something, that
we forget the real reason for what we
are doing. This happens with a lot of
photographers, especially when they
enter competitions or travel to far-flung
locations: with great expectations of
what they hope to achieve, they put huge
pressure on themselves and the subject
to be something special, and inevitably
they end up disappointed.

To be able to see what is special in
things just as they are requires our mind
to be calm, open and empty of all its
preconceived ideas about an image that
doesn't exist yet.

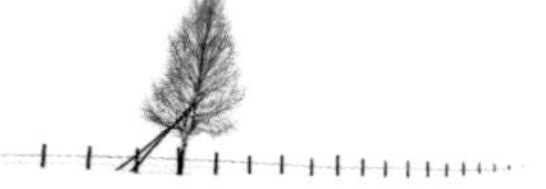

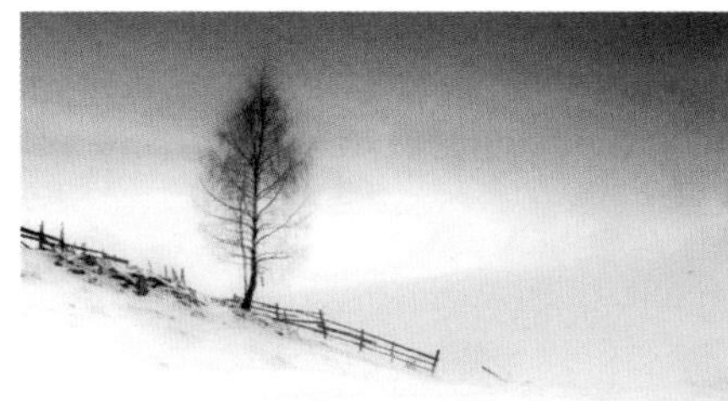

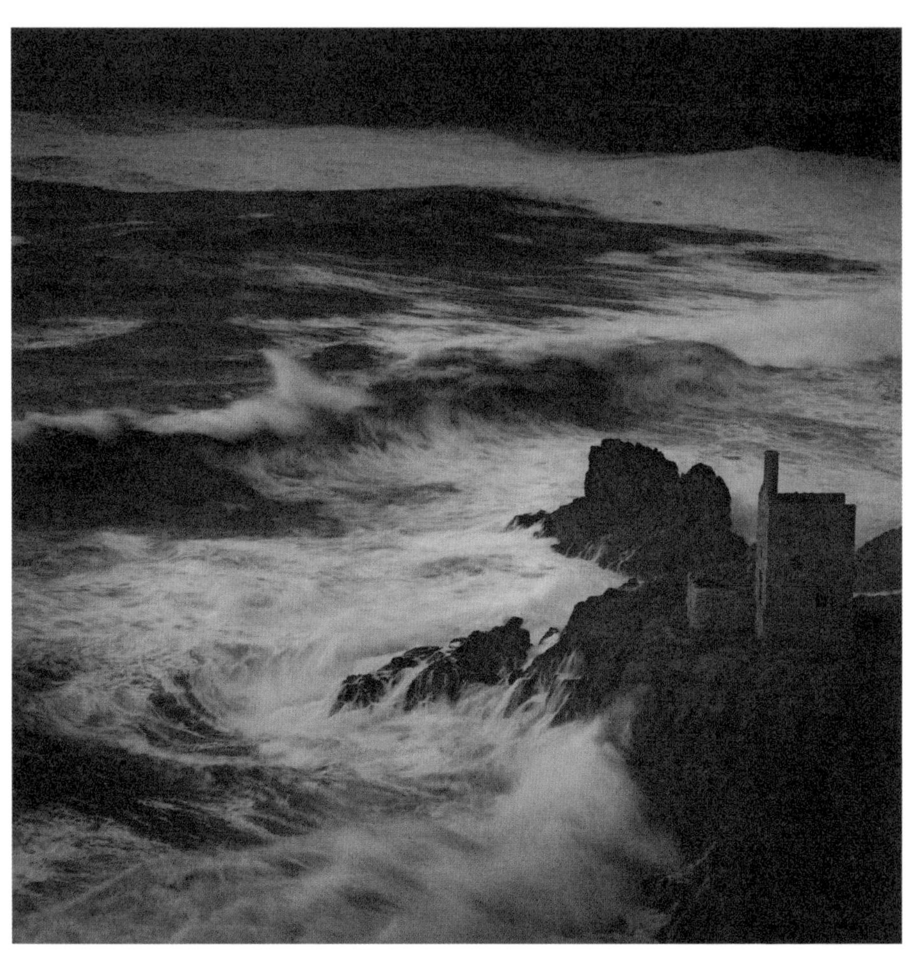

The photographer Edward Weston photographed the area around his home in Monterey, California, in just such a state of openness and emptiness. Deliberately turning his back on the pretty picture-postcard seaside vistas, he let the kelp beds, rock pools and trees speak to him, and shared his own, authentic vision of the beaches. Visiting the area of Point Lobos almost daily, each time he saw it anew.

'The camera should be used for a recording of life, for rendering the very substance and quintessence of the thing itself, whether it be polished steel or palpitating flesh,' Weston wrote. In being empty of all ambition save to see right through to 'the very substance and quintessence of the thing itself', the images he made reveal the beauty in the most mundane and ordinary scenes.

I have been to Weston Beach near Monterey and observed photographers 'looking for' pictures – trying to work out where the great photographer stood to make his images. What they fail to realize is that they are trampling over the very things he might have noticed, because he wasn't looking for photographs; he was observing the changes and the smallest details in the landscape he knew so well.

We can achieve this receptive, empty state first by not reaching immediately for our camera or phone when we arrive at a location or set eyes on our subject. Take your time to relax and become attuned to the environment. It can help to close your eyes and try paying attention to all the things you *can't* see – the sounds, the breeze against your body or the stillness of the air, the feel of the ground beneath your feet, and so on.

When you are ready, open your eyes and let them explore the scene with gentle curiosity, forgiving any flaws and looking closer at the things that intrigue you.

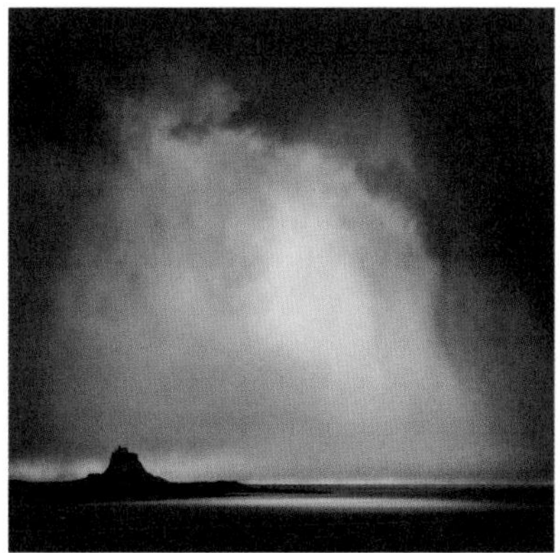

breathe in, breathe out

In any endeavour, the ability to stop and focus yourself internally is incredibly powerful, and one of the best ways to do this is by doing something we've done every day of our life without a second thought – breathing.

For thousands of years, various groups of people, both spiritual and secular, have recognized mindful breathing as one of the best ways to harness a more serene and aware state of mind. Our minds and bodies are intricately connected, and by becoming aware of our breathing we can take control of our responses.

We tend to operate in one of two states left over from our evolutionary history – fight or flight, or rest and digest – which determine our responses to the world around us. Fight or flight is a state of tense alertness that helps keep us safe in the presence of danger – we are poised and ready to act, our heart racing and our breathing shallow. The rest-and-digest state, on the other hand, is when we are content and comfortable, happy to be where we are, our breaths becoming slower and deeper, our heart rate dropping.

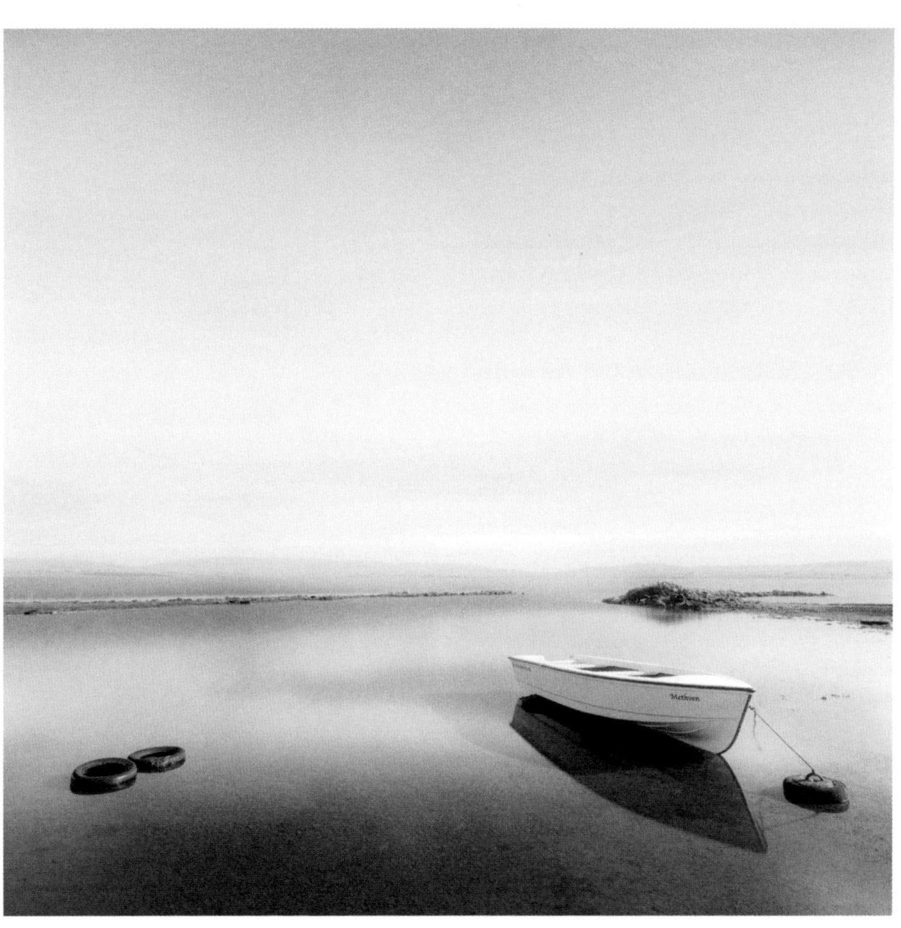

Fight or flight is the state many of us exist in on a semi-permanent basis due to the stresses and constant assaults on our attention made by the modern world. We work, do chores, try to keep up with friends, and get used to the constant adrenaline and little hits of dopamine that make our lives seem worthwhile. It's a lifestyle our bodies get addicted to. Never resting, our overactive minds keep us from sleeping, trawling through all sorts of scenarios...

In life, we need balance. Fight or flight can be great when something arises that requires you to act fast, but how many things really require you to pursue them with that level of urgency? We also need periods of quiet and stillness to recoup our energy, without which we lose focus, become ill and burned out.

Practising mindful photography is a perfect way to break the cycle, but first we need somewhere to start – which brings us back to breathing.

When I arrive at a location or find myself interested in a subject, I stop and breathe, counting five seconds while I breathe in, and another five seconds while I breathe out. For a few minutes, I pay attention to only my breath, bringing my thoughts back whenever they start wandering off. Before long, I feel my heart rate slow and whatever anxiety or daily pressure I might be carrying dissolve.

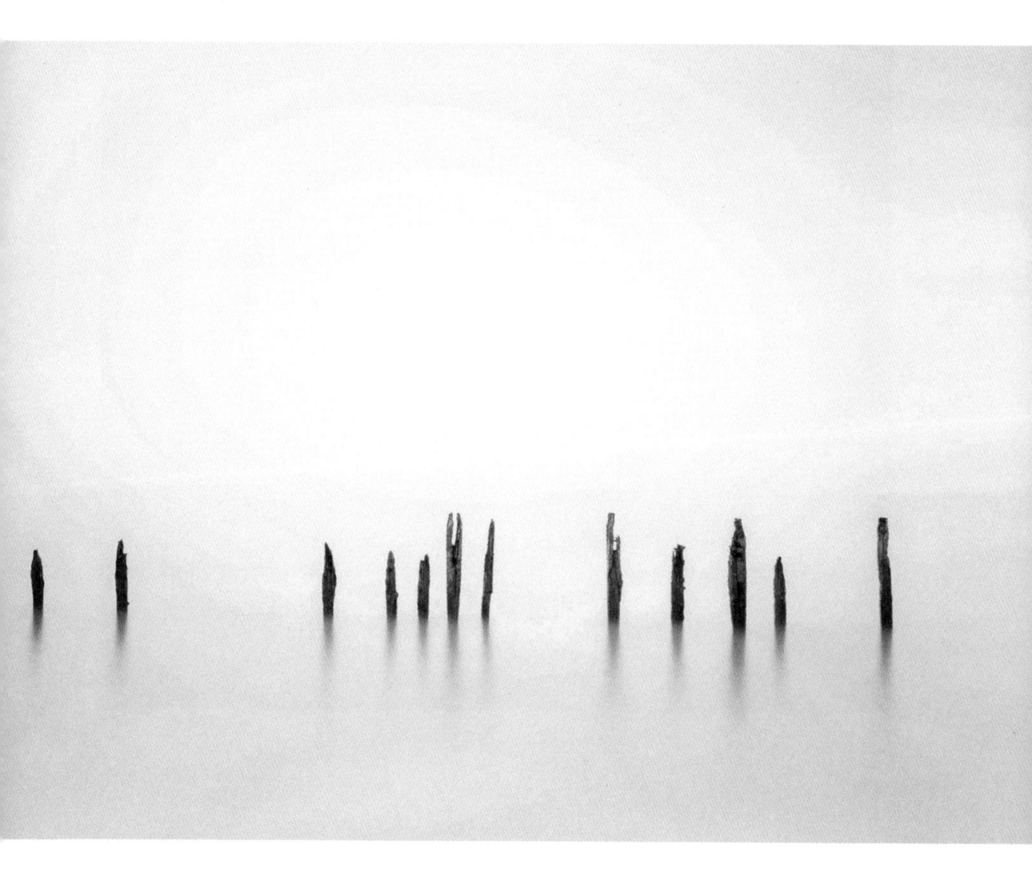

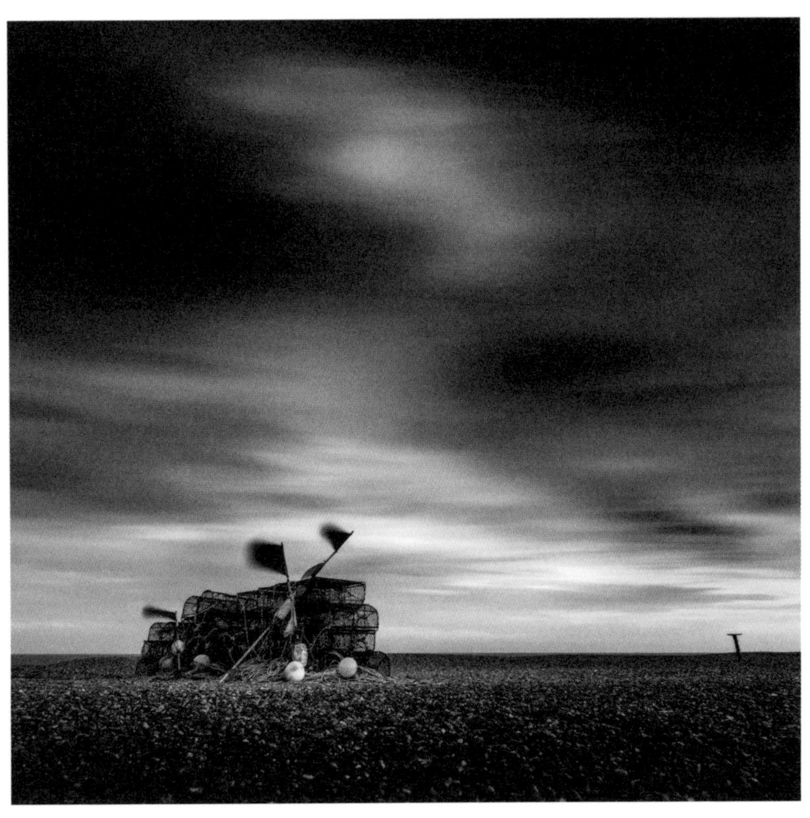

'Flow is being completely involved in an activity for
its own sake. The ego falls away. Time flies. Every
action, movement and thought follows inevitably
from the previous one, like playing jazz.'
—
Mihaly Csikszentmihalyi

These few minutes of breath meditation are crucial to my being able to see, to how I connect to the world and, importantly, to how I receive guidance from my subject. Essentially, I am giving myself time to arrive and settle in to a rest-and-digest state, deliberately seeking that slower, contemplative mode where I can start to pay attention in a deeper way. This paves the way to enter another state: neither rest and digest nor fight or flight, but what is known as the 'flow state'.

This term, coined by Hungarian-American psychologist Mihaly Csikszentmihalyi, describes an optimal state of consciousness in which you feel more connected and less inhibited. In this state, time seems to slow down and you become totally absorbed in what you are doing; the work seems effortless as if it's presenting its own answers, and the lack of any self-consciousness allows maximum creativity and enjoyment.

Csikszentmihalyi believed that the flow state is a skill that can be learned. It requires us to learn to minimize distractions so that we can focus our full attention on the task at hand. Establishing a practice of mindfulness is about building new habits – instead of attempting to multitask all the time, we stop, relax and give one thing our full attention. Instead of trying to impose our will on the world, we seek a state of empty, open receptiveness to what the world presents us with.

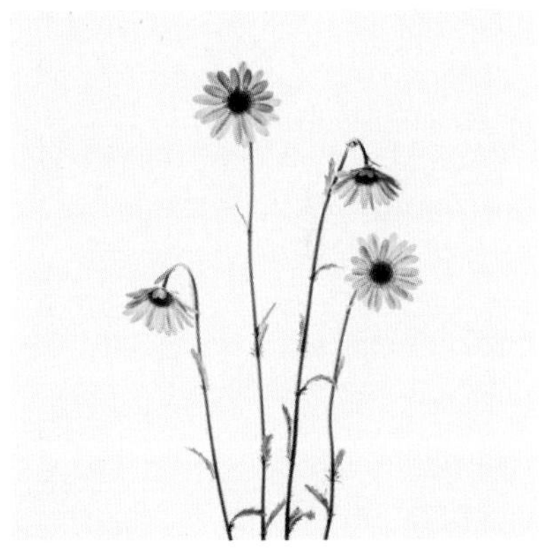

Beginning this journey is as simple and as challenging as concentrating on your breath. We go back to finding stillness, counting to five as you breath in and breath out, quietly paying attention and just being – without the need or demand to be anywhere else.

falling in love

In his book *Essentials for Prose*, Jack Kerouac recommends the writer to 'be submissive to everything, open listening, no fear or shame in the dignity of your experience, be in love with your life.'

The same is true of photography. Making pictures is falling in love with elements and events in your everyday life.

I have often likened photography to flirting: someone catches your eye across a bar or restaurant and you want to explore more. You glance away when you think they might catch you looking, but gradually your confidence builds and you realize that they have been looking at you, too. You move closer to see whether they would be open to starting a conversation. As you talk, slowly you find yourself drawn in – utterly captivated by their smile, their laugh, their easy humour...

Imagine a photographic subject calling to you as powerfully as the partner you've waited your whole life to meet; there's something quite magical about that moment. Now imagine if everything in your life sparkled with that same potential, exerting its fascination and instilling wonder the longer you pay it attention.

True, it might be hard to imagine being in love with the ironing, the washing-up, the trash that need taking out. But these mundane chores are the foundations of the relationship; we need them to be able to appreciate the holidays and high points, and photography is exactly the same. You may find yourself staggered by the beauty of mountains or the golden sands of a beach, but life is more made up of the ordinary than it is of the fabulous trips away. If you reserve your joy, enthusiasm and love for the extraordinary moments, you'll be missing out on an awful lot.

Can you see the colours gleaming in the suds when you do the washing-up? Do you notice the way the sunlight catches the lawnmower as you push it across the lawn, or how the trees cast shadows onto the laundry dancing on the washing line? Learning to love the whole experience of life will increase the number of photographic subjects you will see, as well as the moments of joy.

A few years ago I presented a workshop to a group of photographers in which I encouraged them to fall in love with their subject. The subject: grass! Grass is one of those things that is so ubiquitous we

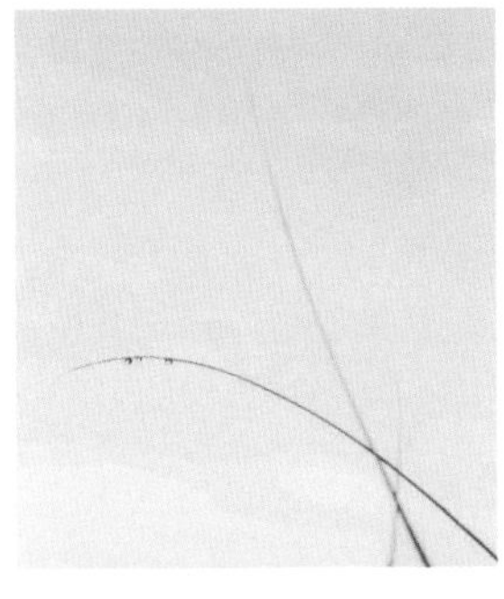

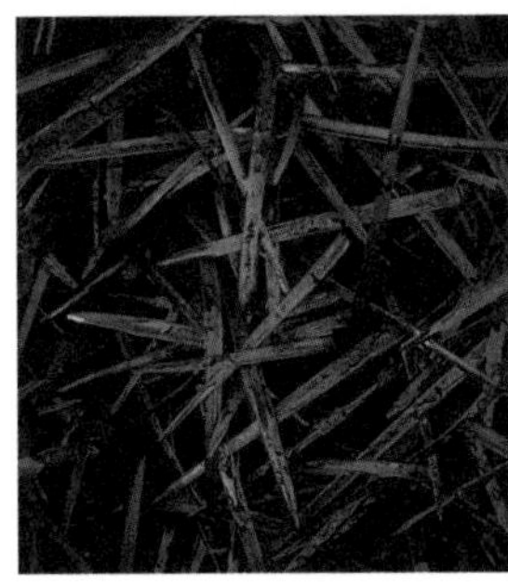

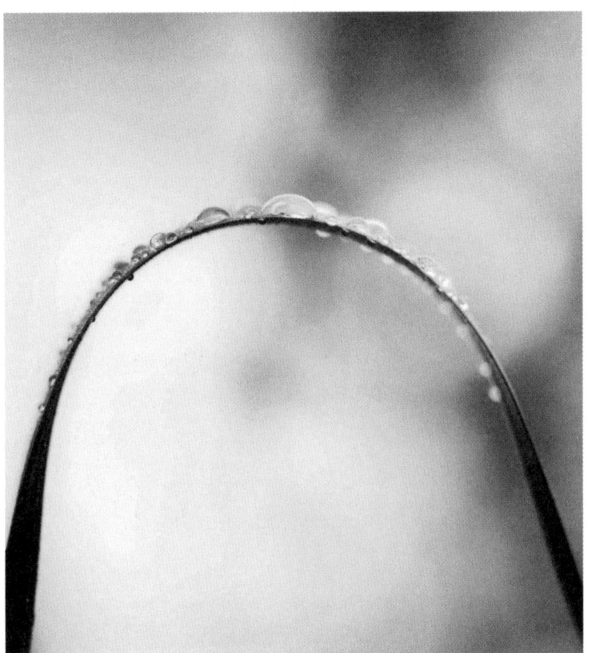

rarely notice how beautiful it is. I asked the group to spend a hundred days exploring grass and finding new ways to appreciate it, and they did. Some wrote poems, others wove baskets from their cut-up photographs (also, of course, of grass), some made drawings or paintings, and all of them ended up finding a deeper love for their subject than they thought possible at the beginning.

Love is not dependent on the camera you use or the number of years you have practised; it cares nothing for awards or status. Love allows you to come as you are to meet your subject in a spirit of trust and openness. It's a relationship in which both photographer and subject offer their best and are honest about their worst to the other, allowing something beautiful, true and transformative to be born.

You may find yourself embarrassed by the fact you have a whole series of images of that washing line, but it's a gift to find riches in the simplest things. These moments will hopefully fill you with excitement; your life will become a visual adventure in which everything becomes an opportunity rather than a chore.

Your life will become a visual adventure.

—

ASSIGNMENT: A DAY IN MY LIFE

We all tend to think our days are mostly mundane, filled with boring moments or tedious chores; at best, we probably consider our lives to be no more than ordinary. Yet our daily lives might be filled with extraordinary moments; it's just that we're not paying enough attention to see them as such. This assignment will change that. The challenge is to photograph your day as if you were making a documentary about yourself.

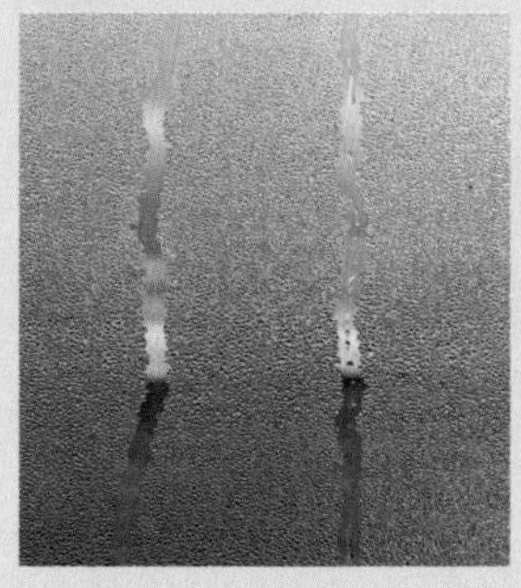 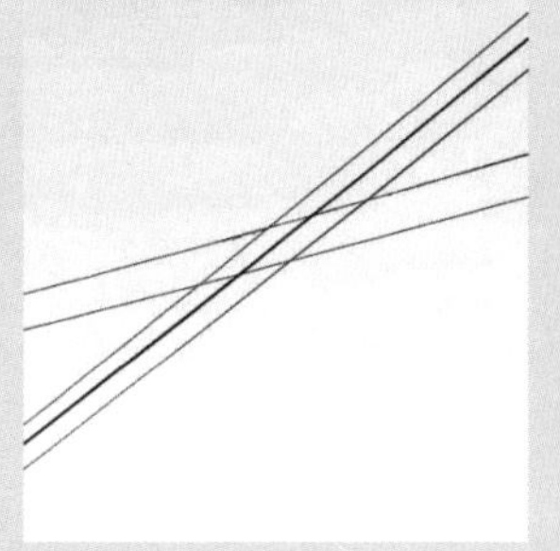 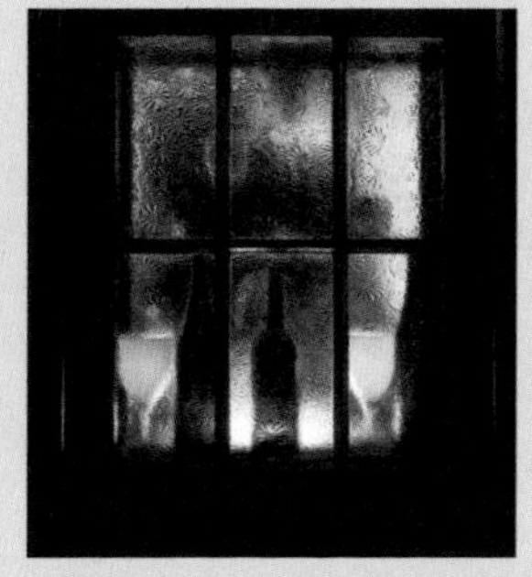

Start from the moment you wake up, with the first thing you notice. Perhaps it's the annoying alarm clock, the cosiness of duvet you don't want to leave, or the light creeping through a crack in the curtains.

As you go about your day, try to photograph every aspect of it: the food you eat, transport, shops, the people you meet and everything you interact with. Record everything – sitting at your desk, a walk or a jog, a yoga class or a lunch in the park... right up to the point you turn out the light at night. It's important to not get into the mindset of thinking watching TV with your feet up in your comfy fluffy slippers isn't interesting enough – remember, this is a fly-on-the-wall documentary about your *whole* day.

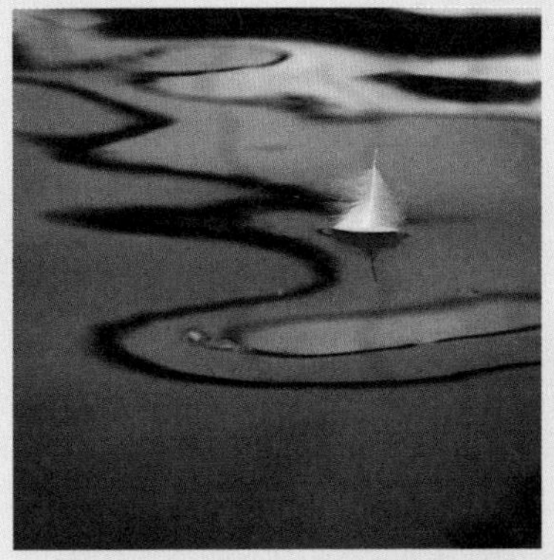

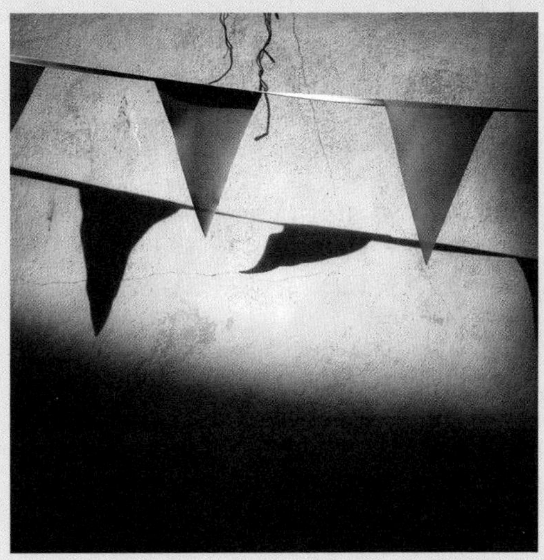

Of course, it is still up to you how you choose to photograph these moments. When I've done this exercise myself, I've always tried to explore interesting ways to convey familiar moments, such as a steamed-up mirror for when I was showering. No one needs to see me in the shower!

If you drive to work or the shops, for example, it could be the reflected scene in the rear-view mirror before you set off. At lunchtime, perhaps you might show the contents of your fridge, or lay your lunch items out on your desk and photograph them all neatly lined up.

Exercise your imagination as much as possible as you go through your day, seeing each activity and encounter as a challenge to your creative skill. It might even stretch you in other ways, putting you out of your comfort zone when you stop to make a photograph somewhere public. Most of all, however, try to see this assignment as an exciting new way look at your day. You'll be surprised how much fun you have doing this, and how extraordinary your day turns out to be.

At the end of the day, make a collection of your images – upload them to a private gallery or print them out if you can, and write captions for each moment. You could try making a booklet or photo story with them

Remember, you don't have to share this with anyone, but do take the time to celebrate every moment you have noticed.

rules

Social media and the internet are replete with lists of the 'rules' of photography. I have never been a big follower of rules, as they often set unnecessary limits and impede authentic seeing.

That said, when taken as a guide, some rules can be useful in helping a new photographer understand some basic principles about composition and using the light – things they might not otherwise have thought about. I'm not going to give you any rules to follow, but a few simple ideas for you to consider.

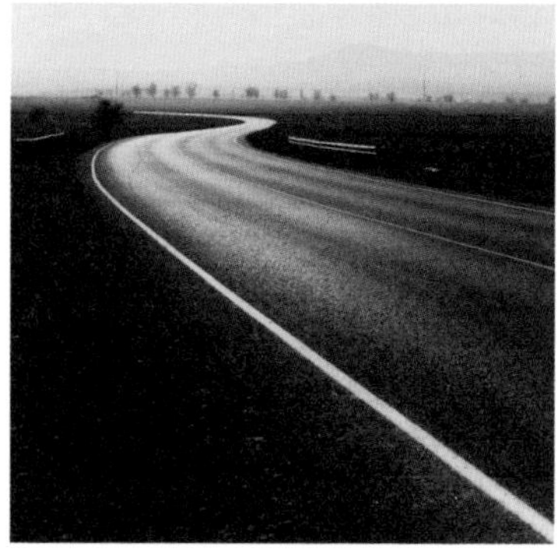

SPACE

One simple thing you can do on digital cameras and smartphones is turn on the Grid view. This will divide the frame into a three-by-three grid, which can help you get a better sense of the size and position of your subject in comparison to other elements. If you have any distinctive vertical or horizontal lines in your scene, turning on the Grid view can also help you get them straight. Most phones and cameras also have a Level setting, which you can turn on to avoid accidentally tilting your camera.

I would say that 99 percent of compositional challenges come down to issues with space. Space allows your subject to breathe, but if your subject is too small in the frame, it can stop looking like the subject. If you mainly use your phone to photograph, it's likely you're photographing with a wide-angle lens that takes in a large field of view. If your subject is looking lost in the frame, you might want to try moving closer.

Getting close can be a great way to notice shapes, textures and details of your subject that you might not have noticed at a glance, but it can also make your subject look squashed. It can also help with cutting out background distractions, but ask yourself whether your subject needs a little context to place it in its environment and understand what it is.

POSITION

A favourite among photographers, the rule of thirds is loosely based on the Classical Greek concept of the Golden Ratio – a theory of harmonious proportions adopted by mathematicians and artists since antiquity. The rule of thirds, which divides the frame in the same way the camera's Grid view does, doesn't equate to anywhere near the complex mathematical equation that gives us the Golden Ratio, yet the basic idea of placing your subject, or the focal points of your scene, on the lines or intersections of the grid can help us achieve more balanced and interesting compositions than always centring the subject or horizon in the frame.

Composition is personal. I will often place my subject at the left or right to give it more of a sense of space or movement, but if you want to position your subject in the dead centre of the frame, then do so. The point is: don't just stick to the first thing you saw when you put your camera to your eye. Play around, explore different angles and consider what feels right to you.

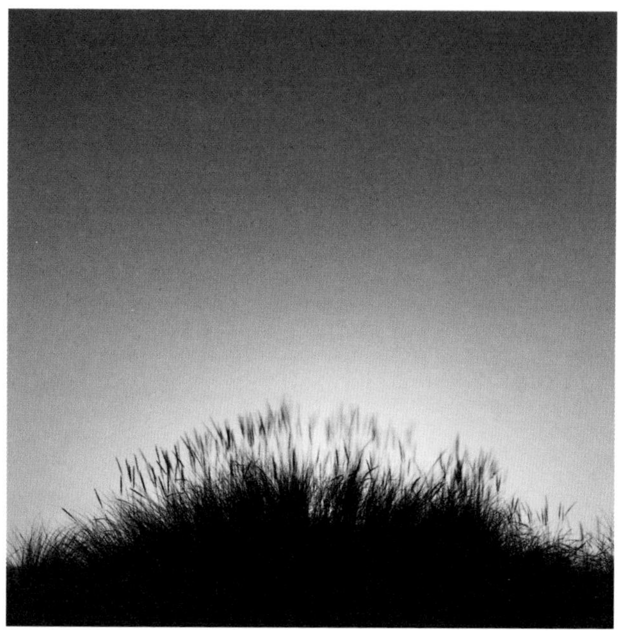

FOCUS

One rule that infuriates me is that your images must be sharp or in focus. It is true that the eye will often be drawn to the sharpest part of a photograph, but that doesn't mean that, if your images aren't perfectly focused, they won't be successful. Yes, your friends and family will probably appreciate any pictures from weddings, christenings and the like being in focus, but when it comes to the way you personally see and respond to the world, the way you approach focus is your choice.

If you don't see with great clarity, for example, achieving perfect focus may be neither realistic nor desirable. Alternatively, you might choose to have only a very tiny part of your subject in focus and let everything else fall into blur. You might even move your camera deliberately to create an abstract composition.

LIGHT

Many photographers believe the best times to photograph are during the golden hours – the hour just after dawn and the hour before the sun sets, when the light has a distinctly warm hue – but there are 24 hours in every day! Aside from the darkest hours of night, each will give a different quality of light – and different again through the changing seasons of the year – that can express something special about the subject you are photographing.

You might hear photographers talking about 'bad light', but there's no such thing. It just takes practice and curiosity to discover how to work with different light conditions. Learning more about the technical side of exposure can help, but, aside from that, we have to learn through experimenting and sometimes making mistakes, and through engaging carefully with what our eyes, our camera and our subject are showing us. We need to be open and prepared to adapt and enjoy what we are given.

You can read a lot about light, but the only real way to learn about it is by photographing in different sorts of light for yourself. Even when you're not photographing, you can still practise observing different conditions – I study light every day, watching how it creates different shapes from the shadows, creating different moods and bringing subjects to life in different ways.

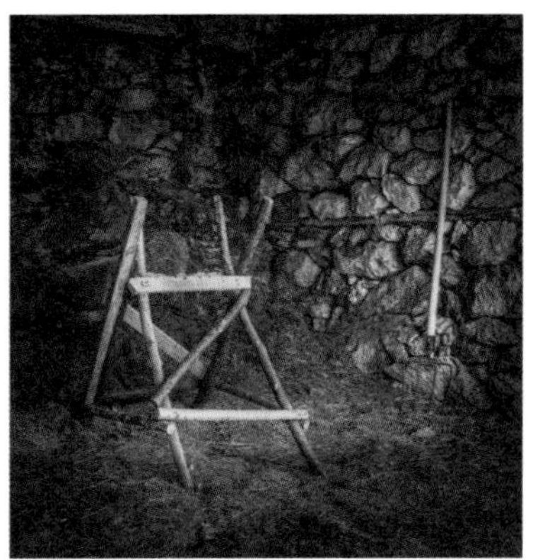

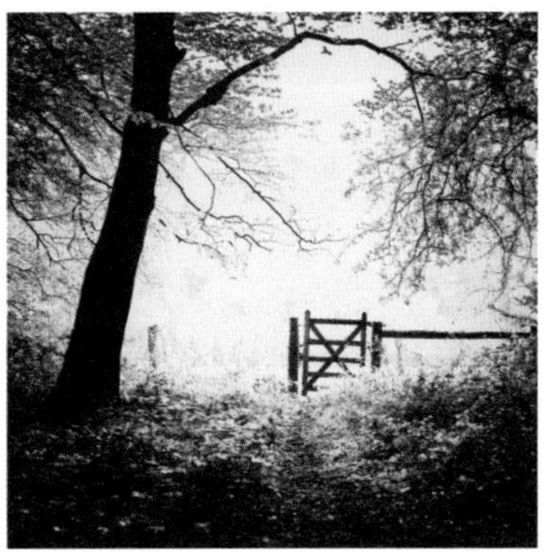

Even when you're not photographing, you can still practise observing.

—

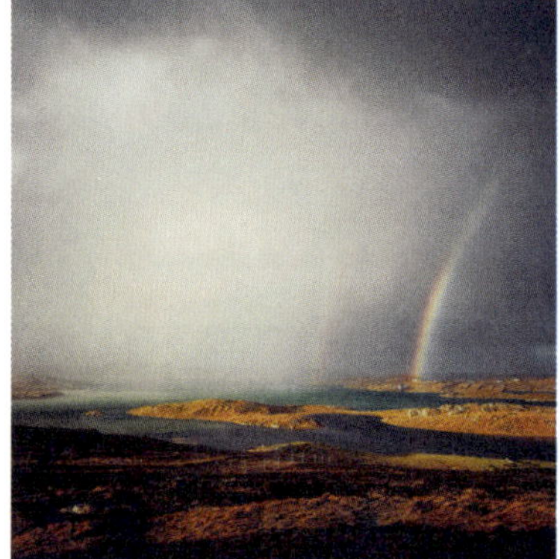

Many photographers love the technical aspects of the art. They might spend time mastering every setting of their equipment or achieving perfect exposure or framing; they perhaps have bulging kit bags. Some have a certain formula or aesthetic they want to conform to whenever they go out photographing. There is no 'wrong' way to do it, but I prefer to photograph from the heart rather than the head. Over time, my practical experience of photography technique has helped me refine what I'm able to see in my subject and convey that in the images I make.

Rules about how to use your equipment and what makes a good picture have usually been established for a reason, but by giving yourself permission to ignore them, you will be free to create unique images that are pertinent to you. If someone tells you that you are doing something wrong but you're happy with what you're creating, keep on doing what you are doing. If someone suggests a 'better' way of doing something, try it and find out for yourself.

Likewise, if someone tells you never to shoot in a certain way, don't take their word for it! You may come to the same conclusion, or you may find a way of photographing something that sets your heart on fire.

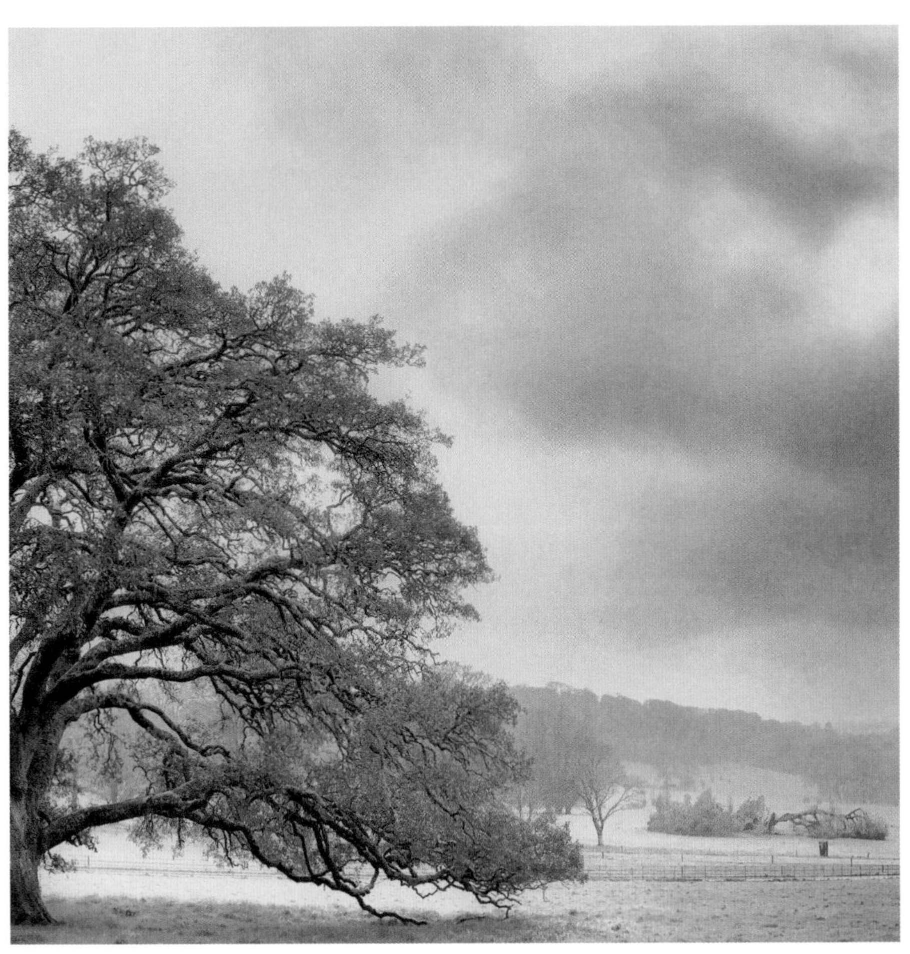

light

Light is the raw material of all photographs. The word 'photography' can be translated from its Greek roots as 'drawing with light', and it is the light that hits our camera's sensor (or the film in an analogue camera) that records an image of what we saw through the lens. Beyond that, light is the tool we use as photographers to convey form, texture, emotion and atmosphere.

There are certain times when you might notice the light having a particularly magical quality, but let's get one thing straight: there is no such thing as bad light.

When I was a child, my family raised and trained puppies to be guide dogs, and I remember reading a book by Sheila Hocken titled *Emma and I*. This is the true story of Hocken, who as a child was blind, and her guide dog Emma, and (spoiler alert) towards the end of the book, Hocken undergoes an operation that successfully restores her sight. Her description of seeing light for the first time, as it touched the grass and flowers, has always stayed with me.

Light, and the things it reveals to us, is a gift we should try not to take for granted as photographers. As it changes through the day, with the weather and with the season, it will cast its magic in different ways on different subjects. When we're struggling to 'make it work' for us, often we just have to pay attention to the subtleties, use all our skills of seeing and choose our subjects carefully.

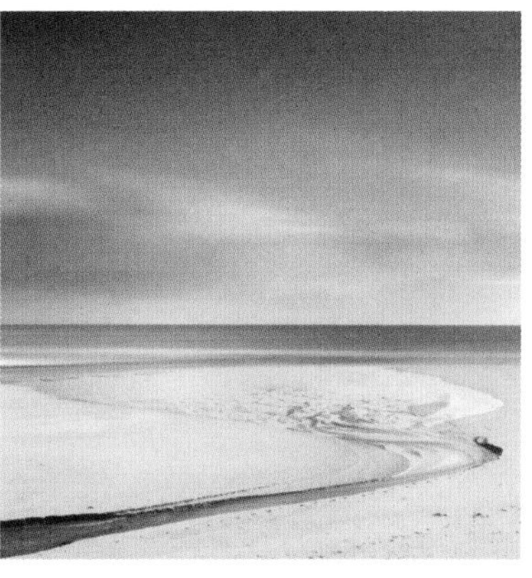

'Wherever there is light,
one can photograph.'

—

Alfred Stieglitz

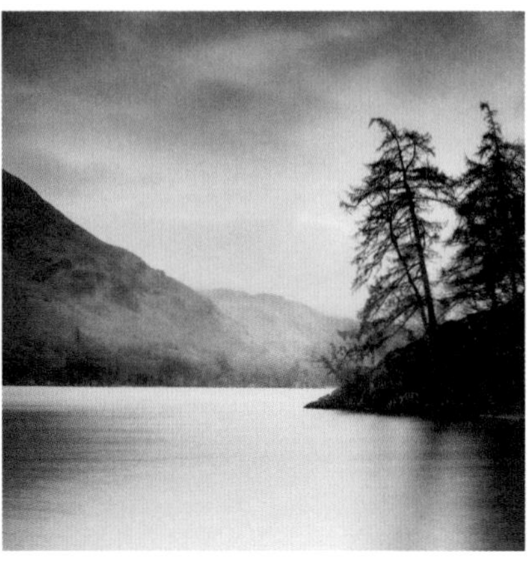

QUALITY OF LIGHT

First, we can observe light itself, in its various forms. There is *direct light*, such as when the sun shines on a wall or sparkles on the ocean, often casting stark shadows if there are no clouds in the way. *Reflected light* bounces off another surface and illuminates something nearby, sometimes taking on some of the colour of the reflected surface. *Diffuse light* is typically softer than direct light, having been scattered and smoothed by clouds or blinds, and giving gentler shadows.

One of my favourite times to photograph is on cloudy days when the light is diffused, soft and flat. There are no hard shadows or over-bright highlights, so in some ways it's the easiest light to use. It won't be ideal if you like a lot of tonal contrast and deep shadows, but it is a beautiful light to photograph details of plants, flowers and woodlands. Since we find diffused light where the light source is shielded by something translucent, which disperses the light through a wider area, it can be replicated with gauzy fabric, or even white baking parchment, which I used for the photos of flowers scattered throughout this book.

Reflected light might not be the most obvious thing to look for, but it can be extremely useful to photographers, and, like diffuse light, can be – and often is – artificially created and manipulated. You may have seen photographers using a piece of white card or a white disc to bounce the light onto their subject, which can brighten up areas of shadow, add a greater sense of dimension, and give more separation from a dark background.

Most surfaces will reflect light to a greater or lesser degree – apart from black, which absorbs the light – and reflected light can be exciting when you use a coloured surface to reflect the light. In professional settings, photographers use gold reflectors to cast warm tones onto their subjects and silver ones to shine a cooler light, but you can experiment with all kinds of colours for different effects and atmospheres.

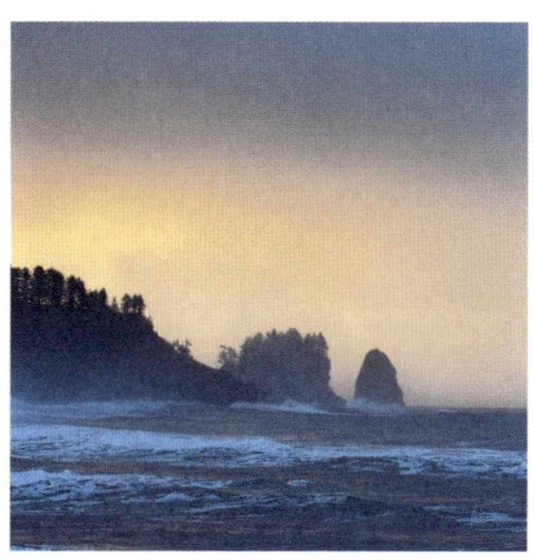

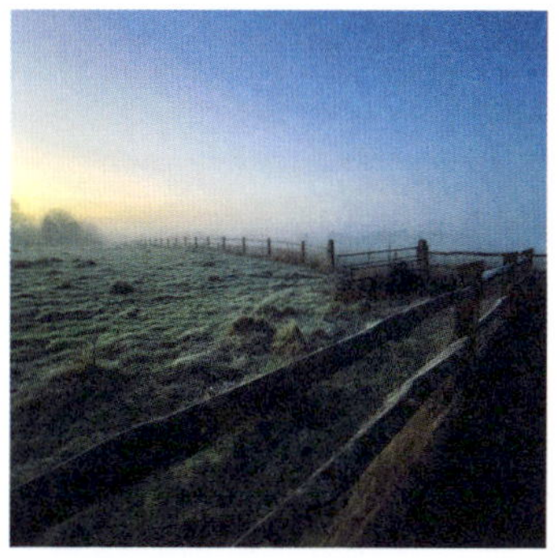

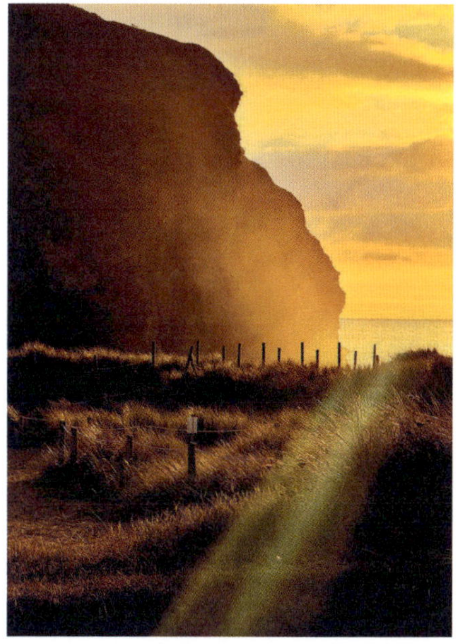

COLOUR OF LIGHT

Light also comes in different colours, or 'temperatures', which are measured in kelvin (K). When it comes to natural light, the sunlight will move through a spectrum ranging from cool blue through neutral white to golden yellows, oranges and hot reds. Many photographers love the blue hours that come around twilight, before sunrise and after sunset, and the golden hours that follow directly after the sun rises and just before it sets. Not only are the colours often quite magical, but the angle of the sun is low to the horizon, lending a dreamy quality with long shadows that can model the landscape and other subjects beautifully. It is also particularly flattering for photographing people.

On the other hand, there are some who will tell you to avoid photographing at midday, when the sun is at its highest and can give hard, unflattering shadows and when perhaps the light is less 'interesting'. Yet there are ways to work with all kinds of light. The challenge for the photographer is to find the right subject or the right angle for the light they are working with.

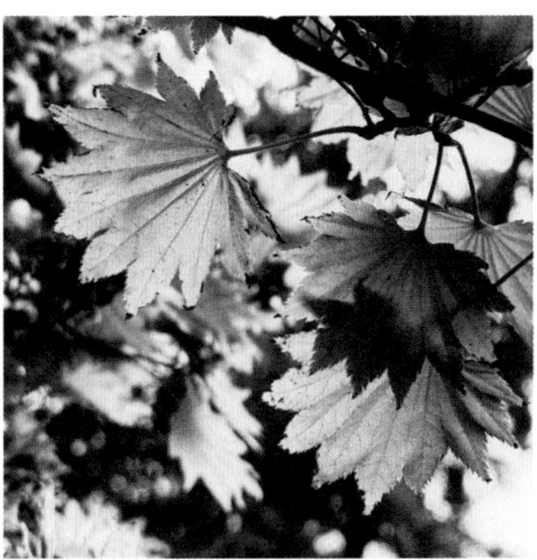

This brings us to another point. Save for physical or geographical restrictions, there are many ways to position yourself and your subject in the light, all of which, once again, bring different qualities, opportunities and challenges. *Back lighting*, for example, is when the light source is directly behind the subject. When you're shooting towards the light, it can be difficult to get the exposure right, but when you do, and with certain subjects, you can get magical results. Have you ever walked through a woodland in spring and marvelled at the vibrancy of the green leaves above you? Or in autumn the gold light streaming through the yellowing leaves, making everything it touches glow and feel more alive, more vibrant? That is back lighting.

Front lighting tends to have the reverse effect. It often flattens out colours and sometimes forms as well; in the woods, the leaves no longer glow. Light from this angle has its own qualities, however. The sense of flatness can be useful, while shadows may still give texture and modelling, and if it creates shadows behind your subject, you can often used these to isolate it from a messy background.

Side lighting is when the light is off to one side or the other, which can create sculptural shadows or pick out subtle textures. Light from this angle can give a very physical, intimate quality, making it feel as though you could almost touch the subject in the image. It typically casts deep shadows on the side opposite the light, which can giving a three-dimensional, sculptural quality to most subjects.

Every angle is there to explore, and not only on the horizontal axis but vertically as well, so you can try crouching low or standing on your tiptoes, tilting your camera, and so on.

An easy way to study light is to take a torch and move it around a static subject in your home. The subject could be a vase on the table, a ball, a fork, a flower…anything. You don't even need to make pictures, simply move the light slowly around your subject and really pay attention to the way the differing angles affect the subject. You may not be able to control the angle of the sun, but it will sharpen your awareness of what the light can do when you are out making photographs.

This exercise is also a good way to explore reflected light. Do exactly the same as before, but this time hold a piece of white paper opposite the torch light. As you hold your torch and the paper at different angles to your subject, you will begin to see the power and potential of reflected light to reveal more of your subject.

It's also worth pointing out that when it comes to light, we're not just talking about sunlight. Moonlight, starlight, streetlights, ceiling lights, candlelight, firelight – every one of these offers different qualities.

And then we come to light's opposite and equal partner: shadow.

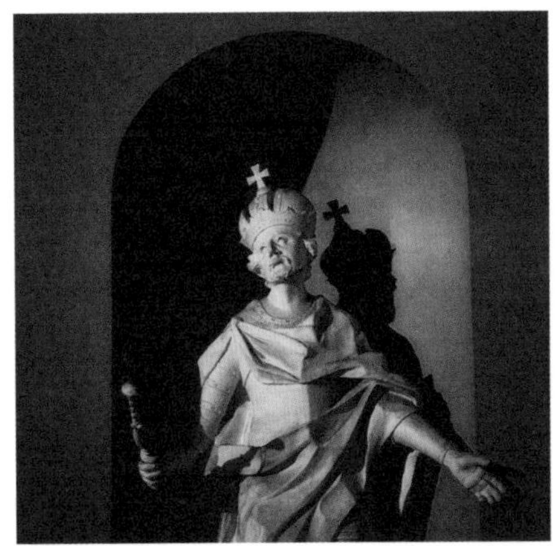

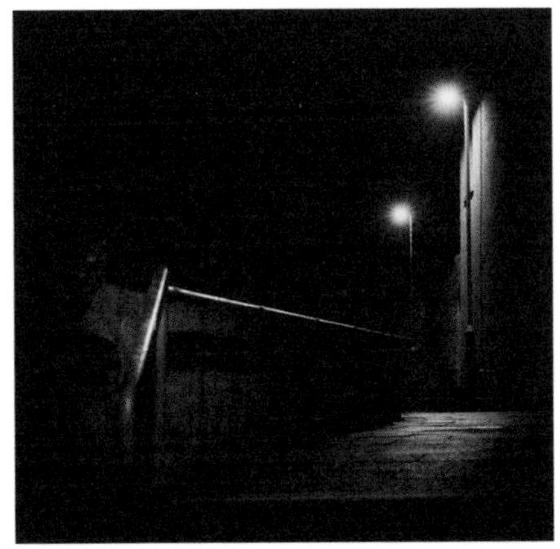

SHADOW

Shadows have as many different qualities as light, and they are just as wonderful to get to know. While our eyes are typically drawn to the brightest part of an image, it's important that we learn to look for the shadows and to see how they play into the images we're making. As I've already mentioned, a clever use of shadows can hide parts of the scene you might find distracting, and they will help convey the sense of shape, form and texture of a subject. Beyond this, shadows also have a powerful effect on mood.

An overly dark image is not incorrect if it has been intentionally made this way. This is called 'low-key' photography. While the tones of the image will be predominantly dark, any bright points will stand out in high contrast, so it can be a wonderful way to draw attention to the subtleties of the light, in the way it plays over a subject. Artists such as Rembrandt particularly enjoyed using this effect, called *chiaroscuro*, to bring a sense of drama to a scene or portrait. You can explore this effect very simply by lighting your subject with a single lamp or torch on a dark evening.

The reverse is called 'high key', where shadows are minimized and the image is predominantly bright, giving an airy, tranquil effect. The optimal conditions for this would be a bright, overcast day, when the light is soft and flat, or by diffusing the light source, as previously described.

Just like light, shadows will vary in size, shape and intensity as the day moves from morning to afternoon and on to evening, as well as depending on the weather. When the sun is low at the beginning and end of the day, as well as throughout most of the day around the winter solstice, it's the long, soft shadows that often add as much to the dreamy quality of a scene as the light, while the darker, sharper shadows of the middle of the day and the summer season are harder, punchier, almost with a form of their own. And then, of course, as the sun moves across the sky from east to west, the shape and direction of the shadows also shifts, changing the appearance of a scene or subject completely during the day.

The joy and challenge of exploring shadows is that they are so fleeting. One of my favourite things to do is watch the shadows on the walls of my home as they shift and change during the course of a morning or evening. I love the way some shadows are hard and dark while others are soft, with the appearance of layers of tone within the shadows. Work as hard to notice the details of shadows as you do the light. Shadows are not just black or grey; they, too, are affected by the surfaces and light around them. If you look closely, the shadows in woodland will have a green hint to them, and at the coast they are bluer. The shadows on snow can range from vivid blue in the morning to red or yellow in the evening.

Another exercise that you might want to try is a 24-hour photograph. Set your camera up in your home pointing through a window. Most cameras have an interval timer, or you can use a cable release to time the photographs. Set the timer to make one frame every hour for 24 hours. At the end of this exercise you will see how much the light changes over the course of a day and through the night. You can, of course, do this just for the daylight hours, too.

ASSIGNMENT: SHADOW & LIGHT

Some might call shadows the poor relation of light. Photographers can spend so long chasing the perfect light that the shadows can be an afterthought at best. Yet without shade – from the pure blocks of black to all the subtle gradations – there would be no form in an image.

Shadows should definitely not be overlooked. In the same way that it can be wonderful to sit and enjoy the quality of the light, watching the play of soft shadows on a wall or the distinctive abstract patterns cast across a pavement in the middle of the day can be just as rewarding.

This assignment requires very little apart from a white piece of card or paper – A4 or letter size is ideal – and a relatively sunny day.

First, get outside and find a tree. Place your card or paper on the ground underneath it, looking for a place with some interesting shadows that will show up well against the white. Look at the way the shadows fall: some will be lighter and others darker; some will move while others will be static; some will be sharper, others more blurred.

Photograph the shadows against the card, filling the frame. You can make a whole series of shadow images, and every image will be entirely unique and unrepeatable.

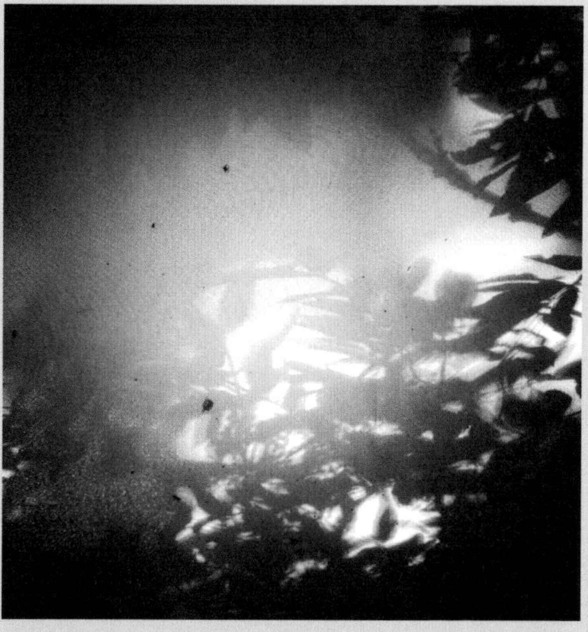

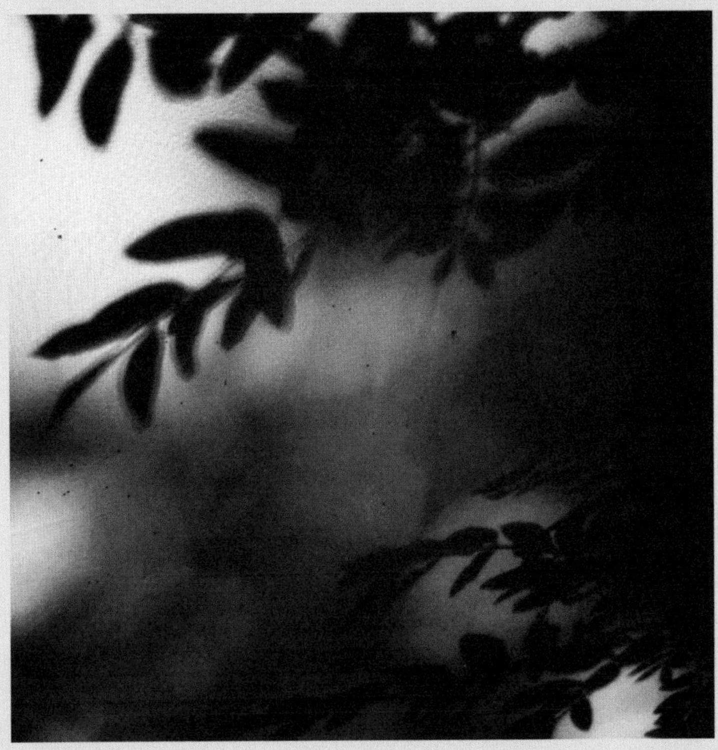

Once you have made a few images, change the angle of the card on the ground. Prop it up, bend or fold it, and see how the shapes of the shadows change. You can also try doing this exercise at the beginning or end of the day, or at regular intervals throughout the course of a day, and look at the way not only the quality of the shadows changes but also the colour of the light reflecting on your card. You can even try this exercise under streetlight, starlight and moonlight.

It can be wonderful to sit and enjoy the quality of the light, watching the play of soft shadows on a wall.

—

4

reflection

start here

During my time in therapy, I found it very difficult to open up fully about how I felt about myself and how I saw myself in the world. With the help of an incredible therapist who encouraged me to express my feelings through photography, however, I was able to start rediscovering a connection to the world, and my identity within it.

To reach this point I had to remove all the armour and the masks that I wore on a daily basis. In our lives, we learn tricks and develop personas to present a different version of ourselves in different settings. For example, you might behave one way among your colleagues at work and quite differently with your friends or family; we learn certain modes of behaviour – social conventions – that make us feel safe from embarrassing ourselves, committing a faux pas or saying or doing 'the wrong thing'. Between all these different masks, and the pressure we feel to fit in, we can start to forget or lose confidence in the person we are underneath, when we're not performing for others.

At the beginning of my recovery, peeling off those masks made me feel more vulnerable than I have ever been in my life, but from that place of vulnerability I was able to observe myself authentically and give myself permission to just be me. Through allowing myself to explore my own sense of self through my photography I started to see the real me, the me I wanted to know and love.

The journey of recovery started with just one image – shown opposite.

Some might imagine that the practice of making photographs from an early age was a huge advantage in being able to explore my feelings visually – and in some ways, they are right. I have a lot of experience behind me. And yet, until 2012, I had always photographed to order or under clear direction – for editors, picture editors and art directors. When I picked up my camera again after leaving *The Times*, I had no idea what kind of photographer I was or what I enjoyed photographing, and I realized that my only real purpose with a camera had been to try to please others.

When I made the image opposite, it was the first image I made that truly expressed how I felt about myself. I didn't intentionally go out looking for the subject, a broken post sticking out of the sea – in fact, I had been to that beach many times and never noticed it before.

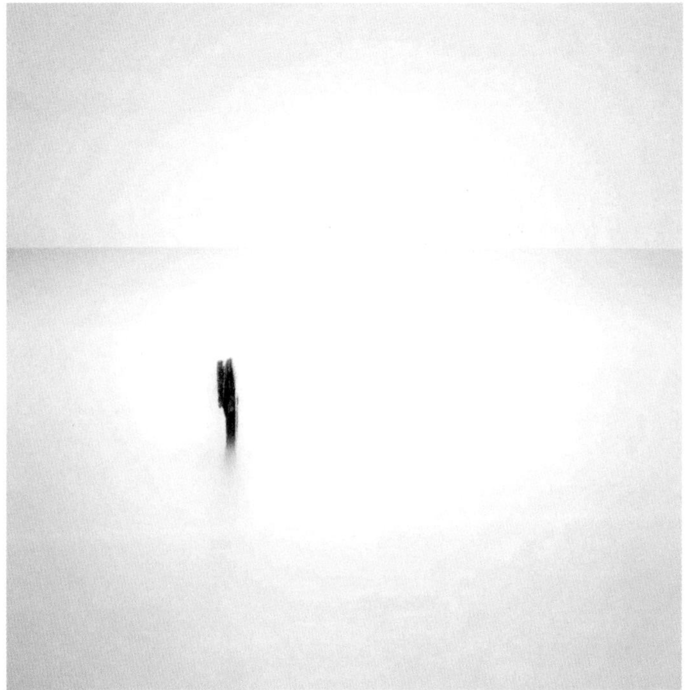

That day, though, I felt it calling powerfully to me. True, when I photographed it, my technical knowledge of exposure and shutter speed helped me achieve a calm, serene feeling, but initially all I noticed was the stick that I wanted to isolate in the image, which led me to using a slow shutter speed for the long exposure that smoothed the water and filled it with light. The result was an image that was me at that moment.

Every photograph we make is a self-portrait when we allow ourselves to be vulnerable, honest and authentic. It is from this point that we can embrace the spirit of openness, being present to both our feelings and our surroundings. Now, with reflection, I can see how every event in my life has led me to this place where I have started to find strength in the person I truly am, not the person I think I should be to please others.

ASSIGNMENT: GRATITUDE

Our modern society has trouble remembering the meaning of gratitude. It races along consuming and discarding without thought or care. In the UK, where I live, and across much of the world, we have more comfort and luxury than ever, and little true appreciation of any of it. Without appreciation and gratitude, how can we take any joy in the world around us?

One of the things photography has given to me is an enormous sense of gratitude for the subjects of my photographs – whether it's a beautiful landscape or a glass bottle covered in condensation. The pursuit of seeing something is truly one of appreciation, and with appreciation comes interest and connection.

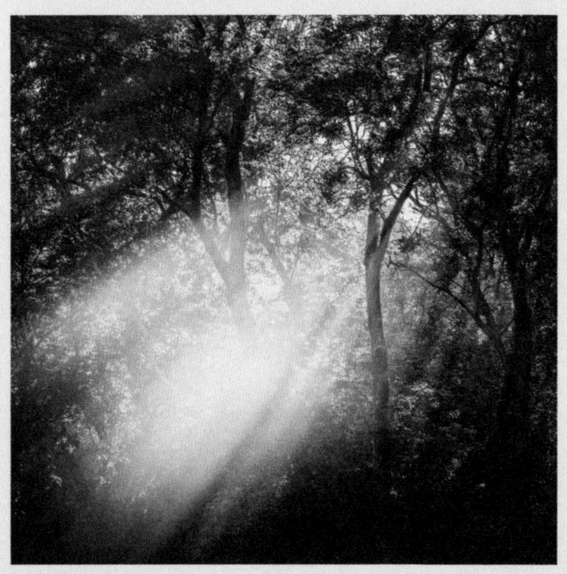

Creativity is also, conversely, about finding the things that connect us as individuals to everything else.

—

When I photograph something, I am not just photographing the appearance of a subject; I am photographing all the people and circumstances that have led the subject to me, or me to the subject. For example, if I photograph a building, I am photographing not only the structure or some detail of its architecture or interior, I am photographing the hand, eye and inspiration of the architects, the skill of the craftspeople, the artistry of the masons, and, beyond that, every person who has used or visited the building, leaving their invisible or visible mark on it.

Each one of those people is responsible for the moment my eye has been caught by something about that building. But it goes further than that. The rain, wind or sunlight; the building's socio-geographical location; my feelings that day – they are also responsible for shaping the way the building appears in that moment.

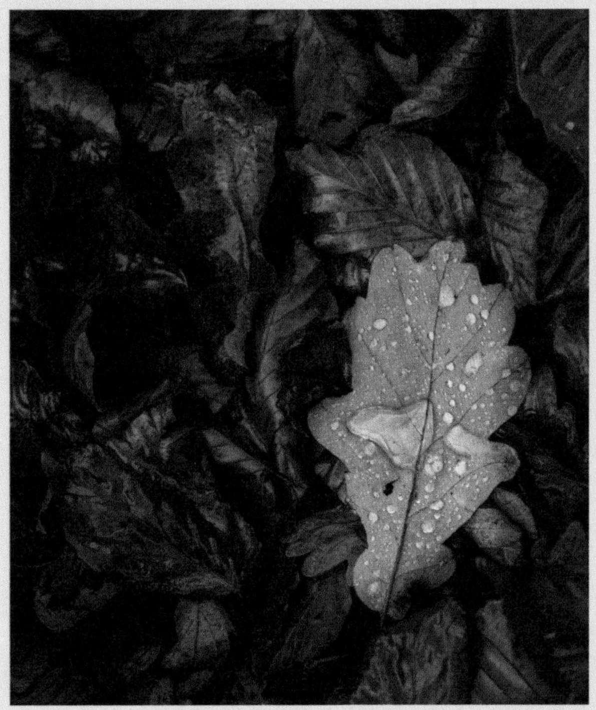

When I spend time acknowledging all that has gone into making the subject ready for me to photograph I feel gratitude for all that effort and time.

Aside from the beauty of discovering what is unique about each of us, creativity is also, conversely, about finding the things that connect us as individuals to everything else. When I think of creativity, I have to acknowledge a higher power; for me that is God, while for others it may be Mother Nature or even a force they can't name. Either way, there is a powerful sense of loving benevolence that comes from following that creative energy into gratitude, connection and peaceful acceptance.

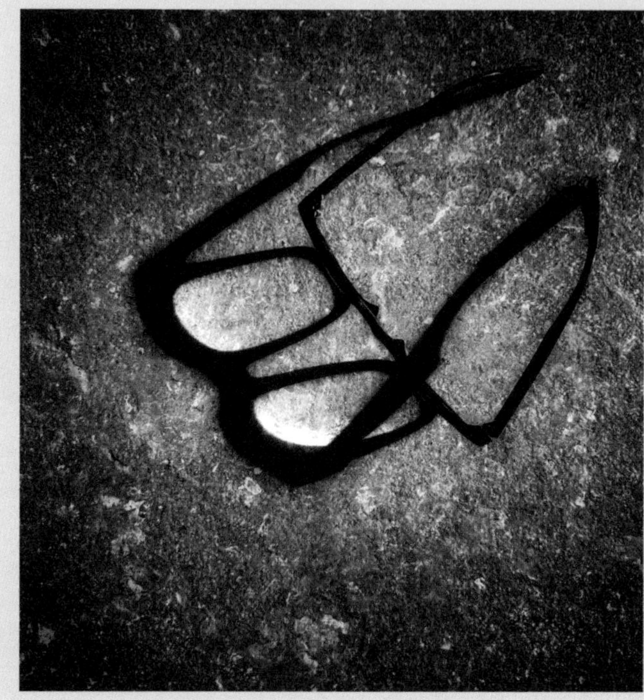

For this exercise you will need an object. Anything you have lying around nearby will do – it could be a fruit or vegetable, an item of cutlery, a glove, a stone or even a screwed-up piece of paper. Anything so mundane that you almost fail to acknowledge its existence.

Hold the subject in your hands if you can, or otherwise touch it, feeling its weight, form, texture. What does it feel like?

Close your eyes and, breathing deeply, turn it around in your hands. Take your time to discover as much about the subject as you can, letting your fingertips communicate all the different qualities they notice.

Open your eyes and let your gaze start to see the colours, patterns and detail of the subject; are there any scratches, tears, creases or other marks? Observe how its shape changes at different angles and how the light (and shadow) moves across the surface.

Now let yourself think about everything and everyone that has bought the subject to you, here in this moment of time. If your subject is a made object, where did it begin? What processes and hands did it pass through to be shaped and to arrive where it is now? If it is something natural, such as a stone, where did it come from, and how did it come to be as it is now, here in your hand?

Sometimes the answers you find will be beautiful; at other times, less so. It might not be very pleasant to think of the sweatshop workers' part in what you're holding, for instance, but these people deserve our attention and gratitude, too. Photography makes me appreciate everything to a much higher level than I ever used to. With gratitude naturally comes love, compassion and empathy, and, ultimately, a greater sense of who you are.

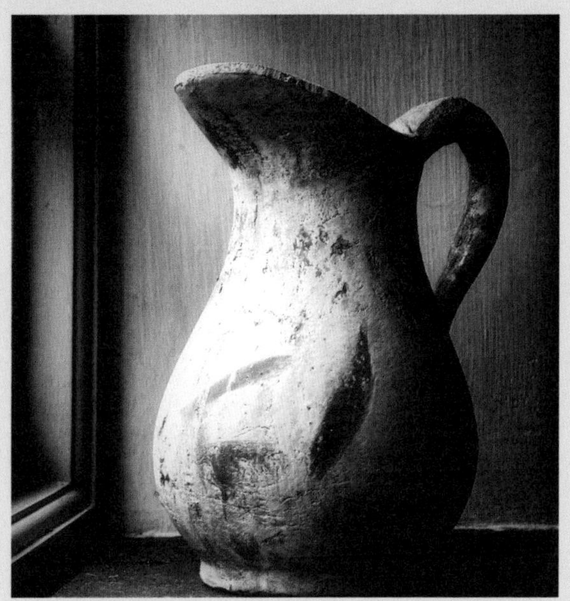

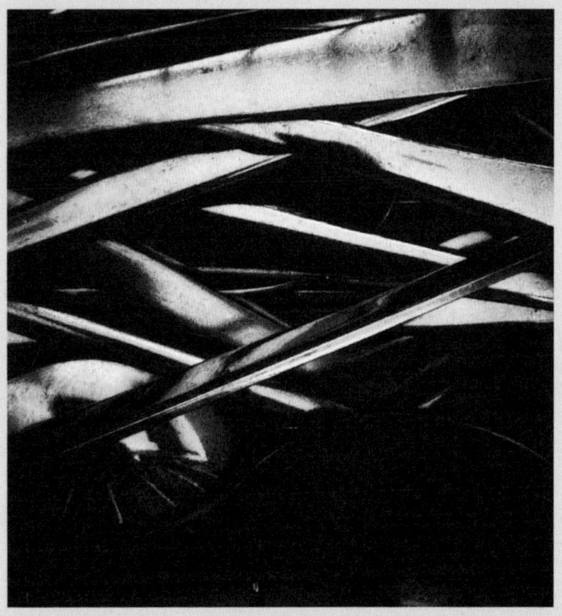

imperfections

Photography is the perfect vehicle for mindfulness, which, if sustained as a practice, can bring a sense of overall wellness, gratitude and happiness into your life.

I can honestly say that photography saved my life. After my attempt to take my own life, I had to find a means to reconnect with the world in a healthy way. Photography became the only thing that enabled me to make sense of the noise of the 'real' world and distil it down to quiet moments.

'Be still with yourself until the object of your attention affirms your presence' is a quotation from American photographer Minor White. I would add to this: reveal yourself to the subject, and it will reveal a moment of gentleness. The experience is so uplifting that, if I hadn't experienced it myself, I wouldn't believe it.

Rarely are we open about how we feel, or the state of our lives, instead hiding behind the masks we use to present a 'more acceptable' version of ourselves. Photography offers us a way to create a habit of stopping and reconnecting both with our authentic selves and the world around us.

You can think of it as a kind of meditation – not one that requires you to sit down, cross your legs and close your eyes, or do anything else that you might find unnatural or others around you might consider weird. No one ever notices people taking photographs these days, or if they do, they usually just want to see what they're missing. Photography is the perfect opportunity to stop and quiet the world, to create a meditative moment between self and subject.

'Be still with yourself until the object of
your attention affirms your presence.'
—
Minor White

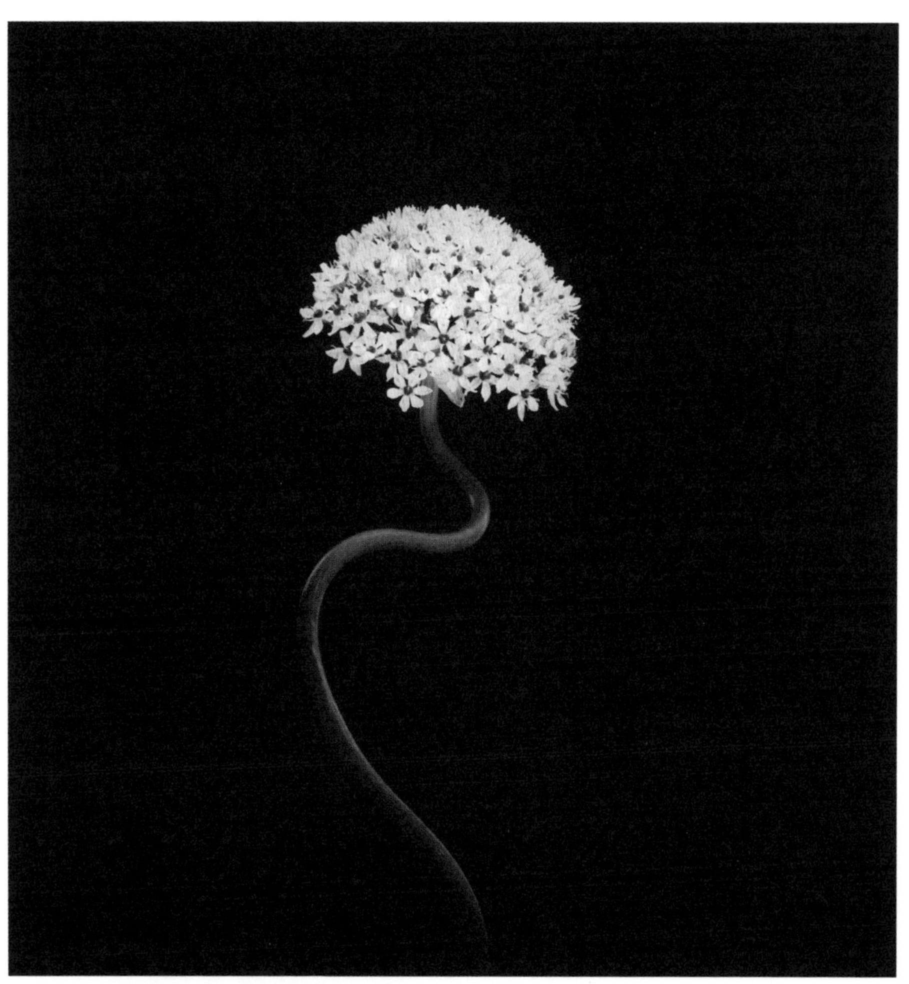

127   imperfections

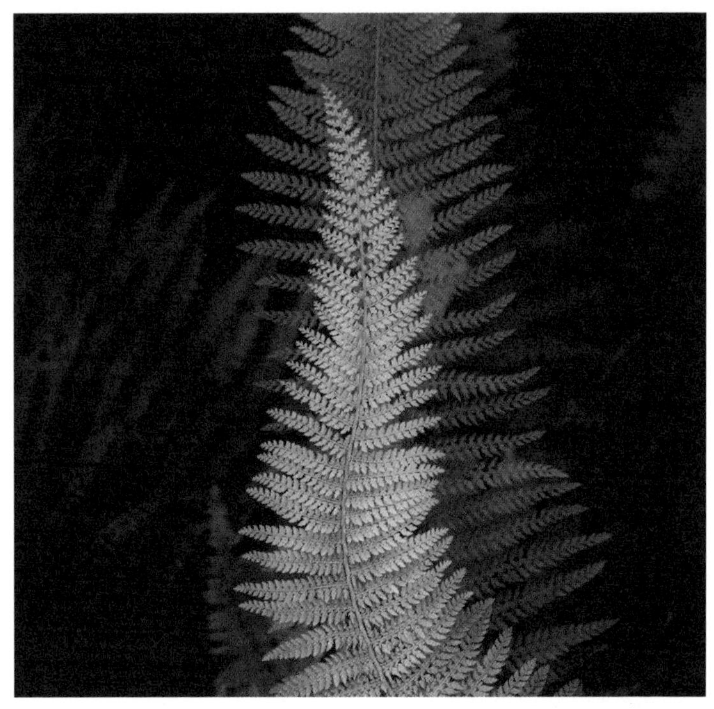

'Awareness that arises through
paying attention, on purpose,
in the present moment,
non-judgementally [...] in the
service of self-understanding
and wisdom.'

—

Jon Kabat-Zinn

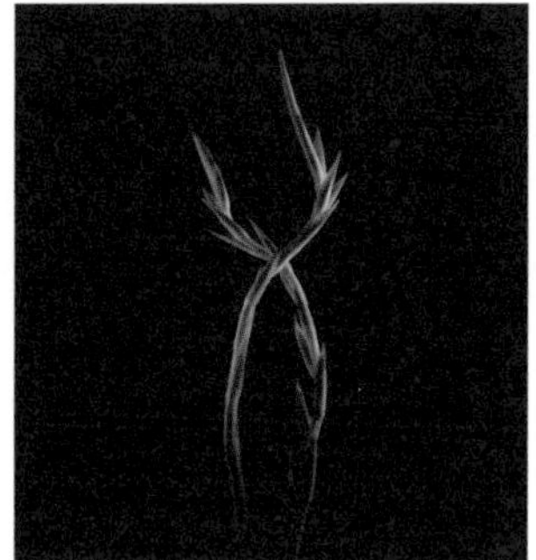

Every day can be filled with five-minute visual meditations. Meditation is a practice that involves focusing or clearing your mind using a combination of mental and physical techniques, which can help you relax or reduce anxiety and stress. When you make a photograph you automatically clear your mind of all the clutter. Like any skill where you need to pay attention to what you are doing – running, knitting, woodworking and all sorts of activities can have the same effect – you become so immersed that everything in that moment seems sharper, while internal worries and external distractions fade to irrelevance.

Jon Kabat-Zinn describes mindfulness as 'awareness that arises through paying attention, on purpose, in the present moment, non-judgementally. And then I sometimes add, in the service of self-understanding and wisdom.' For me, the key to attaining that 'self-understanding and wisdom' is being non-judgemental both with yourself and with your subject.

Gratitude is a big part of it. These days, I always try to treat my subject as I would wish to be treated myself, with kindness, gentleness and an appreciation of the unique beauty that each of us has.

This approach involves accepting the fact that no subject is perfect and neither is any person. Our flaws and struggles, the dents and scars, are what make us unique. It's never just the appearance of something that makes it beautiful; it is the story it tells us that catches our heart, emotions and imagination, and like the shadow to the light, it is the imperfections that tell the story.

In traditional Japanese aesthetics, *wabi-sabi* is a concept based on the acceptance of imperfection that is inevitable with the transience of life. The aesthetic is sometimes described as one of appreciating beauty that is 'imperfect, impermanent and incomplete' in nature. It is prevalent in many forms of Japanese art, including *kintsugi*, a technique of repairing broken pottery with gold, which renders the reassembled piece more exquisite than it was before the break.

Taking time to acknowledge and appreciate the story your subject has to tell you through its flaws and imperfections means you almost inevitably start to acknowledge and accept your own flaws and imperfections in the same way. It changes the way you see the world and how you see yourself, and it can be a powerful way of moving from suffering to recovery.

ASSIGNMENT: IMPERFECTION

Perfection does not exist. As a perfectionist, I can tell you I searched high and low for perfection – in myself, in everything I did, and in every person I had a relationship with. I constantly compared myself to others. Working at *The Times*, where my work was constantly compared to every other newspaper's image choice, exacerbated this tendency, and I was left with no uncertainty that most days my work fell short.

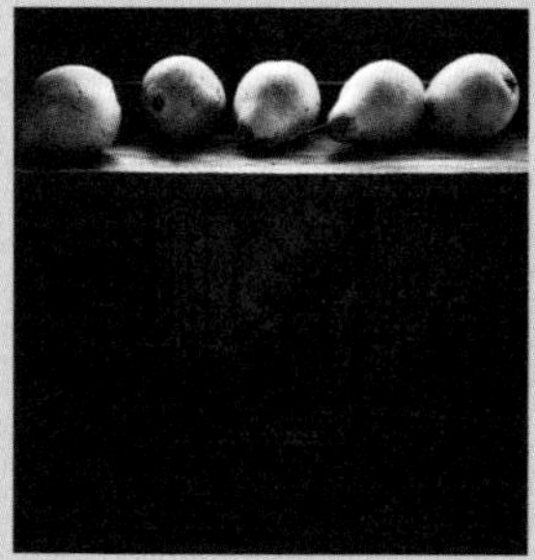 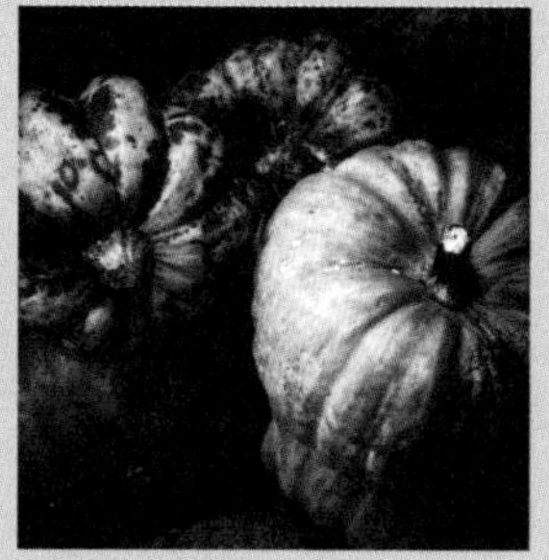 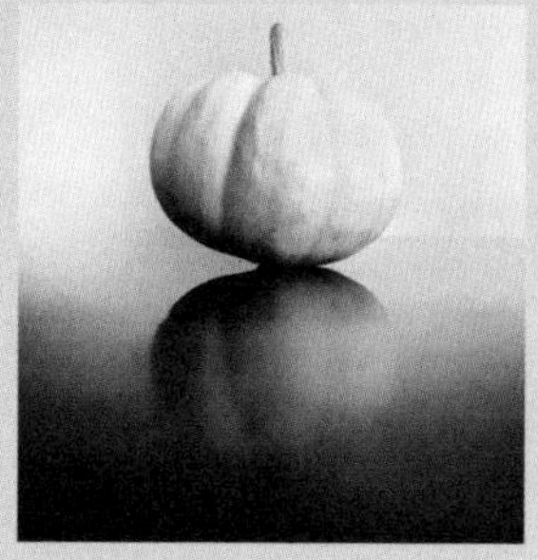

The truth is, none of us are perfect and nothing we come into contact with is either. Even if you can't see the flaws, they will be there. Many photographers painstakingly edit their images to erase any imperfections, just as most people will sweep away the messy clutter of daily life before making a photograph to share online.

For me, however, the imperfections are where we find the beauty, the truth and the uniqueness of a subject. If you look closely at a tree, is there any leaf that is completely perfect? Does the trunk grow straight, or does it twist, bend or lean, precariously balancing using its limbs? Does its bark appear flawless from bottom to top, or is it gnarled and scarred, covered with moss or full of holes? Nothing is 'perfect' in nature, and yet everything is. This includes human beings.

It is easy to point out our flaws to ourselves when we look in the mirror, and easy to judge other people for theirs, too, as this may make us briefly feel a bit better about our own insecurities. But it is

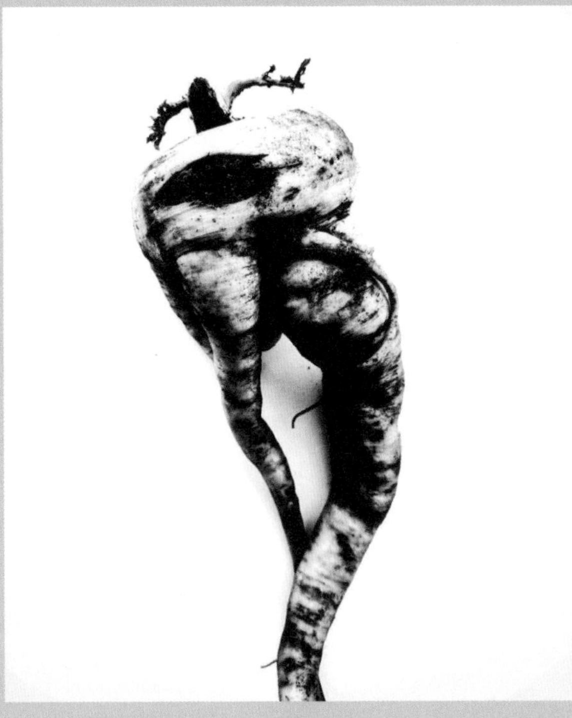

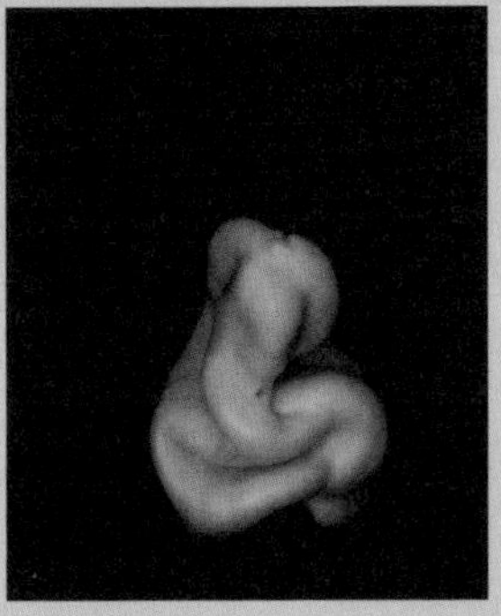

If your subjects have any flaws — be it a wrinkle, bump or dent in the skin of a fruit, a chip on the rim of a wineglass, a tarnished spot or discolouration — you will likely find yourself drawn to these areas, because it's these things that can't be replicated but come from natural use, wear and ageing, and it's these things that make your subject unique.

In his song 'Anthem', Leonard Cohen sings, 'There is a crack, a crack, in everything. / That's how the light gets in.' There are things about ourselves we may want to change, but we may first need to change the way we think about our flaws.

also possible to understand our own and others' flaws in a more positive and generous way.

For this exercise you will need two items that appear very similar — slightly wonky fruit or vegetables work, but it could also be a pair of different wineglasses, loaves of bread, stones from the garden and so on. The aim is to make a pair (or series) of photos that celebrates the ways in which things are different.

At first, you will probably see more similarities than differences between your chosen subjects, but keep looking, practising all the skills of seeing to notice as much as you can. Look at the colour, the tonal variations, the shape from different angles, how your subjects catch the light.

5

visual pauses

A series of images with written reflections

In nature, I am reminded to sit in silence, to be open and receive whatever is offered, for it is only in silence that we can truly see or learn to simply be. To photograph, it is essential not only to be, to look around you and inside yourself, but to do so with quiet wonder and fascination in every moment.

It is only in silence that we can truly see or learn to simply be.
—

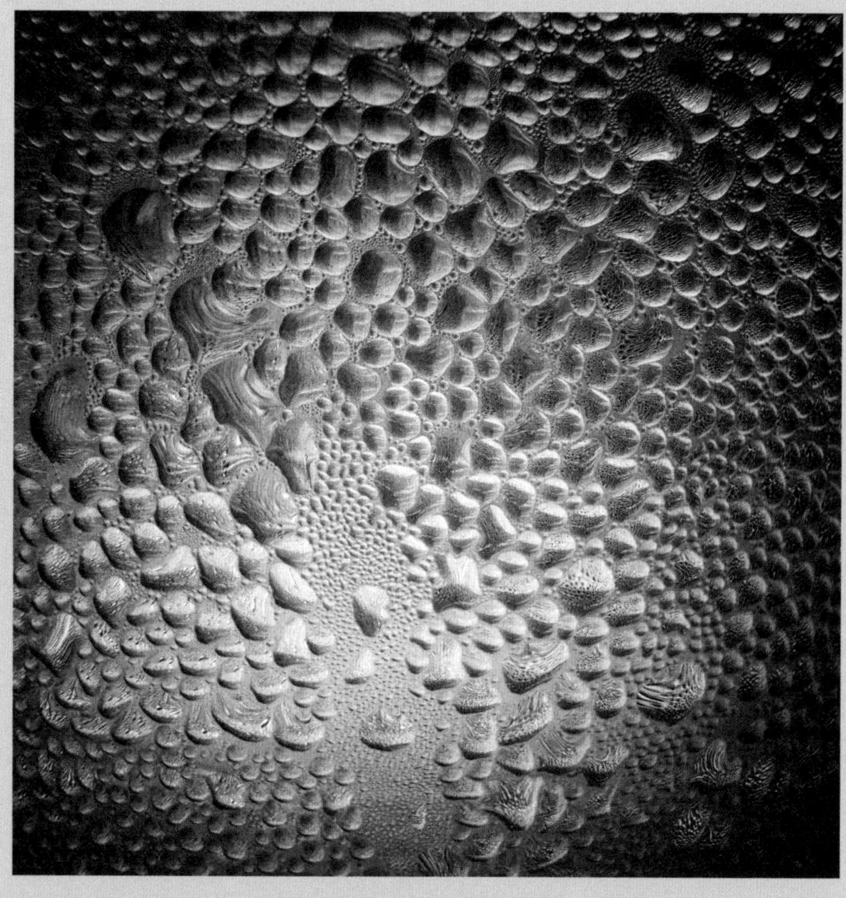

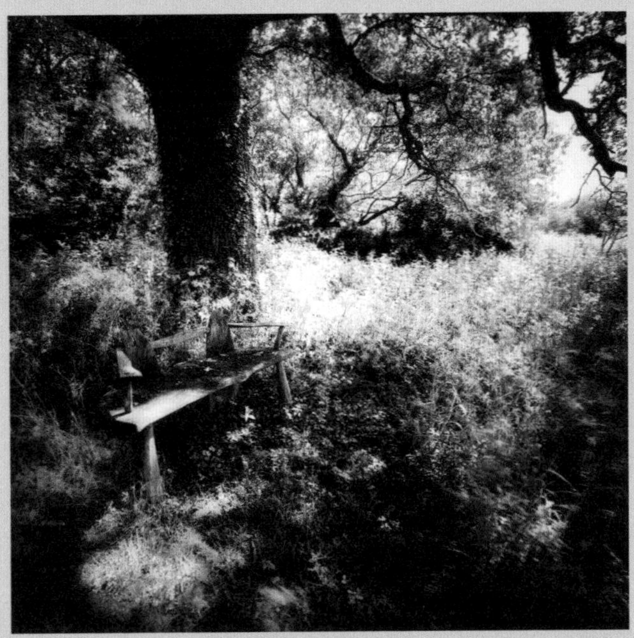

To find a spot and rest without guilt or shame is a blessing in life. How often do we feel awkward about stopping, checking to see whether anyone is looking, perhaps apologizing for taking our time to sit and stare? Being bored, sitting and looking at the world as it races past is not a crime; it is an important exercise.

Stopping, resting, taking five, can be powerful creative time. It allows your mind to settle and drift aimlessly. Just sitting without purpose allows calm and space to permeate through your body and mind. All too often, though, we apologize for being lazy if we are caught or spotted, instantly feeling guilty for appearing to be doing nothing, when in fact we are doing the most important thing for ourselves – just being intentional about being.

Find a place today where you can stop, sit and intentionally do nothing – with no phone, coffee, book. Just stop and watch the world carry on without needing you for a few minutes, breathe in deeply and sigh each breath out as a release. Then, after a few minutes, get up and walk a little more slowly and enjoy the feeling of you being in control of your day and not the day being in control of you.

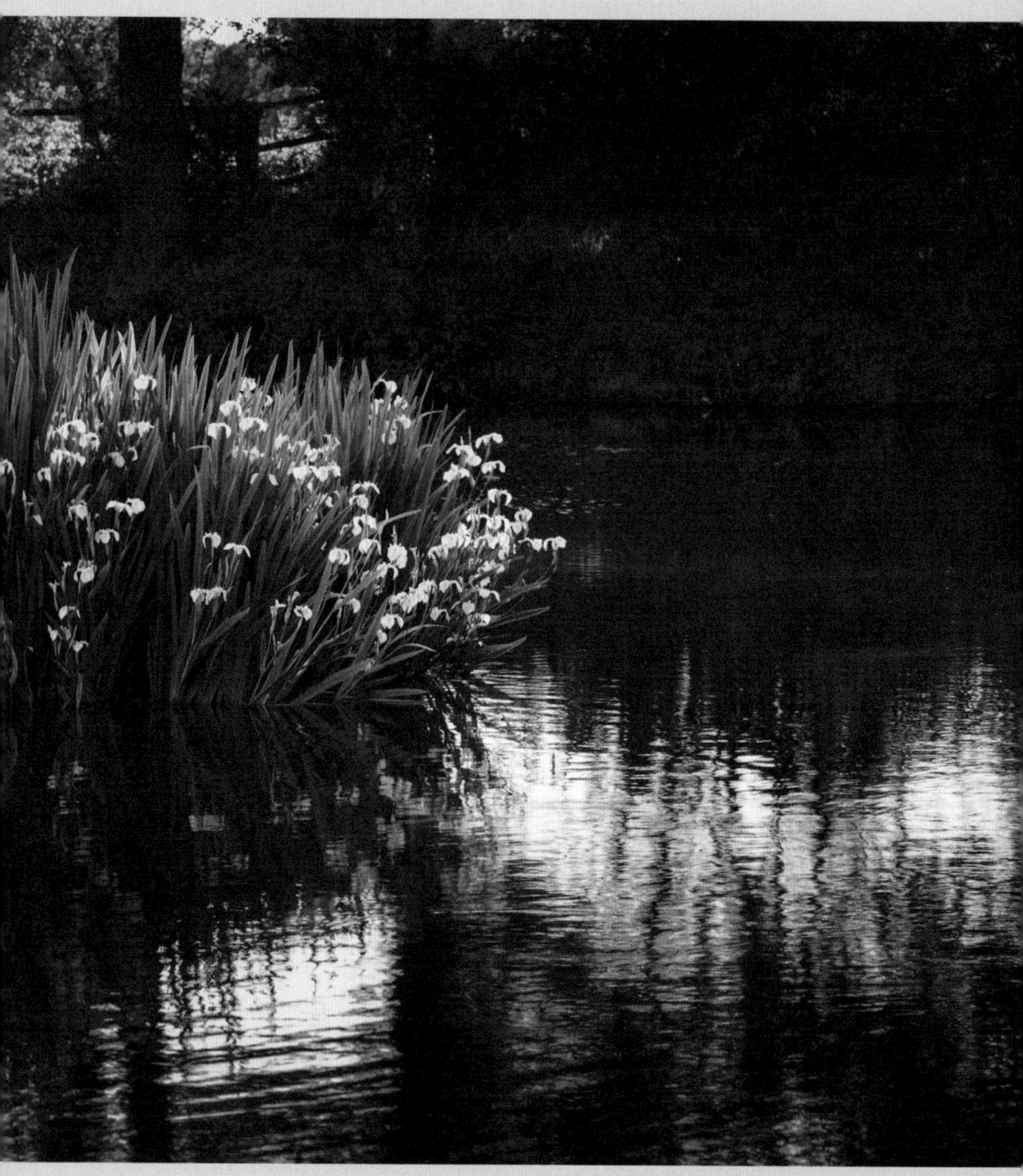

I often wonder whether beautiful things view themselves as we do. I know that sounds daft, but take the irises in the photo opposite, surrounded by water, competing for the energy of the sun, their reflection permanently distorted by the wind and the busyness of the wildlife using the pond. In many ways our constant search for validation is much like the iris seeking the light and warmth of the sun, our beauty becoming distorted by the world we live in. The mirror we view ourselves in is shaped by the social context of our upbringing.

But, unlike the iris, we are conditioned to doubt ourselves. The iris comes back every summer, but do we bounce back from the constant criticism from self and others? These days we seem to pay more attention to our failings than to our successes. Perhaps we should take a leaf out of the iris's book of life to just be our best selves everyday. What if, instead of spending our time gazing at the distorted reflections around us, we could turn our faces to the sun and use that energy for good – radiating beauty outwards, sharing it with the world without needing validation, just knowing we are enough as we are.

Allow yourself the gift of mindful moments every day. Allow yourself to just be, not do, and you'll find your life all the more beautiful.

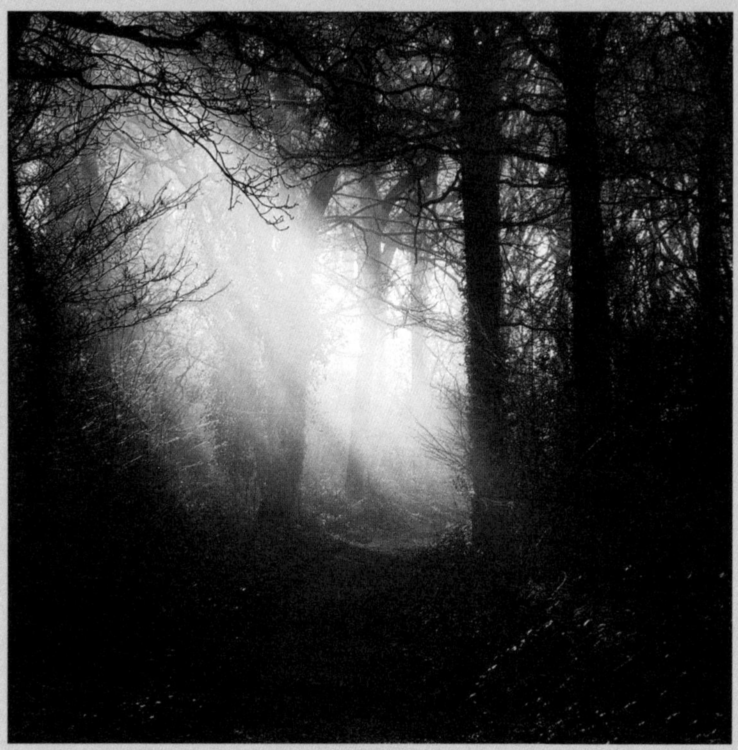

We all have a point in life where the odds are stacked against us, where every step is painful, filled with fear. These are the times when we have to trust, to have faith and to believe in ourselves (and in my case, in God). All too often our self-belief is eroded by the constant noise of negativity that fills our head, a narrative fuelled by today's world's need for us to be perfect or better. Many of us let go of our dreams because of fear, doubt and lack of trust in ourselves or in whatever higher power we might believe in.

There's no easy way through these moments – the doubt, fear, anxiety, demons, all seem insurmountable – but with a simple exercise you can start to turn the tide. Write down in a journal three times every day for six weeks: 'I am enough – I believe in myself and my ability.' Do this every day and after six weeks you will be surprised at how much more you believe in yourself. It takes courage to tread the untrodden path, to make your own path, and to achieve the change you want to see and feel.

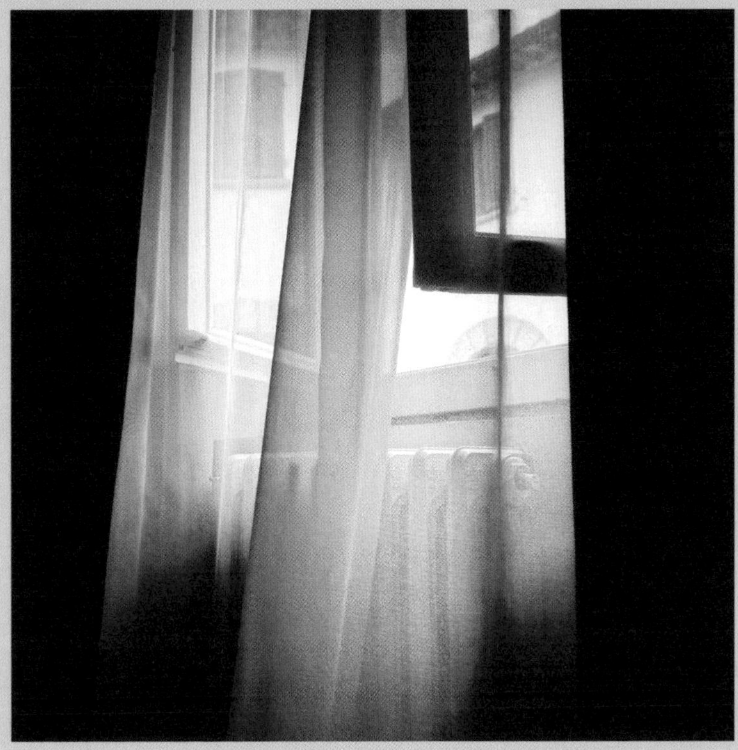

Change comes into our lives in many ways. Sometimes it rages like a tornado, ripping the fabric of our existence to shreds, often with disastrous results or consequences. But it can also creep into our soul, like a soft breeze on a summer's day, refreshing our lives. Both types of change require careful management and will involve discipline, disappointment, frustration, elation, consolidation, but, above all, an openness to adapt to, and adopt, the fluidity of the situation we are facing.

Change is one of the very few things that is continuous across our lives. If we resist change, we risk stagnation. Change is really evolution. It is us growing as we try out new ideas, situations, people, places and processes. Those most offended by change are often not the ones changing, but those watching it happen. Many people are fearful of change in others, preferring the comfort of what has always been and not embracing what others are becoming. How do you view change, both in yourself and in others?

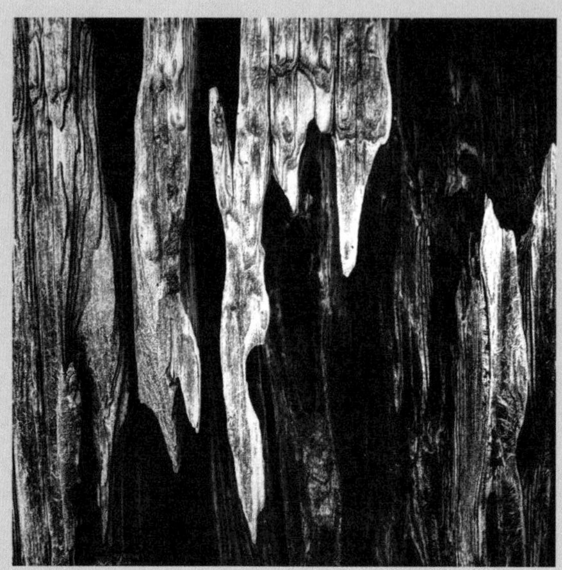

How much of our true selves do we hide, as we try to fit into a world that demands we lead perfect lives? Our days are filled with judging, or comparing our own poor existences to the social media lives seemingly so full of riches. Our eyes stare from empty sockets as we believe we never have, or are, enough, and so fill our lives with meaningless stuff.

If only we understood we are already rich beyond measure, that it is when we let go of the need to seek material treasure that we will find fulfilment and our unique self. Our lines and scars are more valuable than clothes, watches and cars; they tell of a life lived, honest and full, they make us real, not shallow, vapid, dull.

To erase or hide our signs of ageing in search of eternal youth makes us just another victim of a marketing scam. When you next look at the person in the mirror, trace those lines and folds; they are your story being told. They make you who you are; they are your life in all its sadness and delight.

Feel the wind on your face, the warmth of sunlight after dancing in the rain...these simple pleasures are never in vain. Stand tall and proud, holding your head above the crowd as your celebrate learning to lead your own life.

When I look around at people going about their lives I often wonder whether they believe in or feel joy in the everyday mundanity of life.

Are you the battered tattered door bolted against life or are you the daisy dancing in the morning breeze? Despite shade, wind, rain and the unfavourable terrain, the joy and beauty of the daisy remains the same.

Even on your most trying, troubled day, take a moment to acknowledge and appreciate that there are moments of joy in the everyday.

—

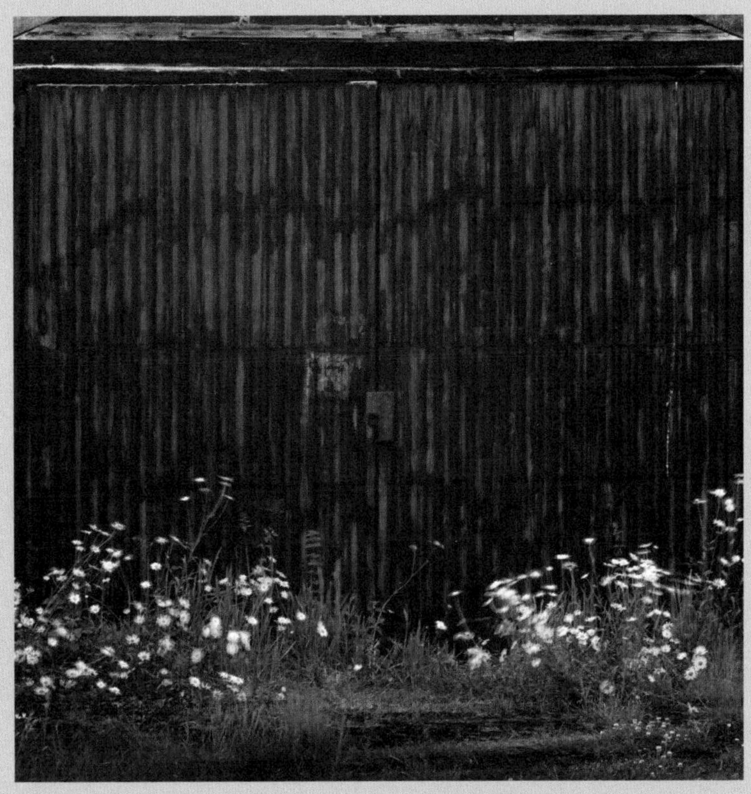

Trees are incredible – I'm a sucker for a tree. This yew (opposite) is about a thousand years old. Legend has it that the door was fitted over damage from a cannonball, and to this day villagers held meetings inside its massive trunk. Imagine how resilient it has had to be, how adaptable.

Although none of us will live to be a thousand years old, we need to learn the art of survival. Not so we will live as long as a yew, but so we can navigate our own lives, building resilience, perhaps a slightly thicker skin, maybe losing some old relationships or habits that no longer serve us. If you spend long enough with a tree, you will realize that very little fazes them: they adapt and overcome; they support one another; they give new life a chance; they provide safe shelter for animals and bugs, and food for themselves and others. Trees are generous, kind, forgiving and patient – oh, the lessons we could and should learn from trees.

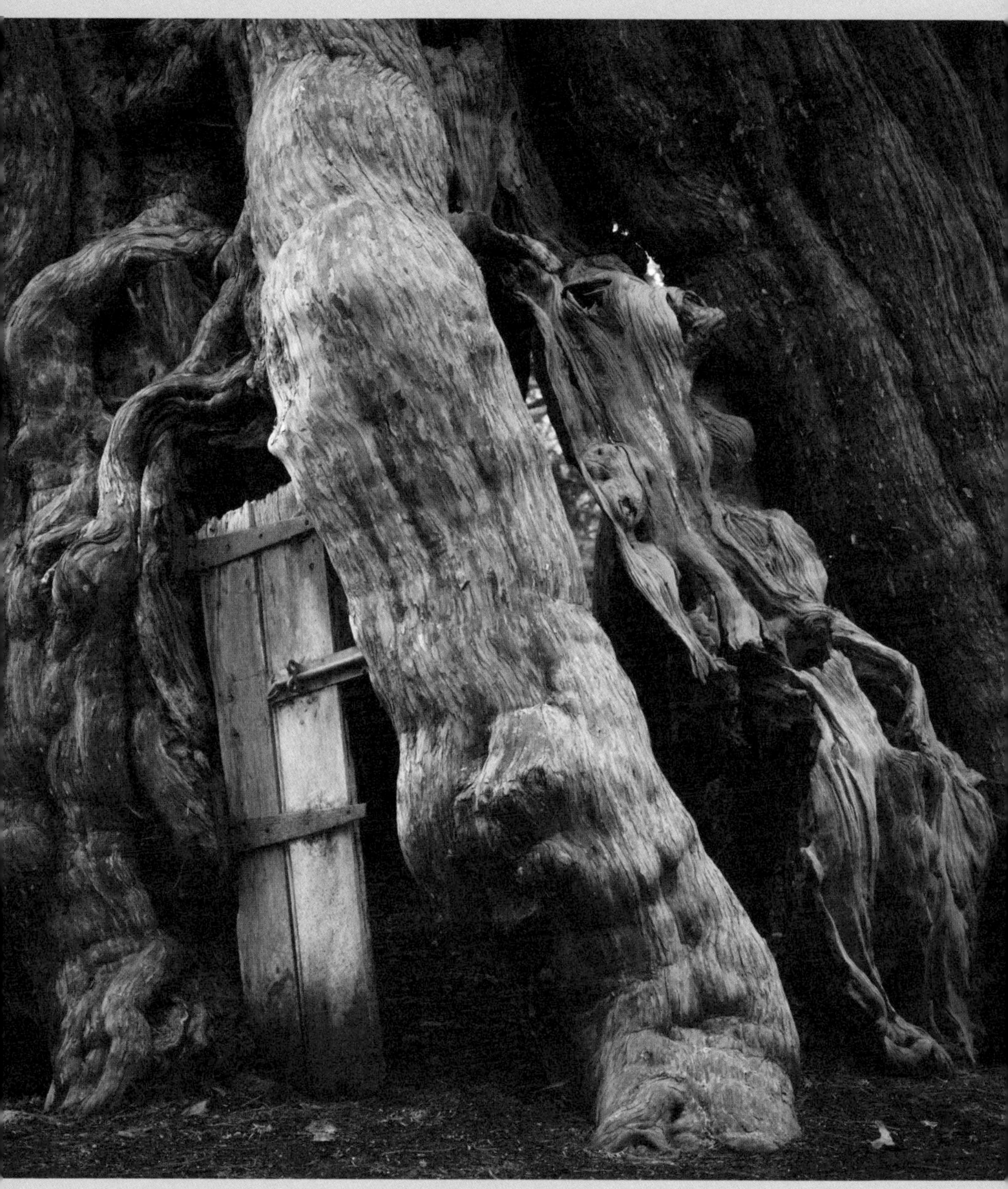

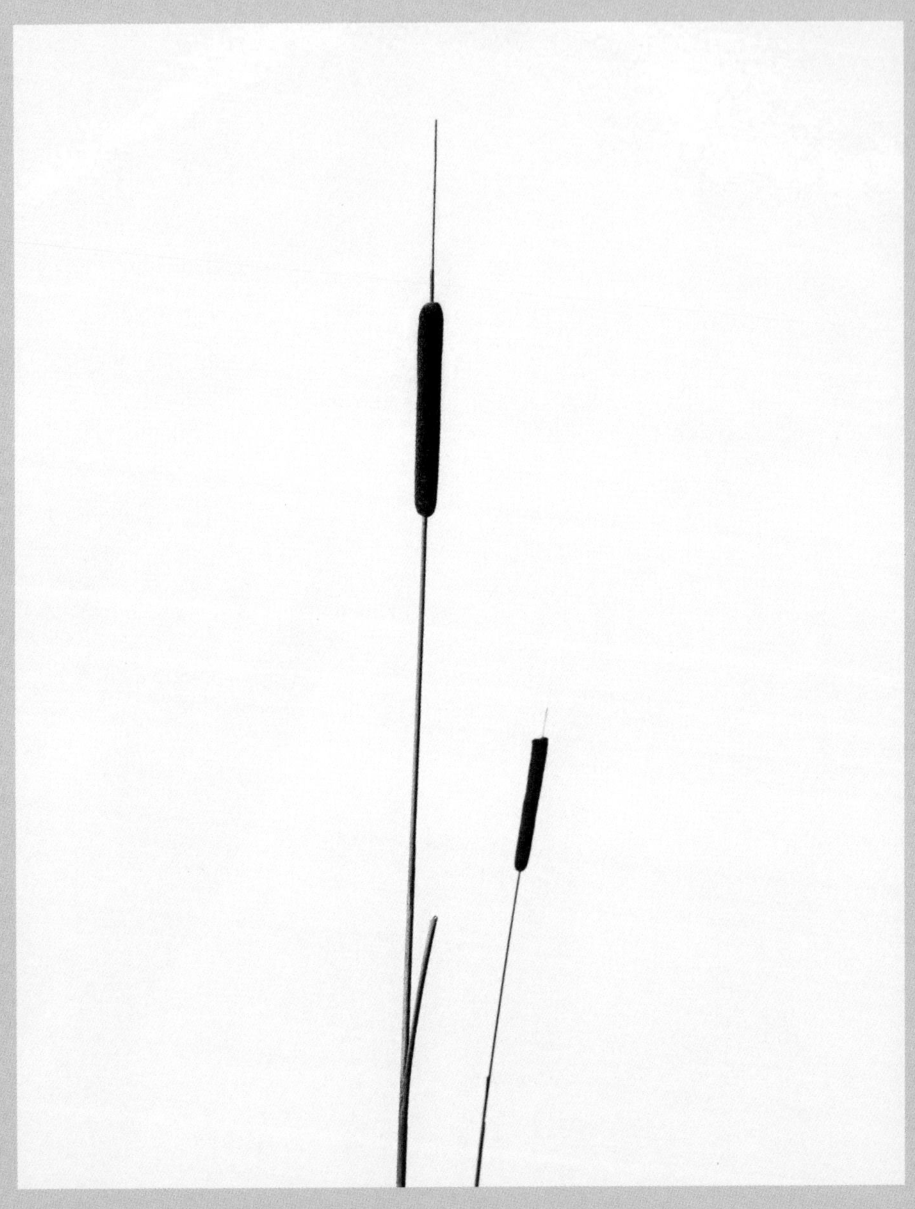

Bulrushes have an outward elegance, but inside, deep inside, a battle for survival is raging. In winter, they stand on the edge of a lake or river, their roots frozen solid, and yet somehow still alive at their core, waiting for spring so they can flourish.

Outwardly, many of us seem calm, with smiling faces, appearing caring, interested and engaged, but under the hard surface of our armour a battle is raging, unnoticed by even our closest friends. The battle we have within ourselves is a bloody and unforgiving war. The way we often treat ourselves is appalling: we are cruel and unrelenting in our self-destructive mindset.

If you, like me, suffer these internal conflicts, remember you are not alone. All those people around you who look as though they have all their ducks in a line are looking back at you thinking how together you look. Perhaps if this world wasn't so driven by material success, we would all be okay with who we are and how we look, and wouldn't need to wear armour or masks to convince the world we are fine when deep inside we are all longing for just a little bit of sunlight to warm our faces and make us feel okay with ourselves.

It is only in our own stillness that we
can be aware of the true pace of nature.
Nature moves slowly at times, the transition
of movement almost imperceptible. Nature
moves with purpose, undistracted by noise
or temptation. Can you find internal
stillness, silence the distractions and step
off the hamster wheel that is modern life?
The world doesn't need you to seek
validation through distraction; the world
knows you are enough already. It only asks
that you pay attention long enough to
notice how beautiful it is and you are.

The world knows you are
enough already
—

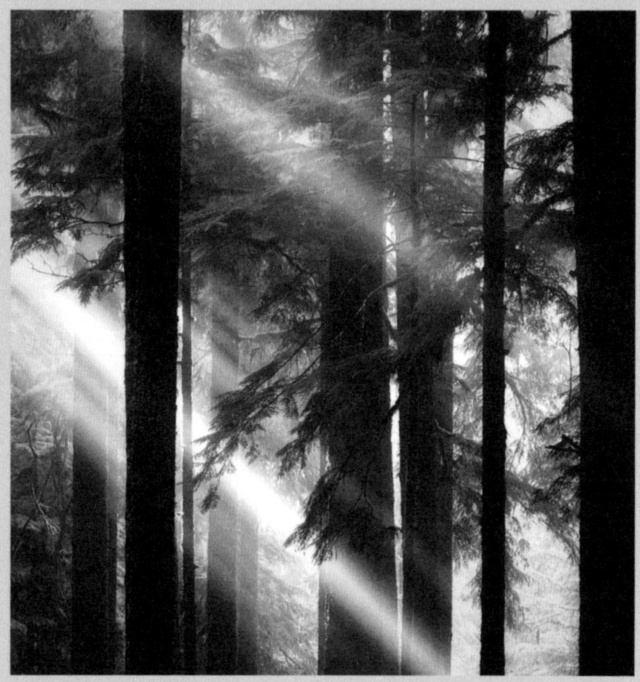

Let's talk about remote working. By 'remote' I don't mean working from home, surrounded by distractions and noise. I mean working in a remote environment, with little or no phone service, no WiFi, TV, radio or rolling news, just nature. I have been embedded in, and held, by the giant Douglas fir, Sitka spruce and hemlock trees, cathedral-like in their watchful silence. I have walked on beaches, making the only human footprints as the Pacific roars over the rocks and driftwood, marvelling as bald eagles, seals, elk and otters have crossed my path with curioisity. I have lost myself and the need to be something in the enormity of the rainforests and the smallness of who I am. By inducing silence in myself I have come to deeply appreciate the beauty in silence. There's no secret to being happy, but it does require each of us to switch off the chatter and tune into the interconnectedness of nature and listen to our hearts.

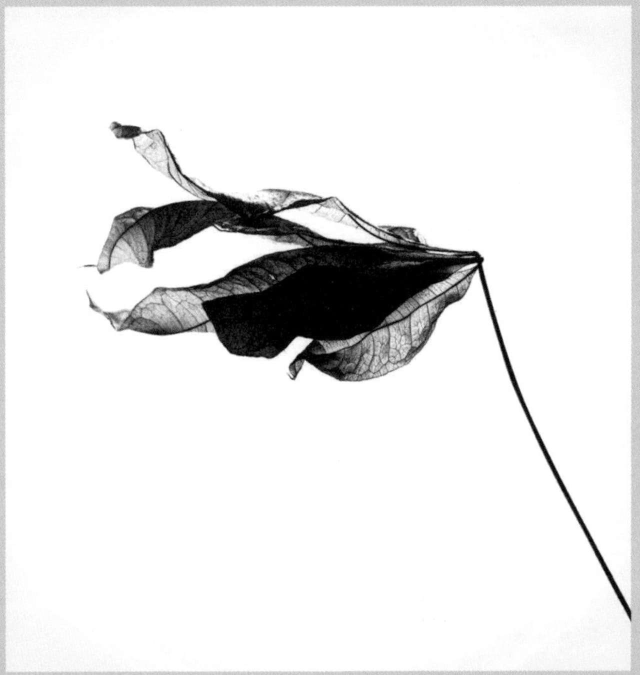

As the leaves fall from the trees I wonder whether the trees let go of the leaves or whether the leaves let go of their parent?

As we make the transition towards autumn, it is a good time to let go of things or people that no longer lift us up or make us feel we can be ourselves. It is never a bad thing to release your hold on something that doesn't serve you, something or someone draining every ounce of energy from you. Autumn is also a time when, in the northern hemisphere at least, parents let go of their children as they either start school, move school or leave home for university. This is an especially hard time for parents as they seek adjustment to the new normal and watch as their child is influenced in ways they can't control anymore.

Sometimes letting go can be as gentle as a whisper; at others it can be filled with nostalgia and tears; and at others again it can also be like having your heart ripped out. Letting go requires self-care, gentle love of your heart and patience with yourself. Letting go brings its own cycle of grief no matter what kind of letting go you are going through.

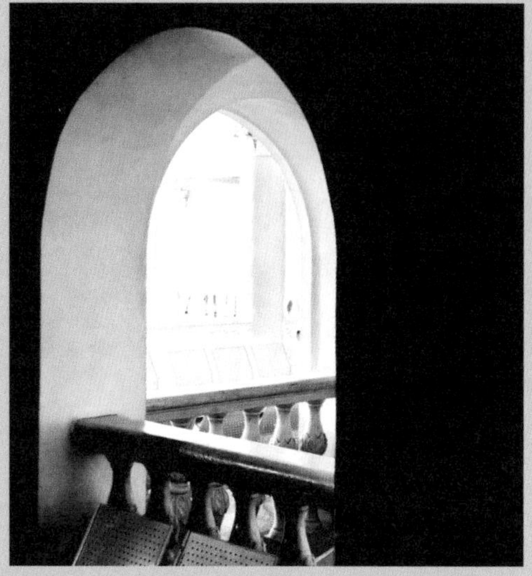

Sometimes things go wrong, things that are totally out of your control. Do you respond, or do you react? The least stressful response is to step back, take a breath, and turn your attention to the beauty that surrounds you. There is beauty, craft, imagination and skill all around us, often created or shown by unknown people. Instead of getting annoyed or stressed, be inspired by the beauty of the place you find yourself in, while allowing that which you can't control to unfold to its own resolution.

The way forward sometimes feels like the most impossible journey, battling low energy, low esteem, lack of confidence, addiction or any mental health challenge that leaves you asking 'What's the point?' The entire journey can be undertaken only one step at a time; you don't even need to know where you are going, just that you don't want to be where you are. Move forwards a little everyday. You will slip or stumble, but that's okay, because you know you have the strength to dig deep and go again.

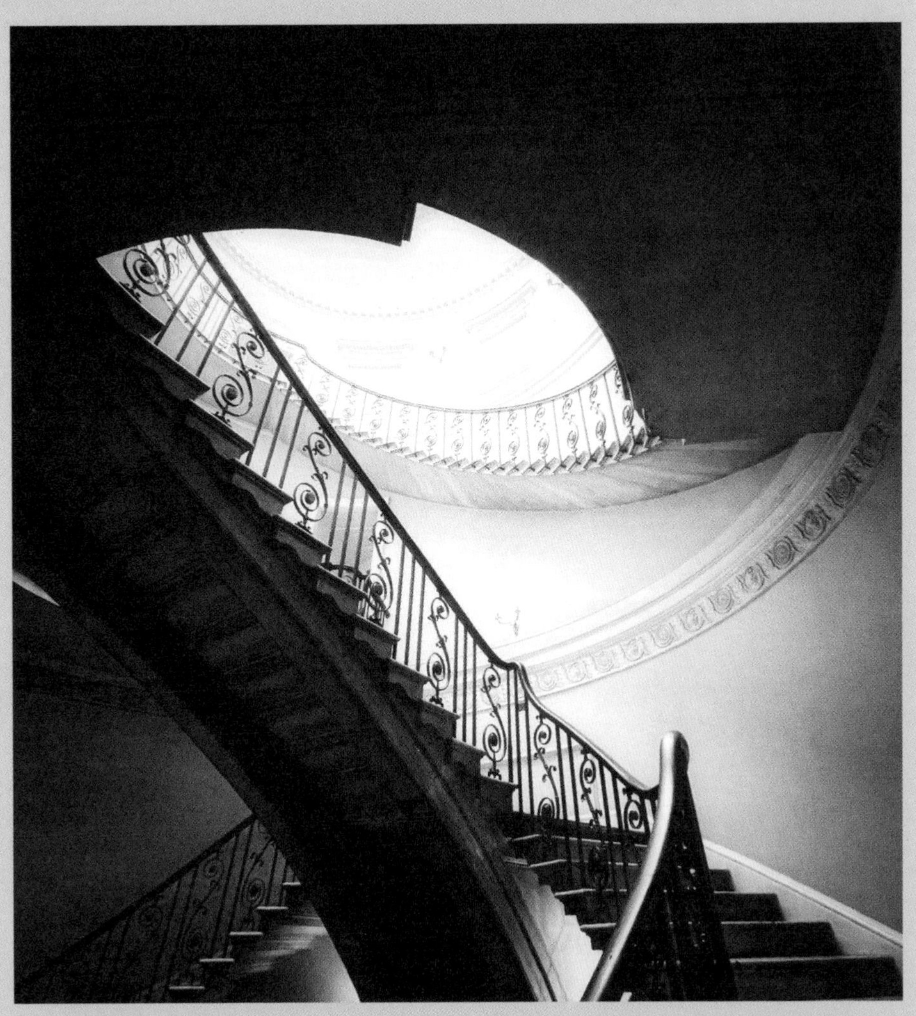

Often, I feel vulnerable and exposed, as if all of my weaknesses and failings are constantly on show. I'm never sure whether this is the case, but my head gives me a high-definition running commentary on how these insecurities are being interpreted by those around me. Even while writing this I can feel my anxiety rising. Why are we hardwired to be so damning of ourselves? Finding a space in your vulnerability for self-kindness is truly important – being able to offer loving kindness to yourself, or a gentle listening ear, can make a huge difference. Out of my vulnerability and insecurity comes creativity, be it writing, photography or drawing. Somehow, being able to create something that reflects how I feel moves those feelings on and out. No, it's not always successful, as occasionally my head is louder than my heart, but learning to love myself, for all of and because of my perceived shortcomings, has been a game changer for me.

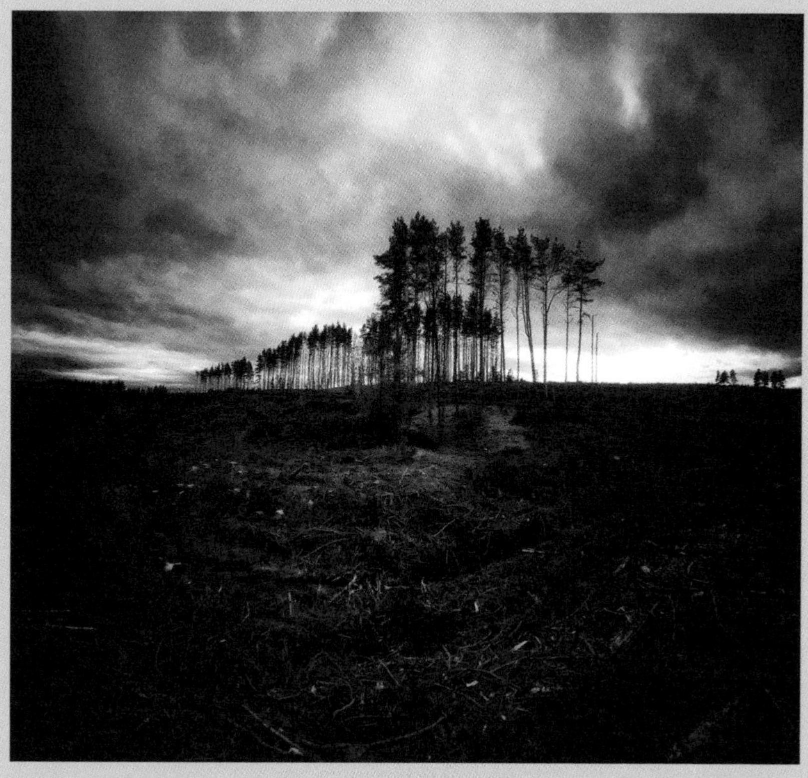

How do we deal with adversity when there seems to be an outpouring of negativity and resentment, criticism and blame?

In the turmoil of the modern world, it is easy to blame, hate, shame and be quick to anger. But in my experience, a quiet response – a prayer filled with love and compassion for those who rant and rage, for those who blame or hide behind those they want to blame – is the best response. In short, I have learned that love is the answer – love that comes with imagination, tenderness, compassion, understanding.

Perhaps there are many people out there who could learn to love in a new way, learn to love those who make mistakes or struggle – because we all make mistakes. If we start to look at situations that cause us pain or frustration with love, understanding and compassion, we won't be consumed by hate and negativity. We will see people trying their best despite what the world throws at them. After all, you never know what is going on under the surface. You see only one-third of an iceberg above the surface, and the same is true of people. Remember to love and be excellent to each other.

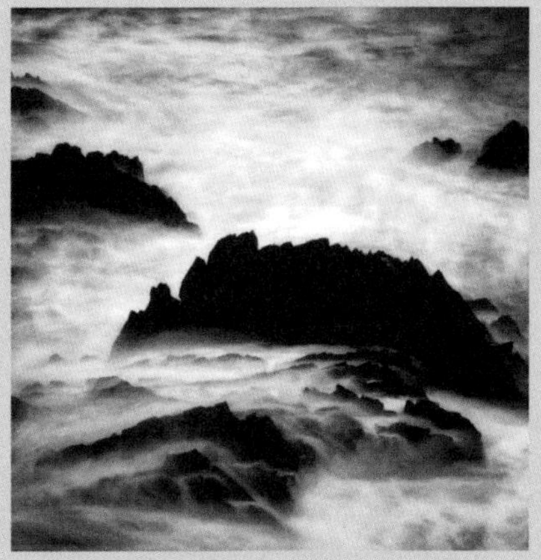

I have learned that love is the
answer – love that comes with
imagination, tenderness,
compassion, understanding.
—

Since leaving my last 'real' job at
The Times, one of the things I have
struggled with most is how to deal with
stress. My life is nowhere near as stressful
as it used to be but now I find that the
tiniest thing takes me to breaking point:
my anxiety rises, my sleep goes, my skin
gets irritated and I am constantly chewing
my lips.

Think of our bodies and minds as
vessels that are constantly being filled with
daily stresses. Eventually, the stress will
overflow and drown us, unless we have a
release value that we can control – not by
indulging in explosive anger or violence or
abusing others, but by reconnecting with
ourselves, letting the stress out slowly and
gently, through a daily practice. For me, it
is mindful photography, mindfulness, sea
swimming and yoga. For others it might
be knitting, drawing, jogging, cycling,
making bread.

Find something that you enjoy, that
you have to be totally present for and in
the moment, that takes your focus, and
let that replenish and relieve you. Then
you can climb out of the pool of stress
and know you are in control because
you have your own release valve.

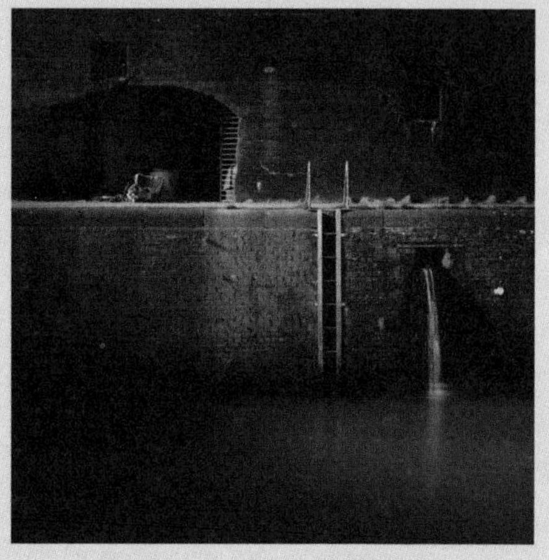

[Release the stress]
by reconnecting with
ourselves, letting the stress
out slowly and gently,
through a daily practice.
—

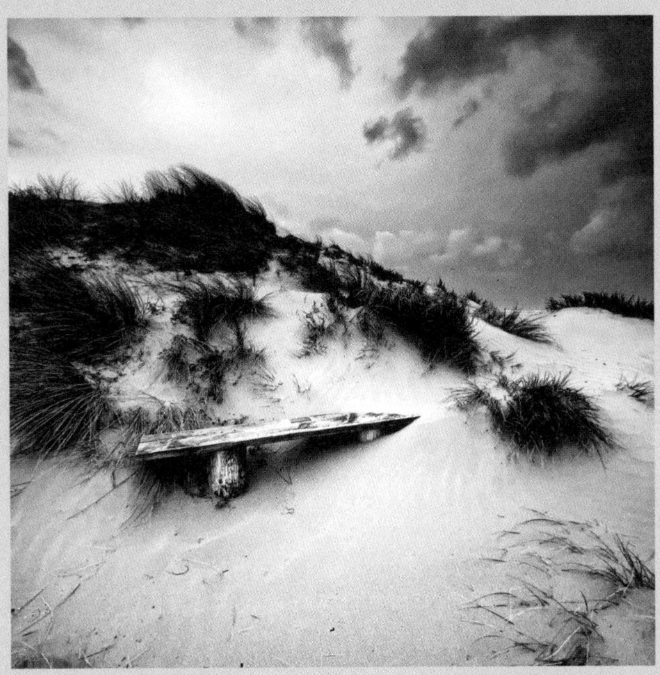

We can easily lose ourselves in the turmoil and overwhelm of life, not knowing where to turn or take shelter. Often, shelter lies within ourselves, not externally. We can find peace through grounding ourselves in the present moment, observing rather than allowing ourselves to be overrun. Grounding yourself means pausing for a second in the maelstrom and focusing on the present moment.

Sit down wherever you are, close your eyes gently, relax your jaw and breathe in through your nose. Feel your breath move through your body to your lungs and your belly. Feel your body expand, then let that breath out, feeling your body contract. Do this ten times to activate your parasympathetic (rest-and-digest) nervous system and to deactivate your fight-or-flight mode, which the modern world insists we reside in.

When you finish, open your eyes and enjoy the simple beauty of something you notice for only 30 seconds, and then carry on your day taking that small bit of calm with you.

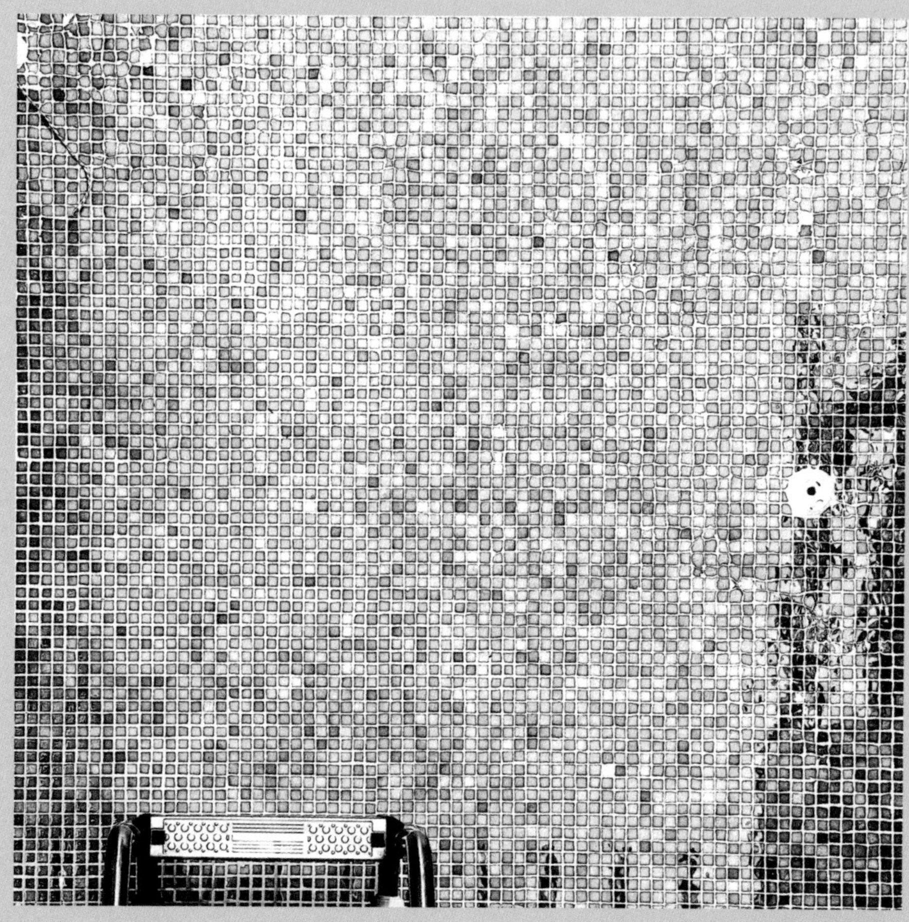

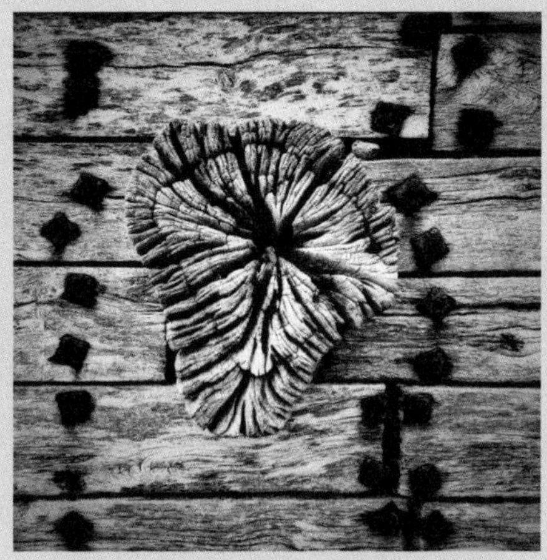

Do you step in gingerly, perhaps feeling as though you are drowning as the water closes over your head, or do you dive in and immerse yourself, feeling the silken texture of the water embrace and enfold your body? The water doesn't change but our approach and experience do. Neither of the approaches above is right or wrong; they are different because we are different.

If you are confident in a situation, rather than laughing at a person who is nervous, anxious or full of trepidation, offer encouragement and support. If you're nervous about a situation, know that it is okay to take things one step at a time, and then, as your confidence grows, allow yourself to fully explore the experience with curiosity rather than fear.

Whether you are a square peg in a round hole or a round peg in a square hole we all feel slightly out of place at times. It is normal, especially when we feel misunderstood or mistreated. Sometimes we can also make ourselves feel out of place or awkward by listening to and acting on our inner narrative.

However out of place you might feel, it is important that you remain authentic to your own values, moral code and ethics – it's very easy to try to fit in by changing who you are, but that will only lead to an even greater sense of unease.

Always be true to yourself and stay authentic. Whatever shape you are, remember that you will find the perfect fit for you soon.

How easily we tie ourselves in knots with our need to please others, compromising everything that is dear to us in a bid to seek the approval or validation of those who in reality don't matter – who don't care about us.

Untangle yourself from people pleasing and those who take from and drain you. Those who really care will accept you as you are.

Recovery from any illness is not a straight line. There are always highs and lows, setbacks, moments of doubt, lack of faith or trust in the process. Mental illness can feel like a downward spiral, as if we are on our own internal helter skelter – only less fun. The feeling of not being in control, of being helpless and afraid, overrides everything else.

The recovery is hard, very hard, as we make every faltering step back up that helter skelter, always expecting to slip or trip, feeling the weight of our helplessness sucking us backwards. But gradually, somehow, we muster the strength to keep pushing upwards into the light; yes, we will slip, stumble and lose our grip, but look how far we have come! That crazy helter skelter is not easy to navigate but we find our way.

The key is one breath, one step, one hour, one day at a time. It's not about where you've been, it's where you are that matters. Be kind to yourself on the days you slip; you're not a failure for falling. Celebrate the smallest victory, and the fact that you are at least trying

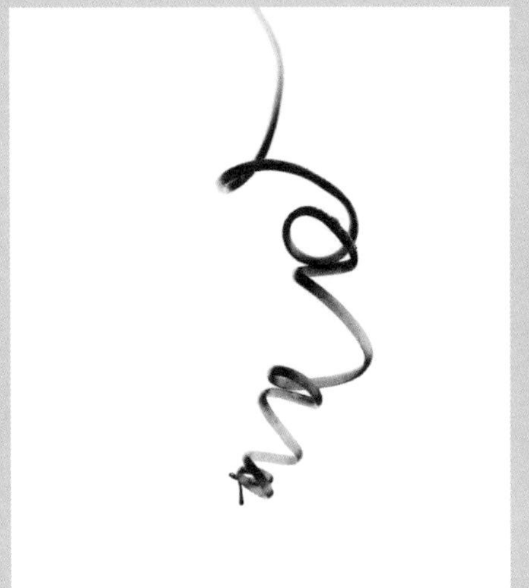

Enjoy each jewel life presents. Even on the darkest days there are miracles of beauty that can fill your entire vision with joy. Embrace the beauty, grace and wonder of each day. Awareness and noticing lead to gratitude for all that you have – and, more importantly, allow you to break away from the *FOMO* (fear of missing out) and embrace the *JOMO* (joy of missing out)!

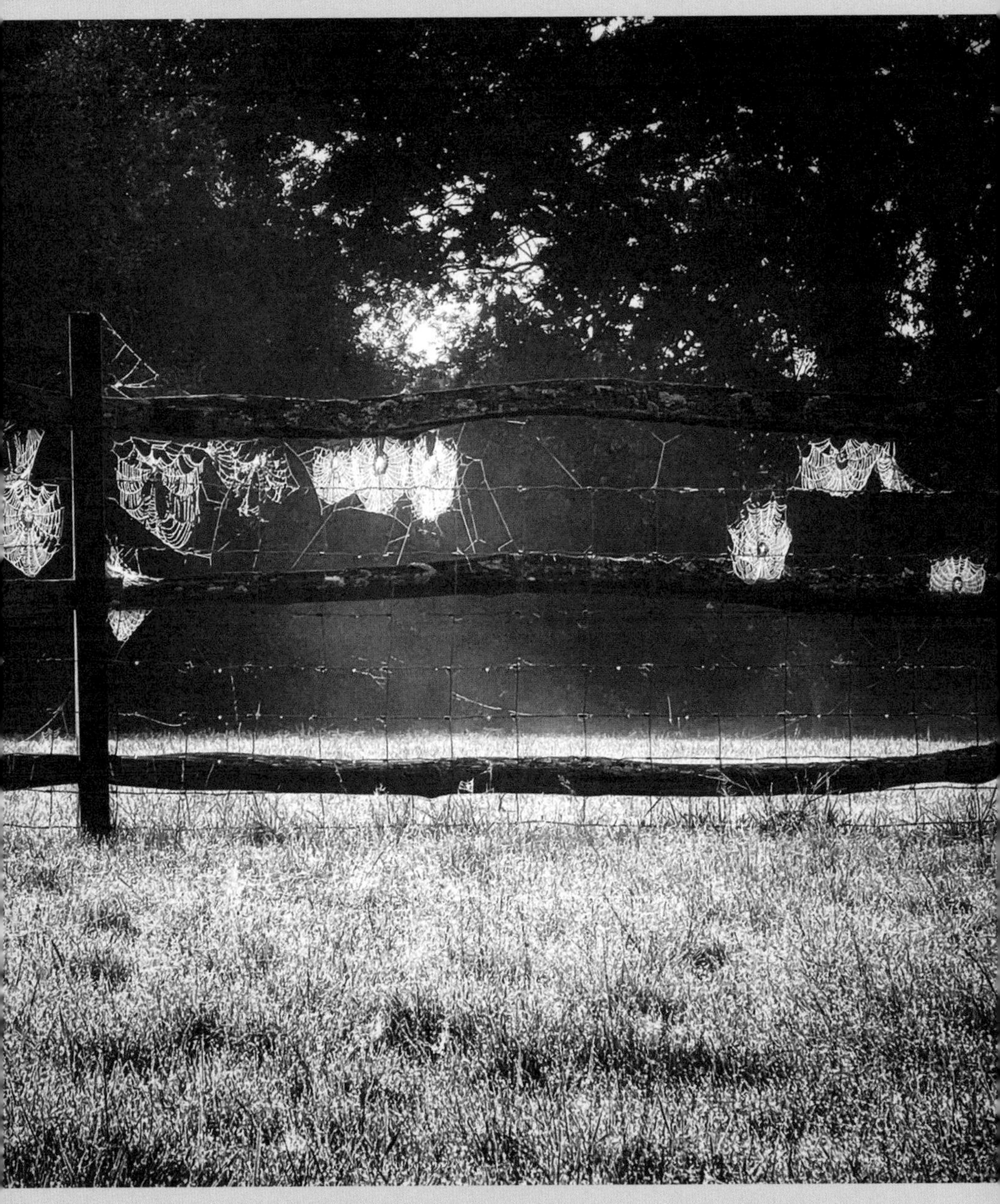

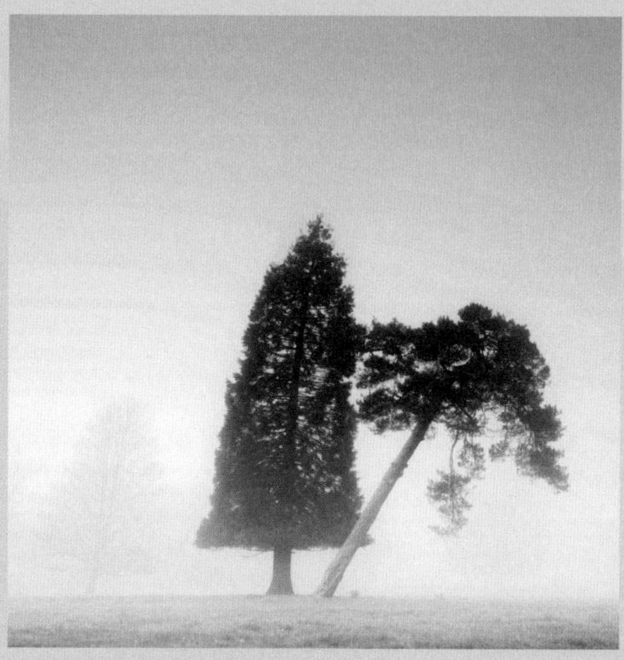

Are you falling or getting up? Is the person next to you pushing you down instead of helping you stand?

Judgement is a terrible thing. We leap to first impressions and make judgements based on our own conditioning, but have we stopped to observe what is really going on? In the seconds it takes to view a scene, we make hundreds of decisions about it – literally hundreds – and often we won't be moved from those thoughts because of our need to prove ourselves right.

Before making a decision about what you think is happening, ask yourself what is actually going on. That person who is seemingly rude or off hand might be having a crisis at home or have lost their job. View others and treat others the way you want to be seen and treated. If your kindness isn't registered or recognized, don't react with anger; just smile and inwardly know you made their day a tiny bit easier.

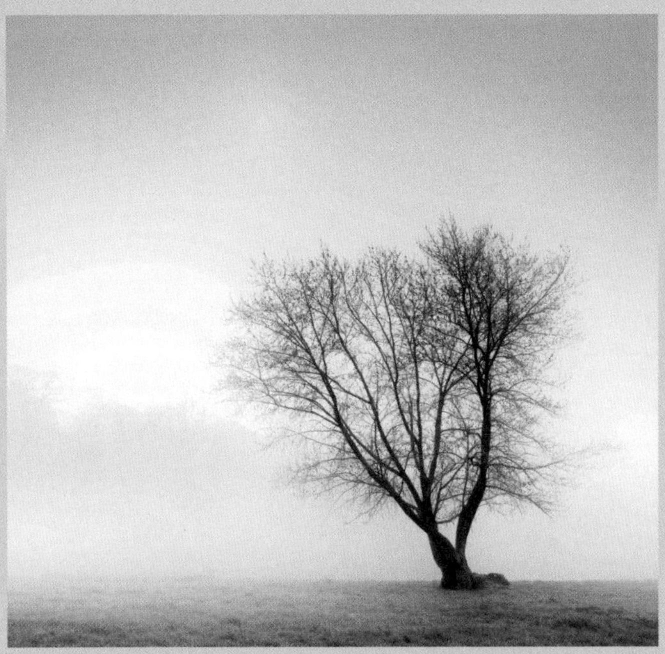

I used to think that trees were bent out of shape, but as I've paid more attention to them, I've realized that the curves, bends, twists and breaks are their story. A tree, given no external pressure – wind, poor soil, perfect light – will grow straight and even, as symmetrical and as perfect as the specimens we draw as children.

The pressure of real life gives the tree its unique beauty, broken by storms, burned by lightning, twisted by wind, bending towards the light. We are so similar to trees: our life experience shapes both our internal and external selves so that our unique beauty becomes visible to the world. We just need to realize it is okay for that story to be seen and stop trying to conform to the unacceptable ideals society demands of us.

Be more tree: be unique, be proud and fall in love with your twists, bends and wrinkles, your grey hair, your spots, lumps and bumps ... your brokenness. You are beautiful, you are strong and you are enough.

Be more tree.

—

6

breaking through

One of the words I recommend you ban from your
life is 'should'; replace it with 'could' and see what
a difference the power of choice makes.
—

creative block

The experience of creative block can be disconcerting, but by being grateful, accepting and generous within it, it is possible not only to work beyond it but learn important lessons along the way.

It is inevitable that at some point you will stop feeling inspired, become bored or disillusioned and want to give up your photography. Finding yourself blocked is really frustrating, and it often leads to a cycle of self-criticism, self-inflicted pressure and overcompensating by trying too hard. All of these things get in the way of any enjoyment, making you feel even less inspired.

Believe me, I have been there many times – so many times, in fact, that I've become grateful for these periods of blockage and started to appreciate them for what they are. Learning to accept a block as a necessary break rather than an obstacle puts things in a very different perspective. Rather than worrying that you really ought to be taking pictures, you can enjoy not having to do that right now and use the time for something else.

Having defined myself largely as a photographer since I left school, there have been time when I've felt this means I should be making pictures all day every day. Choosing not to force it when the desire isn't there, and when I know I'll just be running myself down, is strangely empowering. This is a huge mental shift; you can feel the weight of expectation lift almost immediately.

In fact, one of the words I recommend you ban from your life is 'should'; replace it with 'could' and see what a difference the power of choice makes.

Just because we're not taking photographs now doesn't mean we're not doing valuable work. The chance to rest and reset is itself an essential balance to the periods when we have high energy, and these times offer a chance to reflect on what we have achieved and what else we might want to do. At the same time, these moments can prompt us to examine our art honestly.

Often, a block can mean we have started to become a bit set in our ways; we are overlooking things, judging them and ourselves as not quite right or good enough for the picture; becoming blind to the everyday simple beauty that fills our lives. Otherwise, it might mean we are coming up against a technical limitation. If the same thing is consistently bugging you about the way your images turn out, see this as a good thing. If you can identify what it is you're not happy with, you can look for creative ways to change it.

When all else fails, I find sharing my knowledge and experience with other photographers a really good way of exercising my creative skills without actually having to make any images. Not only do I always learn something from doing this, but it is a great thing to get out of our own heads and spend the time helping others. So many people helped me when I was new to photography that it feels like my duty to pay it forward, so I always try to help those new to

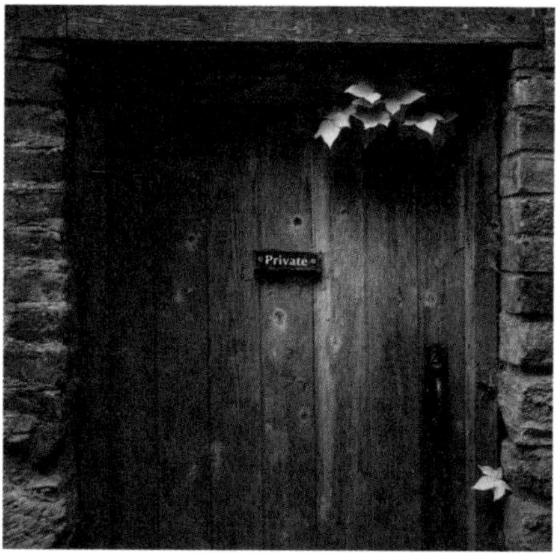

photography or struggling with it, especially when I feel challenged myself. Strangely, these moments when I'm able to help someone else always seem to unlock my own gratitude, making me realize there was something in my photography or life more broadly that I had perhaps been taking for granted.

Gratitude is a habit that takes work to maintain, and when we start losing our sense of gratitude, our vision narrows; we lose our curiosity and become judgemental. What once might have fascinated us is no longer interesting; it blends in, bland and ordinary, so that we can't even see it.

Writing a gratefulness journal helps re-establish the habit of gratitude for the small things in your life. When I feel blocked or frustrated with myself, I carry around a small notebook and write down in it all the things I am grateful for, starting by noting three things on day one and adding another to the list each day. Making this list moves me from self-pitying woe to a place of noticing the good moments of each and every day.

Another way I work with my blocks is by becoming a beginner at something again. There's something wonderfully freeing at being at the start of something, with little idea of what you're doing or where you're going, but no restrictions either – only open horizons and the chance to experiment and explore.

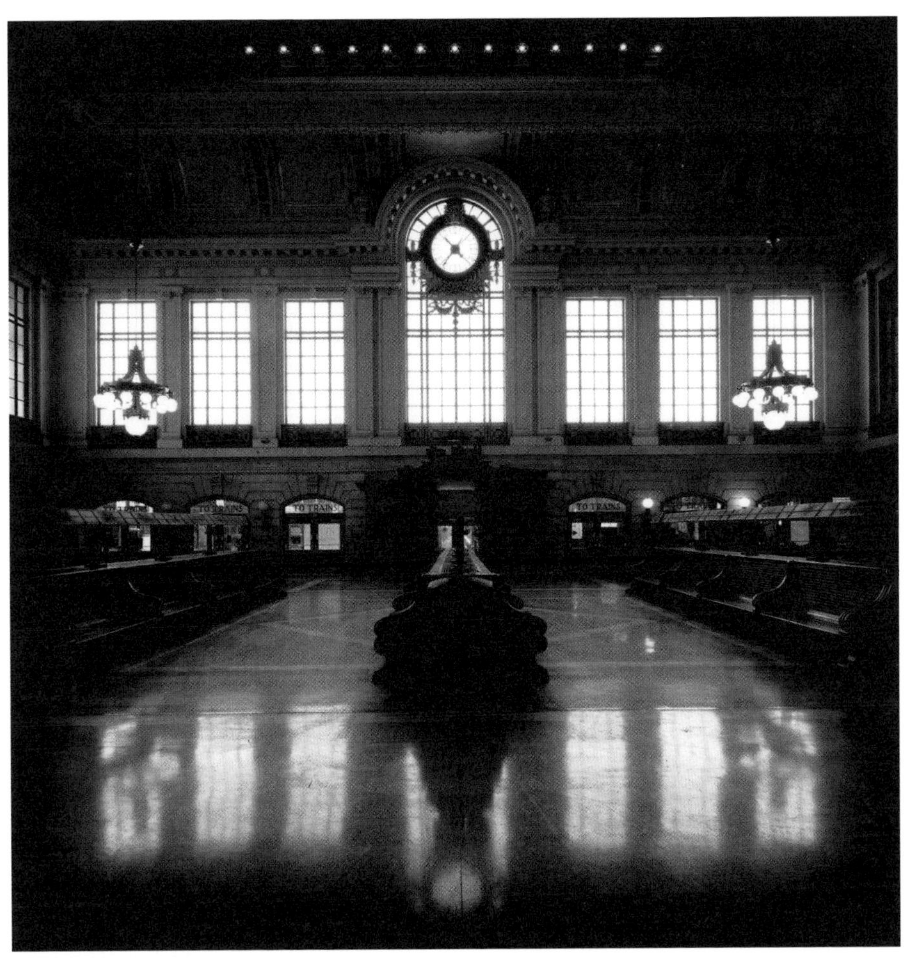
TO TRAINS
TO TRAINS
TO TRAINS

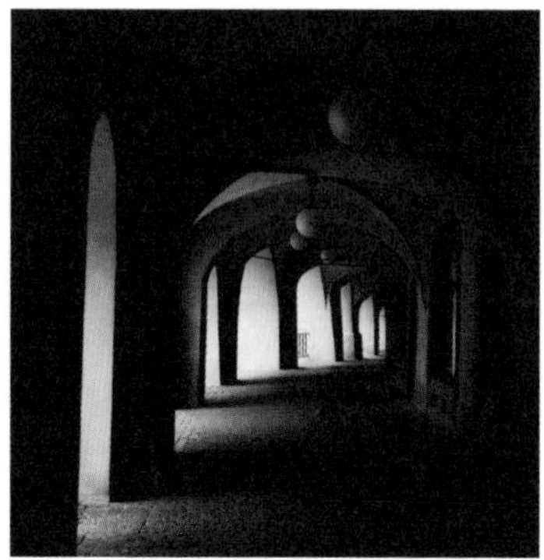

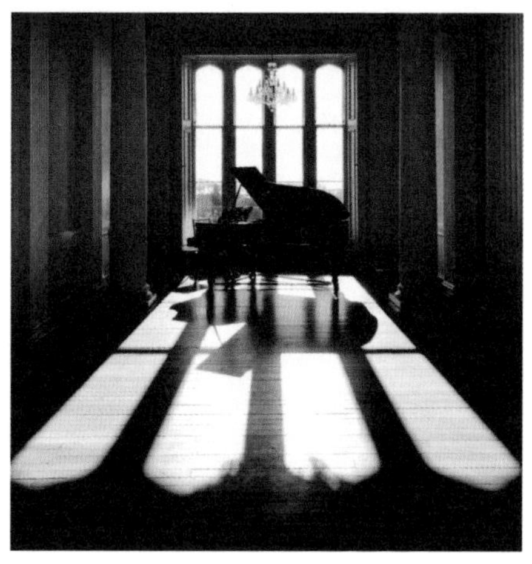

I will pick up a pencil or lump of charcoal and draw, scribbling freely without any particular ambition to be good or better, just enjoying the freedom from my own expectations and seeing what comes of it.

I do the same thing with ink, watercolour and poetry, and every year I book myself on a workshop with an artist or photographer in a genre that I don't have any experience with. Despite all my years of experience, it is fun to start over, and try approaching a new style of photography with a mind clear of expectation. Whether it's a different genre or a different art form altogether, I always come away with ideas and inspiration.

One of the greatest dangers when we become more established and confident in our art is the lure of the comfort zone. By now, we may have hit on a formula that means we expect to come away with good results every time – why would we stray from that? The thing is, we don't practise

Get familiar with
feeling the fear of trying
something new.
—

art in order to be comfortable. If we're no longer feeling challenged, boredom and complacency usually follow, and we end up feeling blocked. Get familiar with feeling the fear of trying something new; you won't fail or lose anything by stepping out of your comfort zone, but there are infinite ways to learn and grow.

My final piece of advice is to enjoy the rest from the work of creating. Put everything to one side and go for a walk or a swim, or sit and read, or do whatever has been on your mind to get around to besides photography. Don't pressure yourself with any thoughts of what it takes to 'be' a photographer or creative. Let rest envelop you, and lean into it just as you would the creative times. I can go two, three or even six months without making any photographs. I enjoy this time of just appreciating my life.

Learning to accept our own limitations, or the limitations of our inspiration, means we can also accept that the world we live in doesn't need us to make photographs of it all the time. Perhaps these times of blockage or dearth are the universe saying, 'No! Just enjoy me as I am for once!'

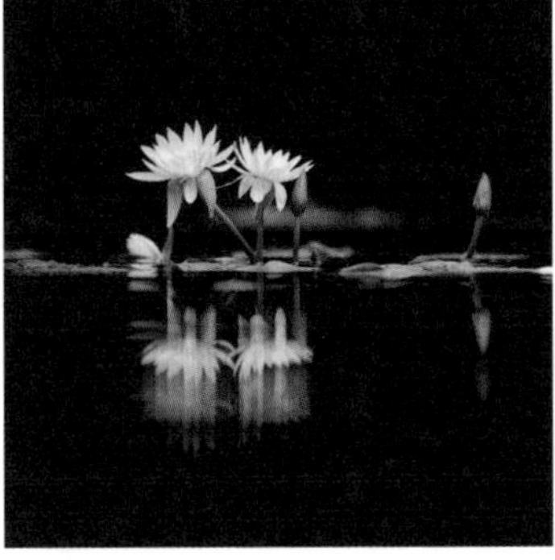

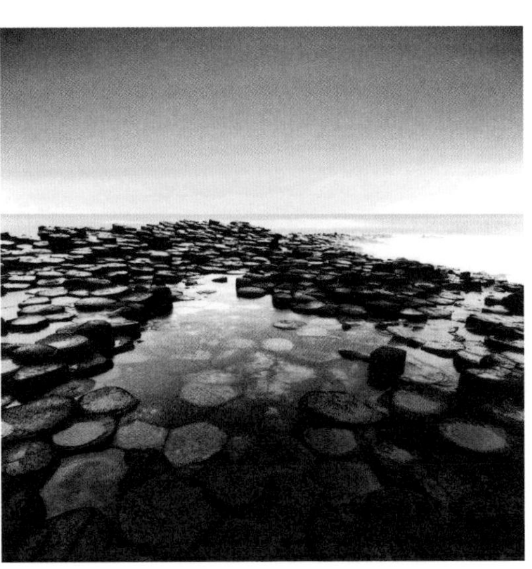

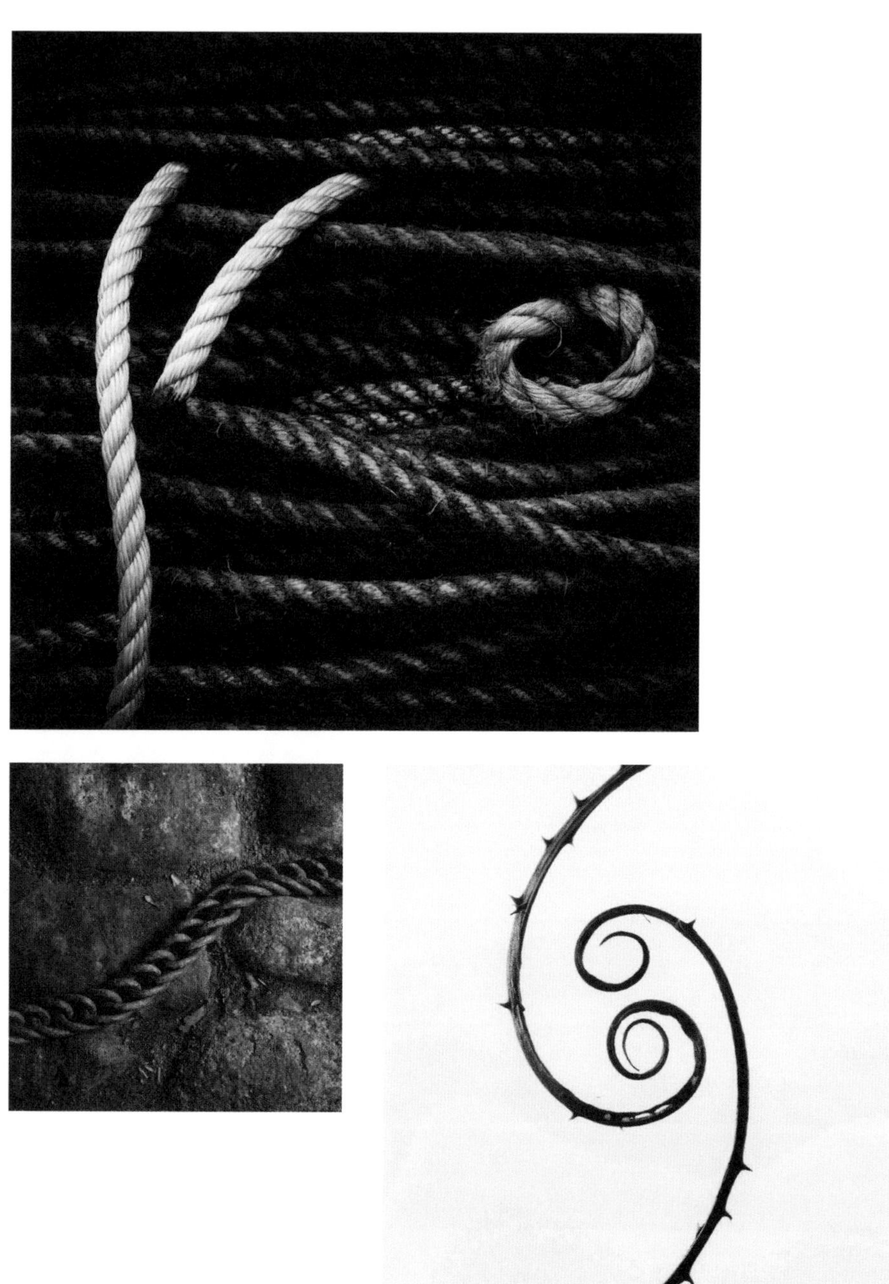

failure

We put so much store in being the fully formed expert or having good
results from the get-go that we forget that failure is an important part
of the creative process.

Not long after I left *The Times*, I started an after-school photography club at the junior school my son attended. I would give the six- or seven-year-old pupils a brief, usually very simple – something to do with light, colour, movement or shadows – and let them run around with cameras for half an hour. One day, one of the children stood staring at me after I had given the brief for the lesson, so I asked her whether she had a question, and her reply broke my heart. 'What if I get it wrong?' she said. 'Will I be in trouble?'

Imagine a child of six worrying about getting things wrong! I explained that she couldn't get it wrong; that you can only learn by making pictures, and this is true no matter what age you are. There are photographs that might come out differently from what you intended, but when it comes to pursuing your own personal vision or experience, you cannot do it incorrectly!

When things don't come out as planned, that is not failure but a sign that you have yet to acquire the skills needed to move on to the next step. However, you wouldn't be able to take that step at all if you hadn't noticed that something wasn't as you wanted it to be.

Let's compare ourselves to a baby learning to walk. When you watch a child learning to walk, they will stumble and fall, shuffle on their behind, crawl on hands and knees, lean on things for support and stagger around like they're drunk. Once they're up and walking, often they still fall. But no one says, 'My child has failed to walk'; they say (with great pride), 'My child is learning to walk.'

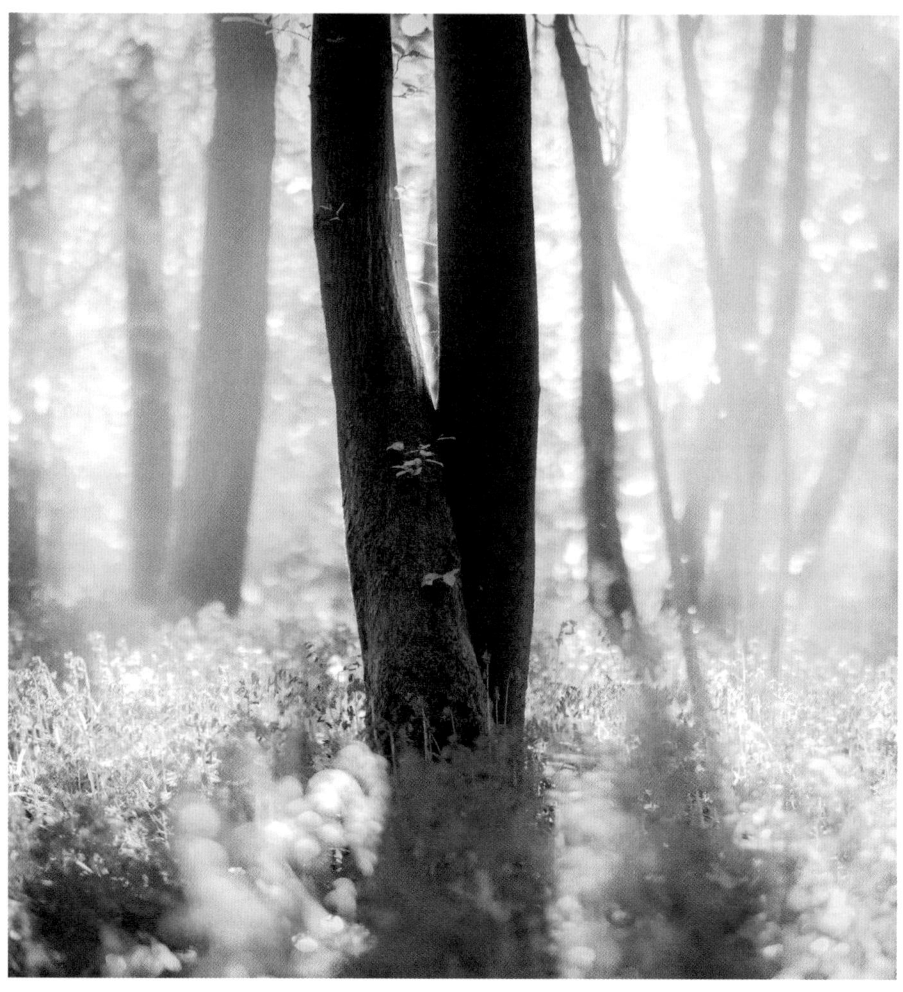

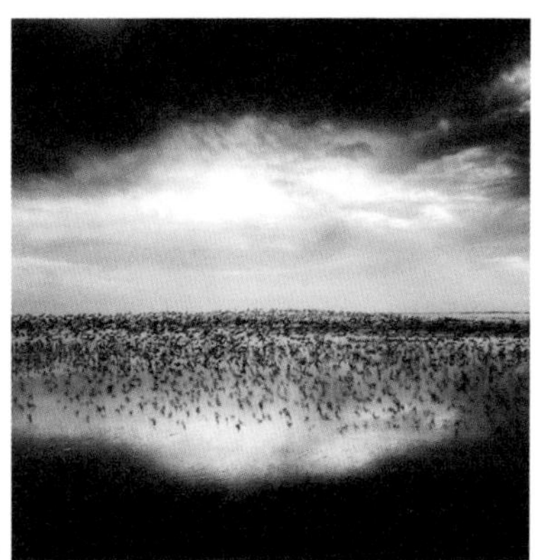

I love failing – failing would
be my superpower, or at least
one of them!

—

The same is true of photography, and particularly mindful photography. I am still learning. I enjoy the mistakes that come into my work; they make me remember to take a step back, to relearn, to understand anew and to revisit ideas so that I can continue to grow.

Don't undervalue those photographs that don't work as you'd hoped – they are the shuffling on your backside as you learn to walk. In other words, they are the key steps on the road to understanding how to interpret the world around you. The challenge with the gap between what you wanted to show and what actually appears is avoiding listening to the internal critic who wants to convince you that you aren't good enough. Again, the toddler version of you offers excellent inspiration. Babies don't have negative self-talk – they want to do something so they keep trying, pushing their boundaries and abilities with sometimes terrifying tenacity until they can.

When the negative talk starts in your head, you can reply to it something like, 'Thank you but I don't need your words at the moment. I am learning something new, and it is acceptable to make mistakes, stumble, even fall – as long as I keep getting up to try again.'

learning from others

When making photographs, it's important that we don't fall into the trap of comparing our work with others', but that's not to say that we shouldn't ever look at other people's work. In fact, looking at what others are doing is a great way to find inspiration and learn the craft.

People flock to iconic locations just to recreate and learn from what others have done before them. In the same way, artists often recreate the compositions, colour palettes, marks, and so on, of paintings they admire in order to discover how something was done. There is no better way to learn than to do something yourself, after all. My own photography was very influenced by the British landscape photographer Joe Cornish. His landscapes seemed majestic, and the light in his work stunning and I admired his thoughtful compositions. As part of my own learning I went to several of his locations and photographed them to better understand how he made the images that captivated me.

The trick is to engage all your skills of seeing, just as you would if you were making an original picture. It's not enough to just stand in the same place as a famous photographer – you have to ask a few questions. Why this location, this direction? What did they include or exclude from the frame? How did they convey that particular detail, atmosphere or quality of light? What is it that intrigued you about the original? No, the subject isn't going to directly answer you, and the photographer is unlikely to appear to whisper their secrets into your ear, but treat it as an opportunity to ask everything you ever wanted to know about it, and you will be surprised how much you can learn!

'Nature is far more curious, incidental, intuitive, organic, asymmetrical, inventive, extravagant, unpredictable and experimental than I could ever be. All I need to do is truly pay attention to it with my whole being.'

—

Joe Cornish

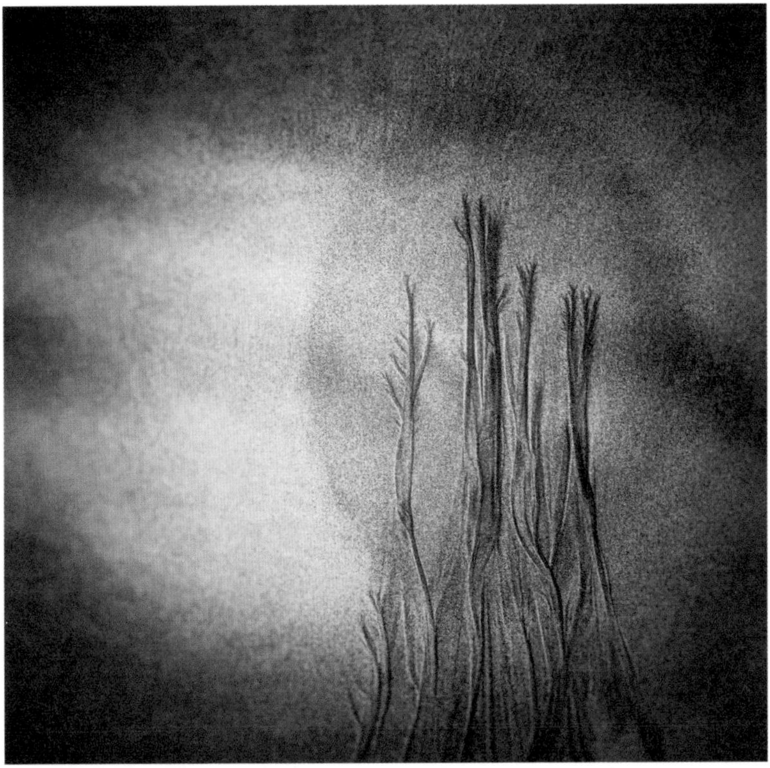

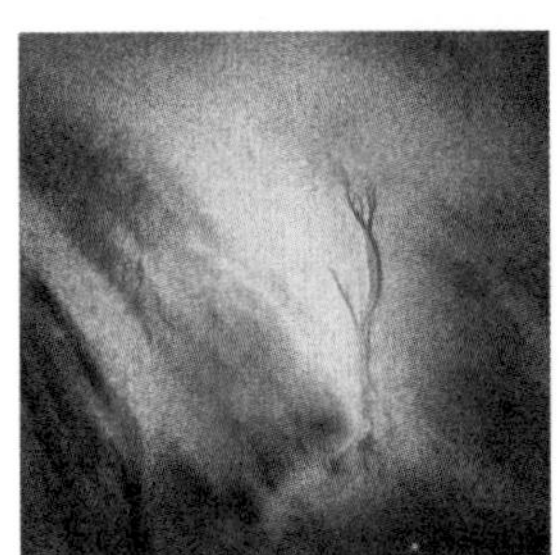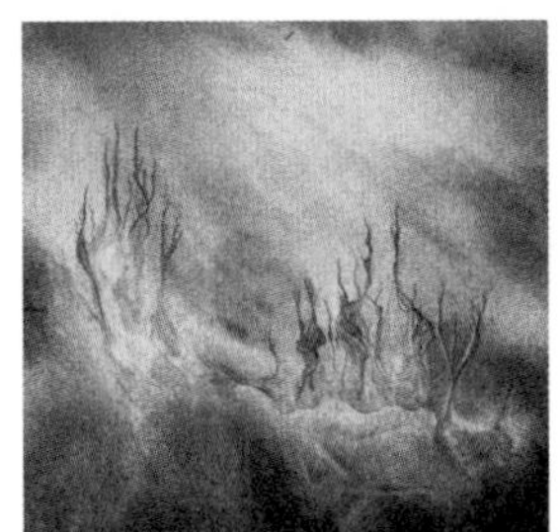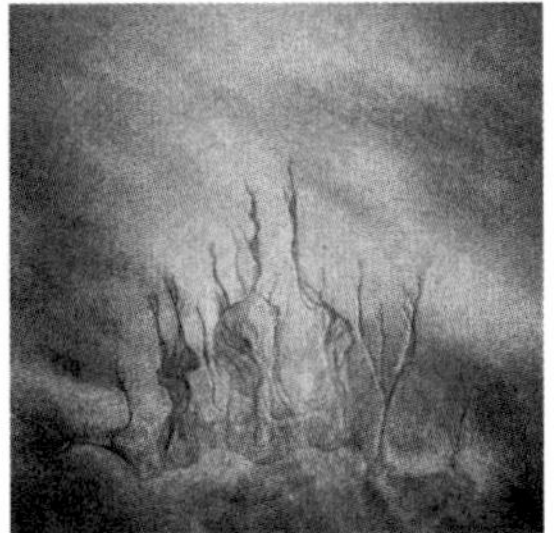

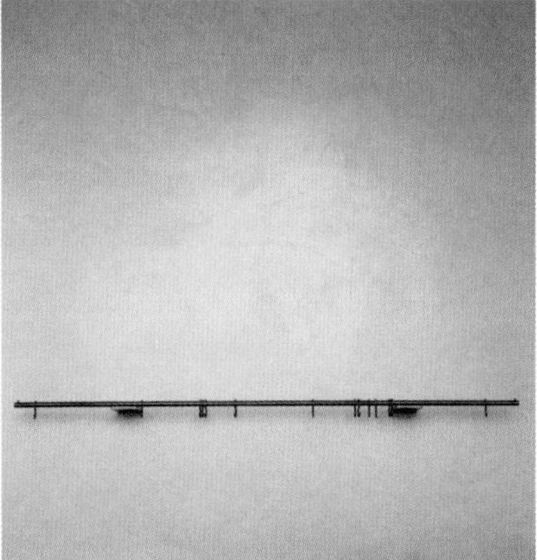

You are not going to recreate every image that inspires you, of course, and simply looking can be just as useful in finding out what you're drawn to in terms of subjects and approaches. In a world as saturated by images as ours is, you're not going to suffer from any lack of potential influences, but you may in fact find the opposite. With so many images, it can be hard to narrow it down and find a series or someone you can really learn from.

When I started in news photography I read everything I could written by photojournalists, documentary photographers and picture editors – my copy of *Pictures on a Page* by Harold Evans is so dog-eared it's almost falling to pieces. There is so much we can learn from those who came before us, not only from the techniques and style they use but also from the context – of the history of photography and also their life and location. In other words, why they photographed as they did. Look at the way they compose their images and use the light and weather; explore the mood they convey in their work and how they tell the story. Don't get hung up on the settings but do explore the techniques.

Every genre has its great names and works, which you can discover through research – online, in books or magazines – and at museums and galleries. Spend a few minutes of your day researching and you will uncover a bottomless treasure trove, as discussions of one name leads to the photographers or artists who

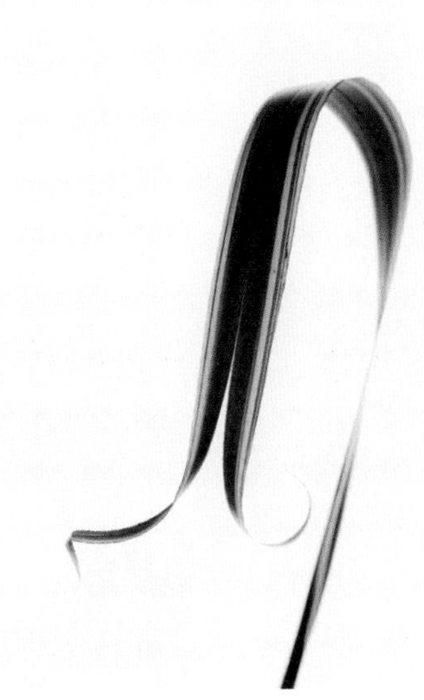

influenced them. It can be fascinating to uncover a 'family tree' of connections – everyone is influenced by someone – and, in doing so, you will almost unconsciously become more aware of the subtleties of their work, and what is possible for yours.

If you need a place to start, some of my influences that I always share with the audiences when I speak at photography events include: Minor White, Don McCullin, David Bailey, Robert Mapplethorpe, Saul Leiter, Henri Cartier-Bresson, Tom Stoddart, Denis Thorpe, Man Ray, Ansel Adams, Robert Adams, Edward Weston, Imogen Cunningham, Joe Cornish, David Ward, Joseph Sudek, Paul Strand, Henry Callaghan, Lee Miller, Anna

Atkins, Fay Godwin, Sarah Moon, Michael Kenna, William Henry Fox Talbot, Sally Mann, Elliot Erwitt and Peter Lindbergh. And there are many, many more!

If you want to take it further, go on a workshop with a photographer you admire. Most practising photographers run courses over a weekend or a week – listening to others speak about their craft is a powerful way to open up new ideas and new ways of thinking about your own. Even if a photographer doesn't publicly advertise workshops, they may well be interested to hear from you. Most people love discussing their craft, and you never know, it could be the beginning of a valuable relationship.

sharing

To share or not to share – that is a question I am often asked. There's a degree of pressure to share your life on social media these days, but we each have to decide whether and how much we're comfortable doing so. It's also worth pointing out that social media is not the only way to share. your work.

Personally, I like sharing my images, but I don't try to anticipate what my audience want. I stay true to myself and share when I feel like it, or when I feel I have something to say. When I share my work, I am saying, 'This is how I see the world and find my place in it. This is how I make sense of the chaos of life.' It is very easy to find others with a similar mindset to you through social media: you can build up a community of people whose work you enjoy and who enjoy yours.

As long as you're not doing it just to count up the 'likes', sharing your work can be a very positive experience. It's nice when others enjoy what you post, even if it's just family and friends. But you will probably find that other people you don't know will reach out to you because your images have resonated with them. A note of warning: when we share our work, we are asking for engagement in some form or other, yet, despite social media being supposedly all about engagement, people tend to spend only a few seconds looking at still images, which can often feel disappointing.

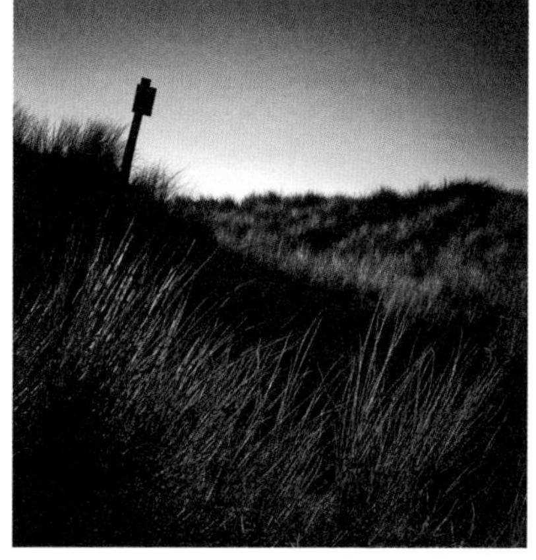

Sharing by way of an exhibition – whether online in a virtual gallery, a café or other venue, or an art or bespoke photography gallery – is in my opinion the most rewarding. While it can be intimidating to imagine yourself worthy of putting on an exhibition, a lot of cafés will be very open to it as a way of bringing extra footfall through their doors, and you don't have to worry about sitting in an empty space, as hopefully people will be coming for the coffee, too!

At an exhibition, people will slow
down and view your work at their own
pace, some will pore over every detail
while others spend only a few seconds
before moving on, but then come back to
linger over their favourites. I find listening
to and watching people as they interact
with my work fascinating. The way they
discuss it often gives insights that
wouldn't otherwise have occurred to me,
and there is a huge sense of achievement
when you see people you don't know
looking at and engaging with your work.

Seeing how others present their work
is a good way to gauge how you might
start to share your own. It is a big step
to start sharing images that mean
something to you, when you are effectively
putting your heart and soul on display.
For me, it is important to go to exhibitions
to see how others present their work.

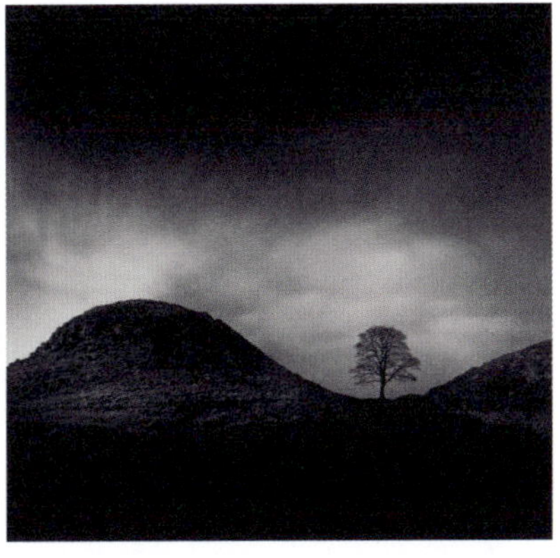

Some people are critical of camera
clubs and photography groups, but these
can also offer an outlet to share your work
and receive feedback and advice from a
variety of people with differing levels of
experience. The social side of photography
comes into its own in this environment,
with many people to learn from and share
ideas with. Regularly looking at the work
of others is a great way to learn the things
you like and dislike and get inspired. It
might also pave the way to taking part in
a group exhibition, which is much less
daunting and less expensive than putting
on a solo show.

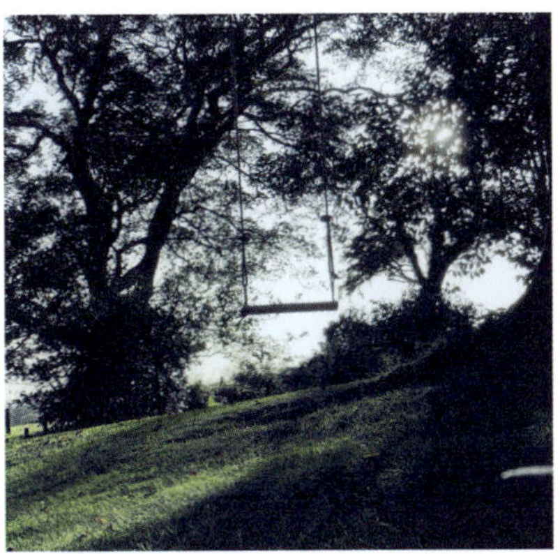

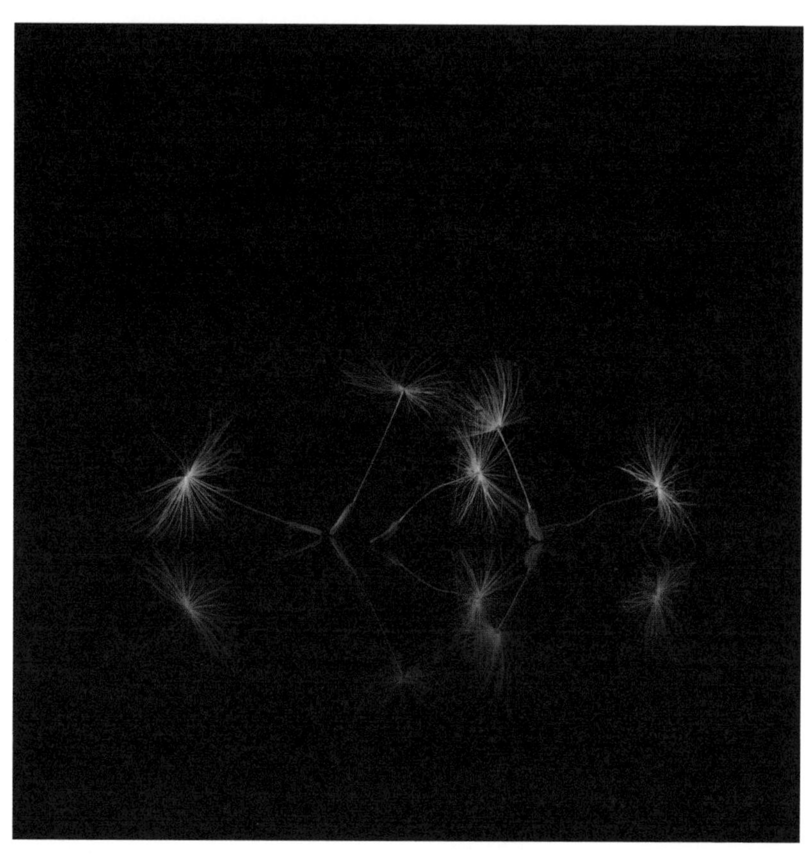

It's important to remember that, when you
share your work, you are setting it free. People will
have their own relationship with your photographs
and they may interpret them differently from you.

—

Perhaps the most meaningful way of sharing your work is to make books of your work. I buy countless photography books – not expensive ones, but the small, often handmade books that are sold at craft fairs, in some galleries and at open-studio weekends. When people have a book or print in their hand, it is impossible for them to rush. They will feel the weight of the book in their hands, they will connect with the paper as they turn the pages and they will view the work in the order you have selected. Images presented in this way often get the most engagement from the viewer – I get more questions about my prints and small books than any form of sharing.

It's important to remember that, when you share your work, you are setting it free. People will have their own relationship with your photographs and they may interpret them differently from you. Some will love your work, some won't like it – if you can treat both responses with the same acceptance it will help you to continue enjoy sharing your work.

Allowing people to have their own relationship with your images is key. Letting go of your emotional attachment to your images allows you to grow and to move on to new ideas. It can also be an exciting and eye-opening experience to discover how others respond to your images, even if they really hate them. Also remember that negative comments are sometimes intended to be helpful. You might not have solicited that advice, but try to see it in the best possible light.

Learning to take critical feedback will help build your resilience – which is something we all need in life. Every creative person has to take a few negative remarks about their work, and on occasion about themselves, too. This is the danger of sharing your work, however you choose to do so, but remember, it is always a personal choice.

If the thought of putting your work out there scares you but you think it could be a good thing, then do it. Moving out of your comfort zone is the only way to grow, and the boost to your confidence and self-esteem because of this act of courage will be incredible. As long as you enjoyed making the work you put out there, it doesn't really matter if no one else likes or admires it – but, in my experience, chances are, more people will enjoy seeing what you produce than don't.

critique

One of the hardest parts of photography – and of any skill – is learning to take feedback, but it's important that we do. If we want to become better photographers, and make images that better reflect our experiences with a subject, we have to be able to assess our work with an objective eye – not to tear ourselves down, but in order to grow.

First, there is a huge difference between non-constructive criticism that undermines you and your work, and a more useful, constructive critique, which helps you improve your eye and technique.

The trolls who criticize and abuse, safe behind the anonymity of their keyboards, generally aren't people who practise any form of creativity. Their words can still be upsetting, but the best course is simply to ignore them, delete them and move on.

When someone can actually explain their observations, this is critique in its true sense. If you can listen to their thoughts without taking it too personally or feeling offended (which can be hard if you haven't asked for critique), it can give you valuable insights into how you can improve your photography.

As an example, I had an editor who liked to be given prints at the end of the day. I would produce a dozen or so prints of the photographs I had selected for the stories of the day, to which he would look at me and say, 'Why?', before proceeding to actually tear chunks off my images. It is awful to have someone rip up your work like this. He would hand me back a torn-up print and tell me that this was how we were going to use it.

After a few weeks of this treatment, I decided to ask him why he ripped up my pictures. At that point, he carefully explained that the pictures were good, but we were a newspaper; space costs money, and my pictures had too much space in them. He added that he was surprised I had not asked before! In a similar vein, while at Reuters, the chief photographer, David Diggers, would always say 'Where is the story? Crop to the story and the images will walk into the pages of magazines and newspapers.'

When we understand why someone objects to something about our image, it can change our entire way of thinking about image-making. Then, again, it's also up to us to agree with them or not.

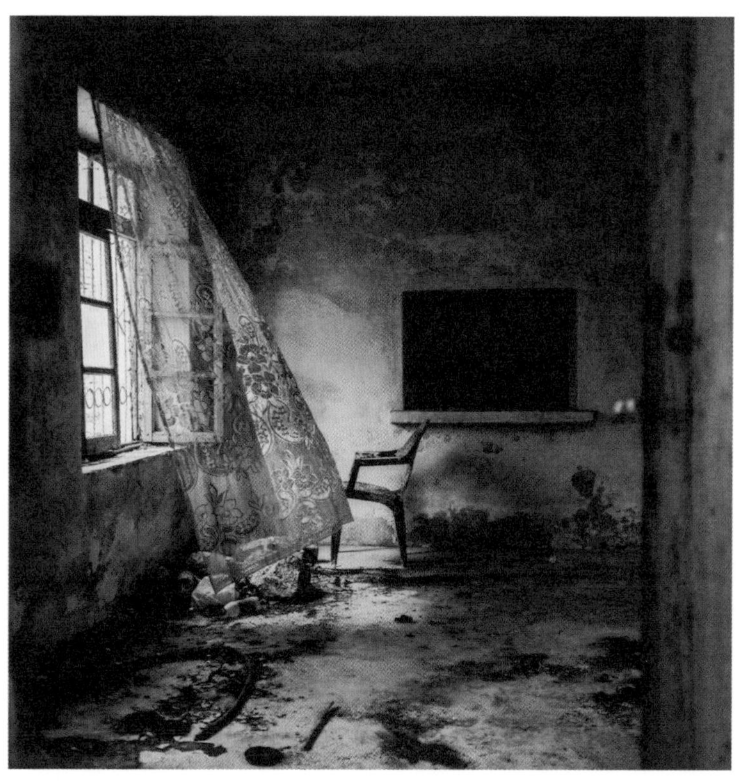

'Where is the story? Crop to the story
and the images walk into the pages of
magazines and newspapers.'
—

David Viggers

We don't have to take every piece of advice we're given on board, and it's equally important to be able to trust in our own instincts. If you like what you're doing, you can respectfully disagree.

Receiving feedback is as much a skill as any, and one I definitely recommend putting into practice. It is a part of being open, and accepting that there is always more to learn. Throughout my career people have given me guidance, even today I still listen to the advice or ideas of others because I know it helps. If you know a fellow photographer you can trust to be honest but supportive, share some images with them, and see where it takes you. And if you're in a position to give feedback yourself, bear in mind how you would like to receive it – I look first for the things I like in other people's photographs; there is always something good to build from.

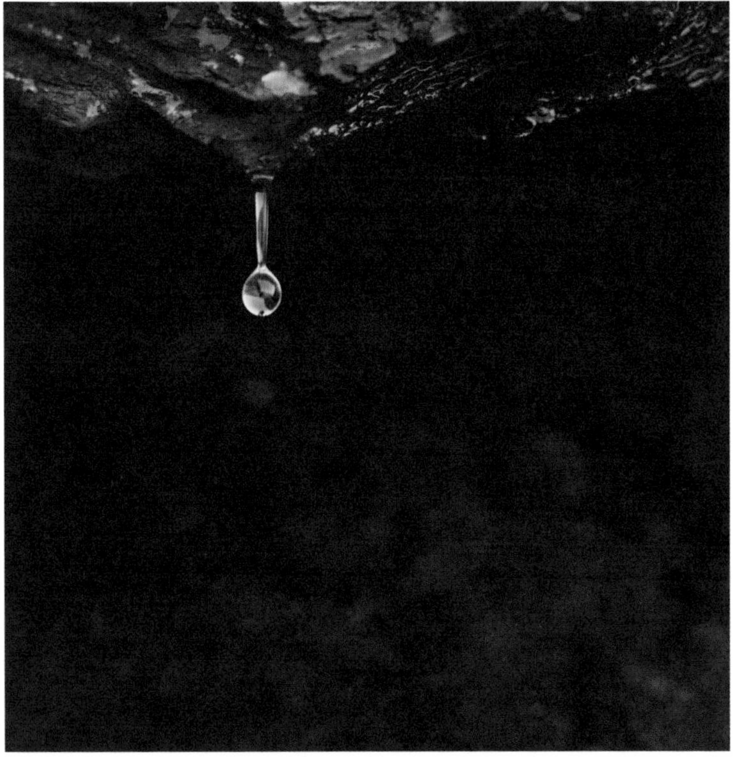

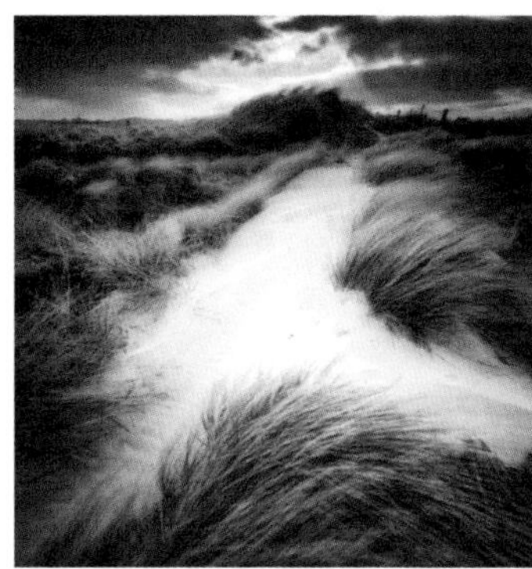

Apply the same generosity when assessing your own work. I look at every image I have made when I get back at the end of the day, going through them all quite carefully, and I never delete an image without first giving it proper consideration and trying to learn what I can from it. Analyzing your images will keep you engaged with them and will also help you evolve as a photographer.

One of the important things to keep in mind when reviewing your own work is not to turn into the critic. This is one of the reasons I avoid simplistic judgements like 'good' and 'bad' about my photography. I decided a while ago that either the images communicated to me what I wanted or they didn't, and if I don't feel they succeed, I simply try to establish for myself what I might have done differently.

With mindful photography, as I see it, technical perfection is much less important than seeing, so learn to look at your work with compassion. Have you made the point, told the story, or shown your subject the way it caught your attention?

At the end of each day, I select the photographs I like the most. The one that best conveys what I wanted it to receives five stars in my editing software, while others get three stars. I then go through the also-rans and ask why didn't that image work as well as the one I chose as the best of the day. I look at composition, lighting, separation between the subject and the background, clutter around the edges, the mood... Asking yourself questions about your work helps you clarify what you're trying to do, and what success looks like.

Selecting one five-star image is a great way to end a day, as well as to track your progress as a photographer. If you make pictures most days of the year, then at the end of the year you could have 300 or so five-star images. At the end of each year, go back over your favourite images, and you will notice a gradual learning curve unfolding as your seeing has become more refined and you've developed new techniques and ideas. It is only in looking back that you realize how far you have come.

conclusion

I have written this book in the hope that you, the reader, will find joy and inspiration in your everyday life. I hope it will help you learn to enjoy seeing your world and your life free from judgement, comparisons with others and the internal dialogue of not being good enough.

When I receive an image, to me, this is a gift from God. Even if you don't believe in God, you can still recognize these moments as gifts – from the universe or just the hand of chance. These gifts are not to be critiqued, judged, compared or necessarily shared, although it can bring both you and others joy to share the moments that inspire you.

Don't be ashamed of what catches your eye – be in love with the moments that life throws at you. Allow fascination and intrigue to develop over cynicism and criticism. Give yourself permission to pause every day; to breathe the air, to feel the earth beneath your feet, to see the world around you and reconnect with it, if only for a few minutes.

Try not to worry about what equipment you're using. More than 50 percent of the images in this book were made on a smartphone, and there's no shame in that. What you make your images on is irrelevant; what matters is what you *see*, not what you see through.

Similarly, don't go chasing 'perfection' – it's a game no one and nothing can win. Every subject of every image in this book is imperfect, and that hasn't stopped me finding the beauty in it. In noticing this, I can see myself as also perfectly imperfect. I am flawed and I am vulnerable, but I am also stronger for that recognition.

The important thing is to pay attention. When you really look at the world, spending the time to be curious and to notice things, and being generous with what you see, you will begin the practice of finding the treasure in your everyday. Before long, you will come to see how rich you are, just by realizing what you already have in your life, rather than perpetually chasing after what you don't have.

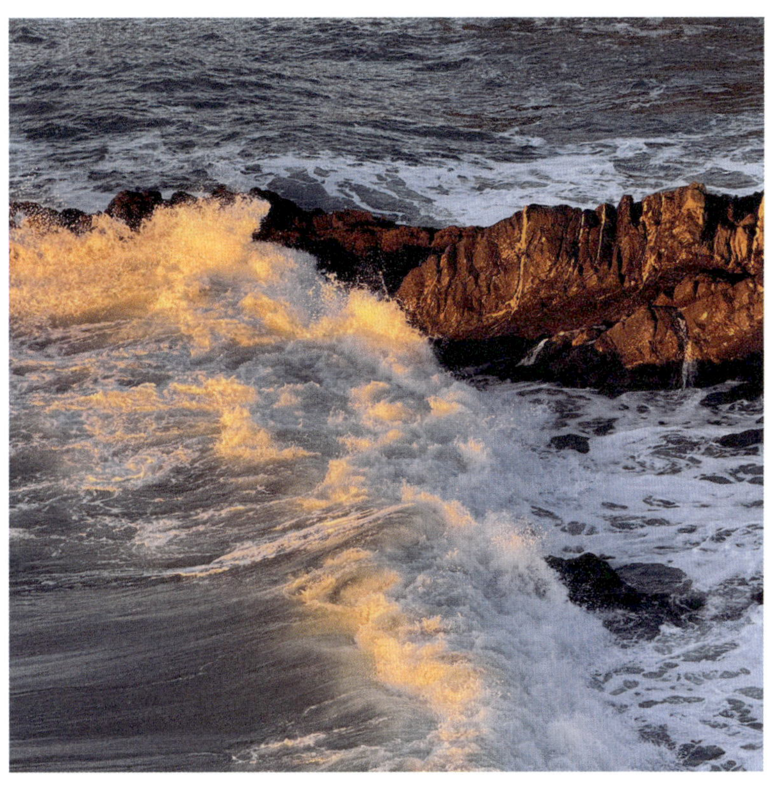

Give yourself permission to pause every
day; to breathe the air, to feel the earth
beneath your feet, to see the world
around you and reconnect with it,
if only for a few minutes.

—

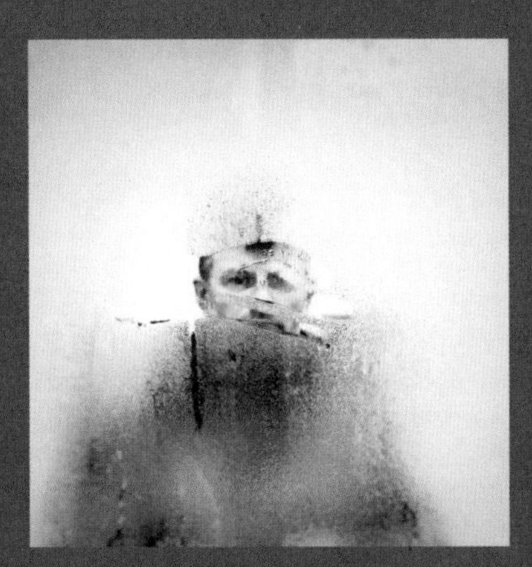

about paul sanders

British fine-art photographer Paul Sanders has been involved in photography for over 35 years, first as a black-and-white printer, then as a fashion photographer.

An opening at a local weekly newspaper for a trainee photographer led to jobs at the *Manchester Evening News*, Reuters, and then as picture editor of *The Times*, overseeing the entire visual content of the prestigious publication.

In 2011 Paul suffered a nervous breakdown as a result of stress and burnout that led to a period of severe depression, insomnia and self-destructive behaviour. He made the decision to leave the role at *The Times* to pursue his love of nature and the landscape and, working closely with a therapist, started exploring how photography could aid his recovery.

Paul's approach to landscape photography is one of mindful connection. After looking at thousands of images every day during his years at *The Times*, his own work is made in response to emotional and spiritual reactions to the locations he visits, and reflecting a sense of stillness and calm.

The initial capture of the photograph is only half the story, as Paul is also passionate about the printing process, and believes that a photograph needs to be viewed as a print to properly appreciate it.

Paul's, beautiful, reflective work has been exhibited widely – across the UK and Europe and in Japan.

acknowledgements

Without the following people this book wouldn't have
been possible:

Rachel Silverlight and Richard Collins at Octopus Books, whose
patience know no bounds. Beth Kempton for giving me the
courage to try. Sue and Jonathan at The Beach Café, Porthtowan,
for the endless cups of coffee and cinnamon buns that have fuelled
my writing. My friends through thick and thin: Hannah and Dan
Belton, Angus Thomson, Martin Scarland and Graeme Fife.
Charlie Ingram and Andy Potter, the ministers at Bessels Green
Baptist Church, my spiritual home. In the photography industry:
Toby, Vince and Tim at Fotospeed; Alison Barclay at 3 Legged
Thing; Sarah Jones at Cambrian Cameras and Alister Bowie at
Ffordes Photographic. There are a great many people who have
helped me throughout my career: the team at Richard Bailey
Photography Ltd in Coventry; Nick Stanley, for giving me my
first job in photography; Peter Aengenheister, the first editor who
gave me a break; Robert Thomson, former editor of *The Times*,
for giving me my dream job; Nigel Iskander of News Team.
Also: Nick Bowman, Kim Scott Clark, Bob Kirwin, Dave
Thomas, Michael Unger, Joe Cusack, Phil Noble, Martin Rickett,
Gary Roberts, David Viggers, Hugh Pinney, Marc Aspland – each
of whom has shared knowledge and ideas with me so openly.
I am forever grateful.

Finally to my dear friend Teresa Houghton for her belief in me
and my work until her dying day.